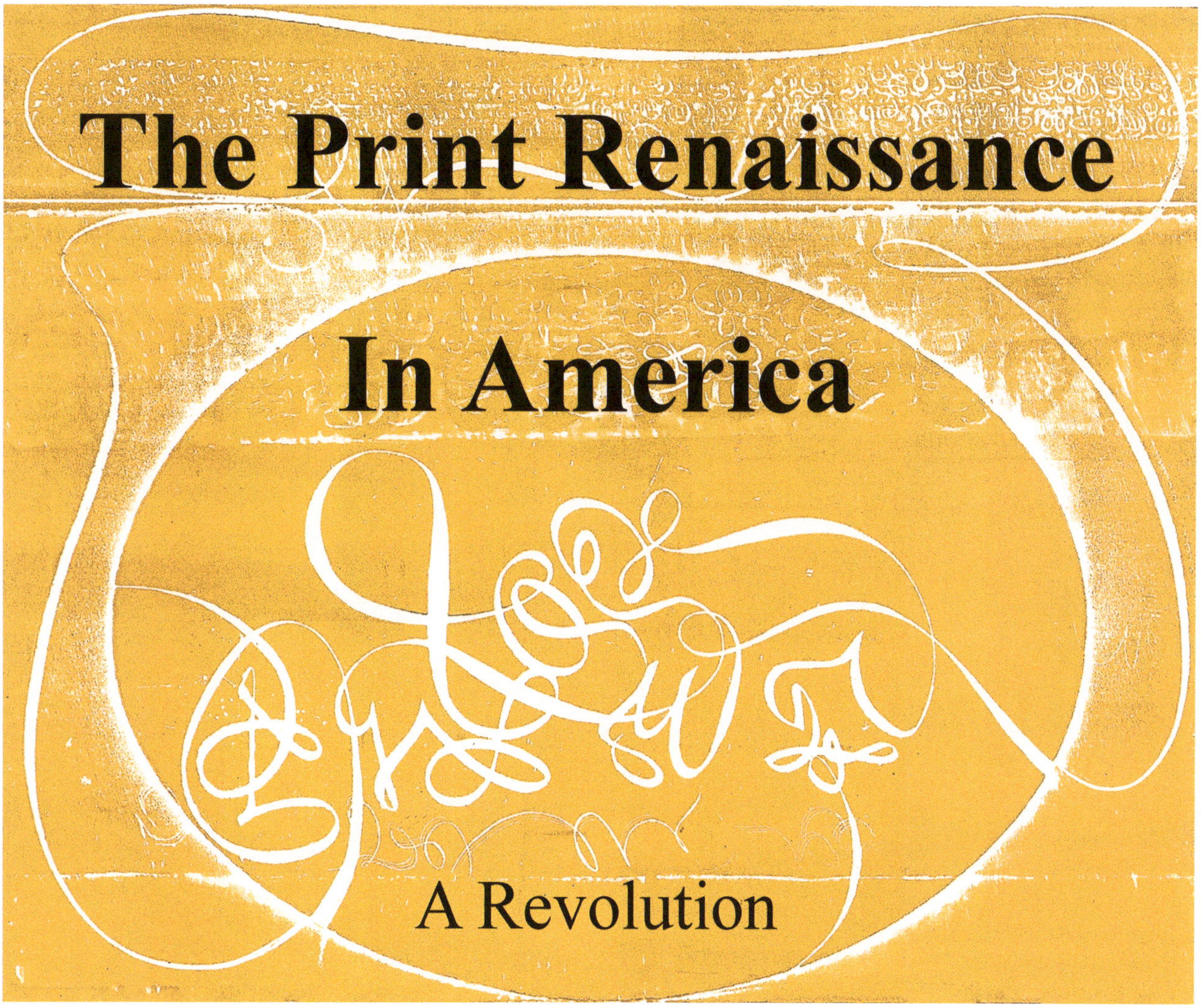

The Print Renaissance In America

A Revolution

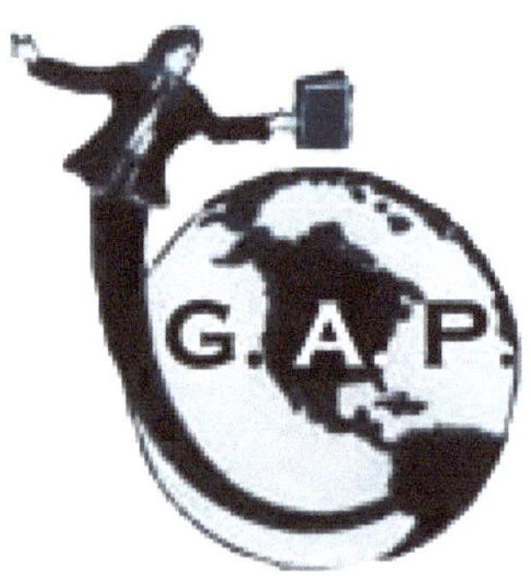

ISBN: 978-0-9861109-1-7

Library of Congress Control Number:2015946132

Published by Global Authors Publications

Filling the GAP in publishing

Interior design by Ronald L. Ruble and Kathleen Walls

Edited by Mary Ruble

Cover Design by Ronald L Ruble and Kathleen Walls

Cover art by Arthur Thrall, "Oval 10" etching/engraving 14 x 16 1/2

Photography by Steve Agard

Printed in USA for Global Authors Publications

The Print Renaissance In America

A Revolution

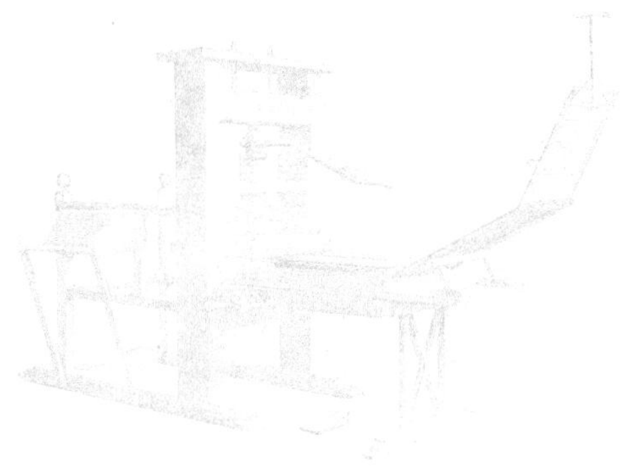

"It is the defining of the historical event that I want to highlight, and a few notables who made it happen"

The Ronald L. Ruble Collection of Fine Art Prints

Dedication

To my wife and best friend Mary Katherine, whose continual support, patience, and encouragement sometimes is not always properly acknowledged in the flurry of my activities. Yet, my love and appreciation are always there each and every day. Without her, there would be no life.

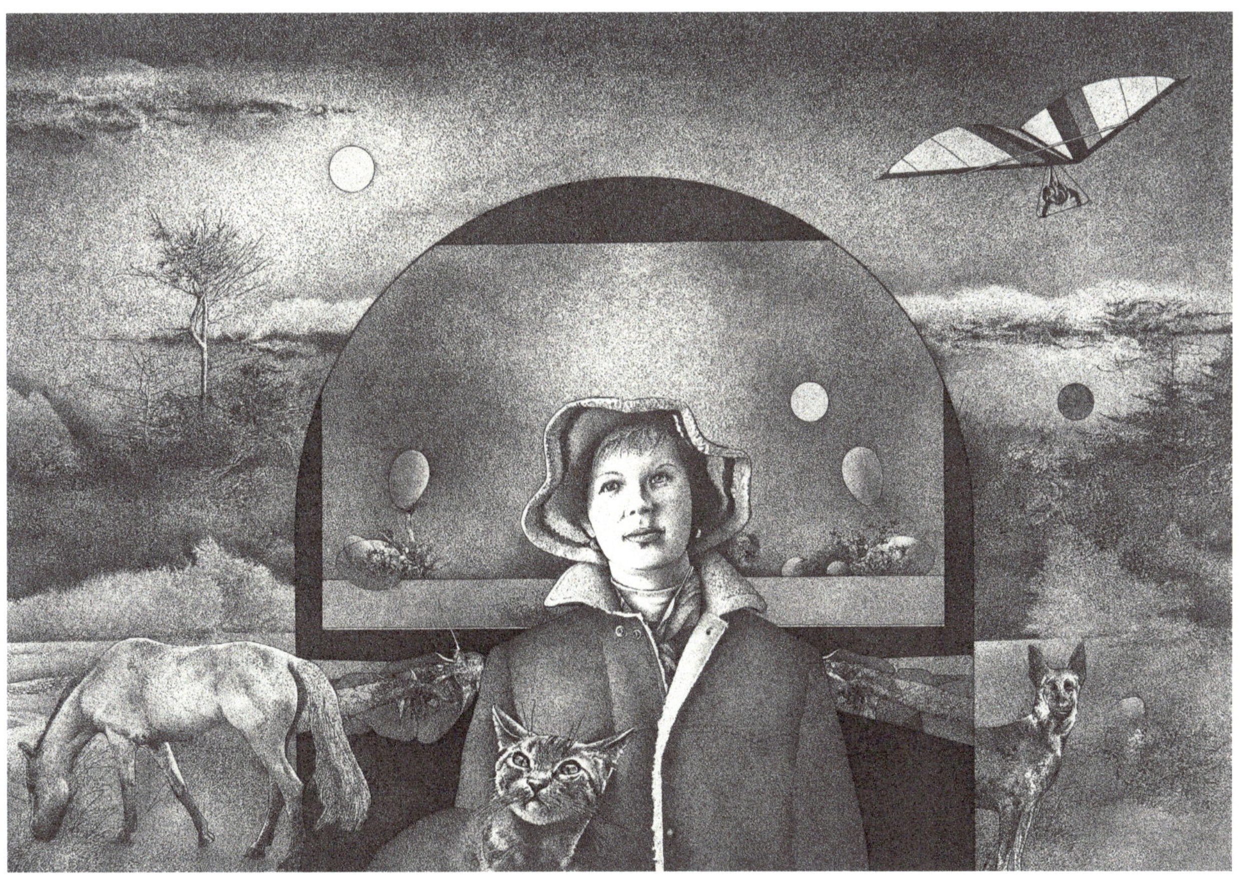

Ronald L. Ruble "Mary Wickens, Mary Wickens" Etching 18 ¼ x 27 ½

There are limitations to any project, and there are regrets for these shortcomings. Mine is the omission of many fine printmakers on these pages, who were a part of this occurrence and deserve to be included. This is my loss, as well as possibly a disappointment for those people who are reading this book. We can all think of additions of noteworthy artists and others in the printmaking field who were players in this significant revival in art history. I express my personal regrets to these wonderful people who contributed significantly, but were overlooked on these pages. In an effort to solidify my apologies, I dedicate this book to you. You are not forgotten, just personal victims of my limitations. I ask your forgiveness, and my thanks go out to all of you.

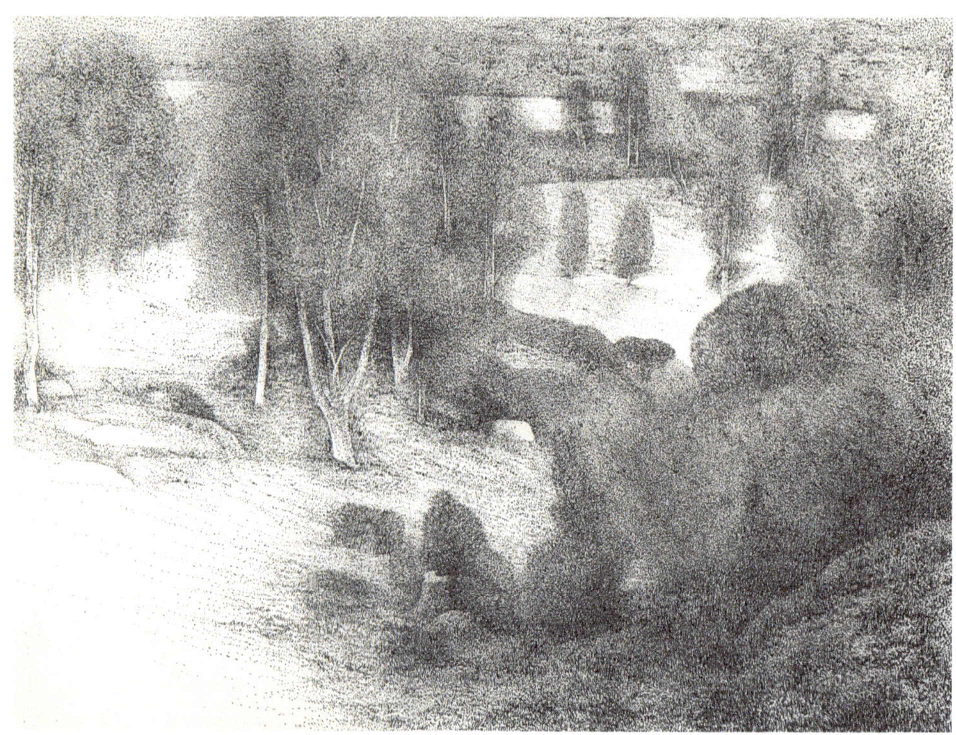

Richard Claude Ziemann "Berkshire Valley" Etching/Engraving 19 x 24

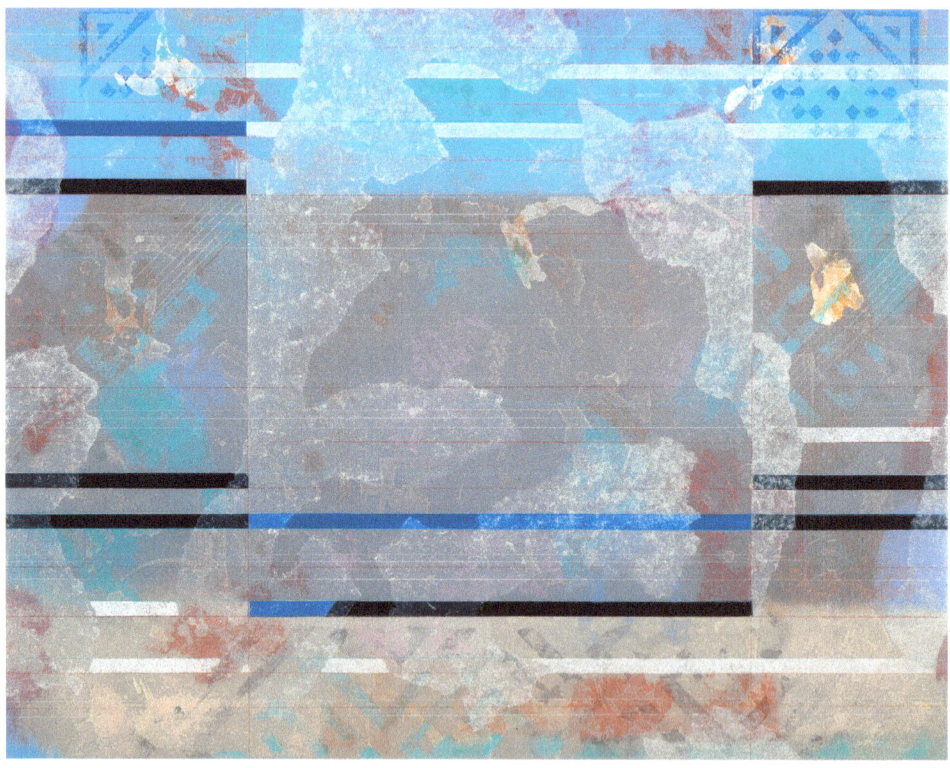

Robert Kelly "Untitled" Etching 25 ½ x 33 ½

Acknowledgements

No project in life is accomplished autonomously. There are always other people involved in one way or another, who provide necessary support to any worthwhile project. I would like to thank the following people who stepped up and gave freely of their time and efforts to make this book a reality.

First and foremost, I would like to thank my editor and wife Mary, for her tireless efforts in plodding through the narrative and the many artist biographies contained within this book. She made them come alive with her abilities to transform my thoughts into words that express what I was attempting to say in a more understandable manner.

Others that helped with the narrative editing and their support were Evan Lindquist, Evan Summer, Shelley Thorstensen and Larry Welo. Win Thrall was also there with her thoughtful suggestions, and background knowledge to share in the area of publishing. Their encouragement kept me going during those times of hesitation towards continuing the project.

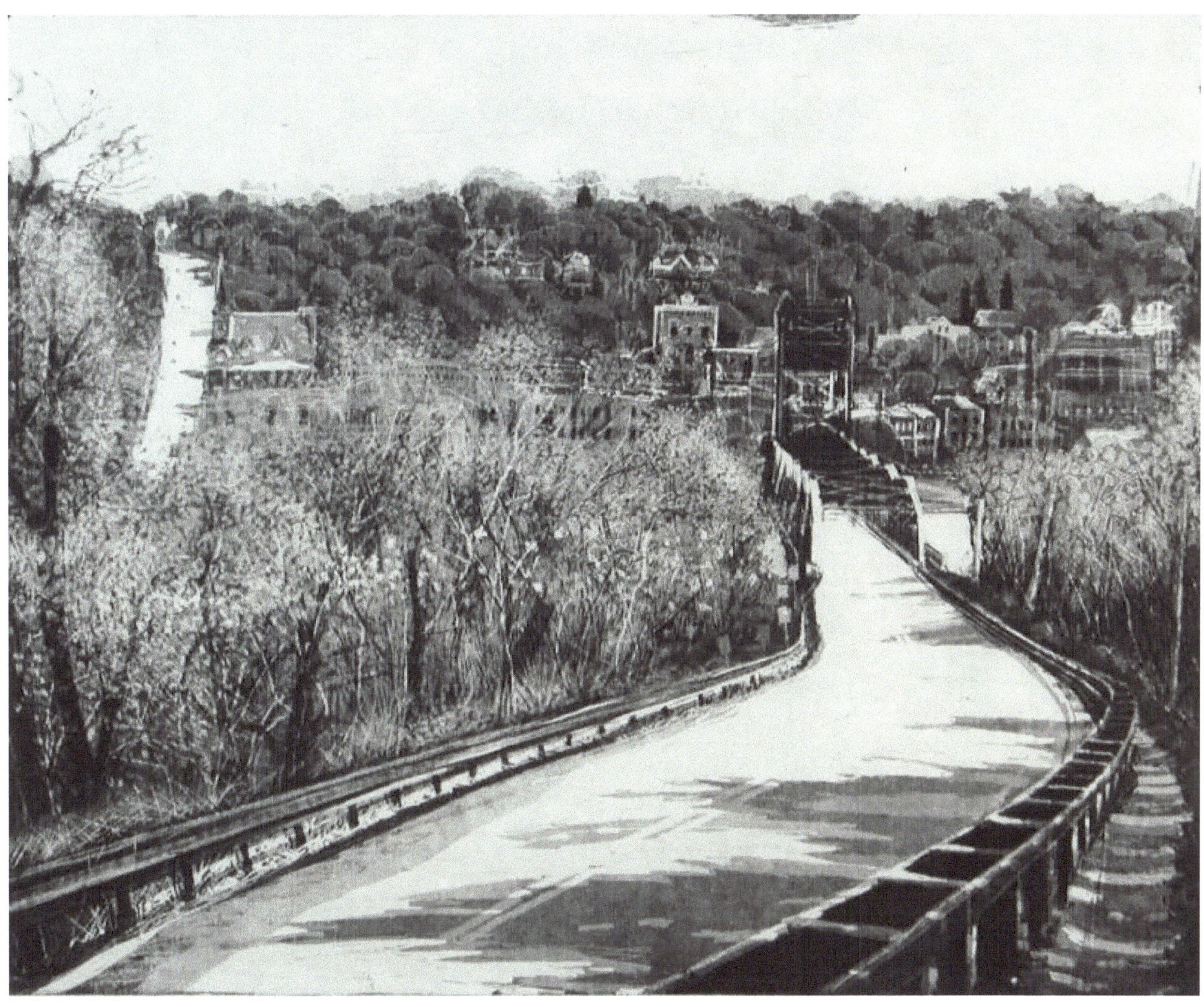

Larry Welo "The River" Etching 16 x 20

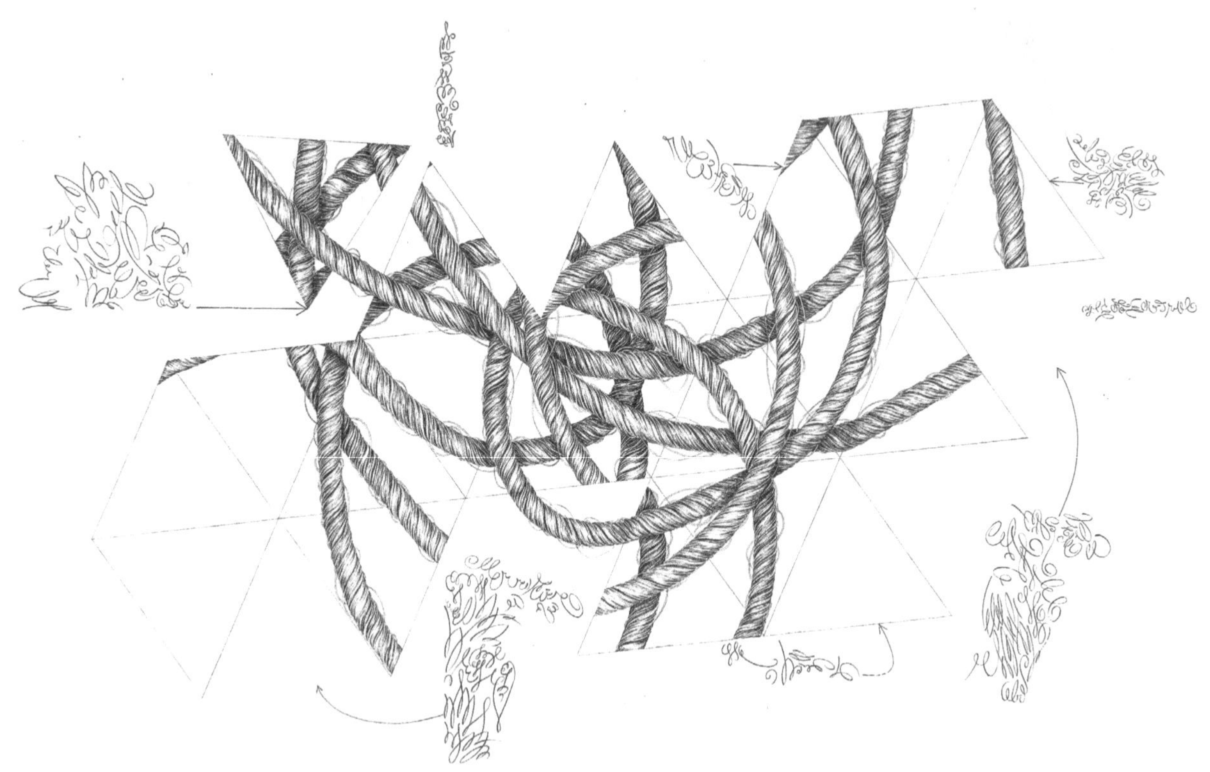

Evan Lindquist "Document" Engraving 14 ¾ x 23 ¾

A special thank you to Warrington Colescott, one of the few notables that I have had the pleasure to meet, who were personally involved in every aspect of the Print Renaissance. Colescott personifies those artist-printmakers who transformed the medium of printmaking into what we enjoy today. His encouragement convinced me of the importance in defining this period of art history as a worthwhile endeavor. His first-hand knowledge of the event and his support was invaluable and greatly appreciated.

Thank you Susan Carter, for always being there when my lack of computer knowledge, causing frustration, was definitely removing years from my life expectancy. The computer is a tool that transformed our world, but it can also take on the role of assisting its user to an early exit from this life. You saved me many hours to be used much more productive with a mere tap of the correct key.

To the many artist-printmakers represented here, thank you for being a part of this educational document for both the use by the student population and for expanding the knowledge of your peers. Without sharing, where would we be? Art is for everyone.

A large thank you to Steve Agard, our photographer, for the wonderful images in this book. Preparing the art work for "print ready" copy was a huge multi-step task, and for one to attempt the representation of the artist's original image is not a job for the faint of heart.

My hat goes off to Daniel Lineau for sharing a copy of the original 1944 catalogue for the "Hayter and Studio 17" exhibit at the Museum of Modern Art. This addition has made that historic exhibition come alive.

And lastly to my publisher, Katy Walls, founder and owner of Global Authors Publications. Without her faith and belief, and the many hours spent on keeping me focused, there would be no book. Her knowledge, suggestions and experience were invaluable and made this book come together.

Table of Contents

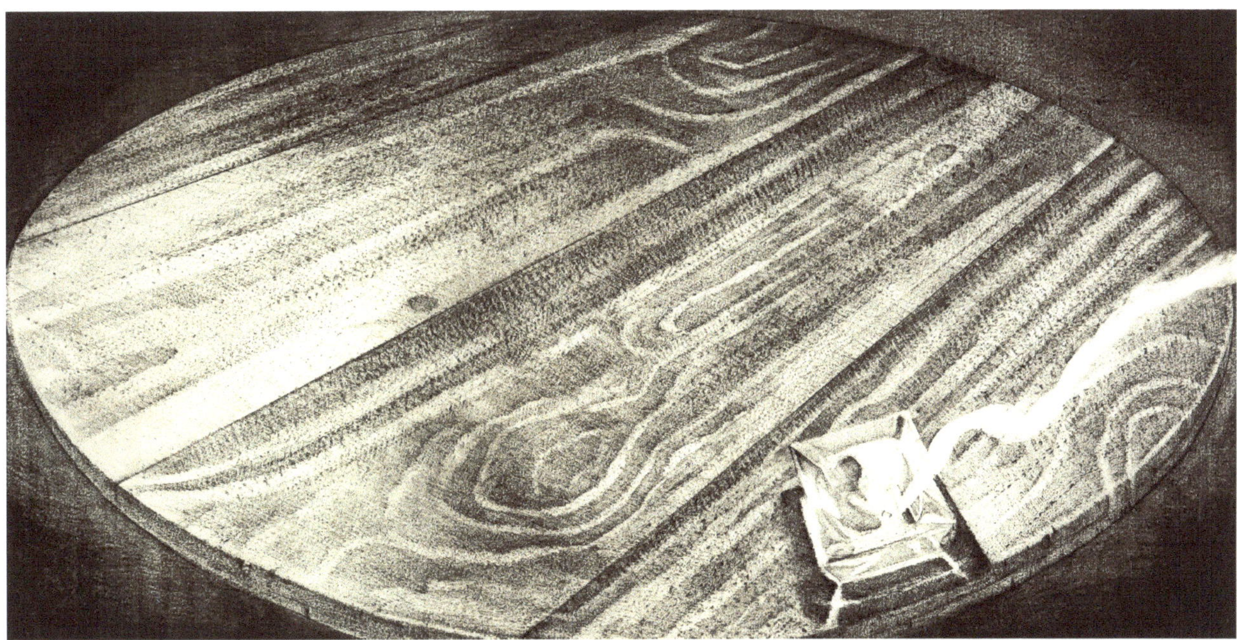

Michael Mazur "Smoke" Etching/Aquatint 17 ¾ x 35 ¼

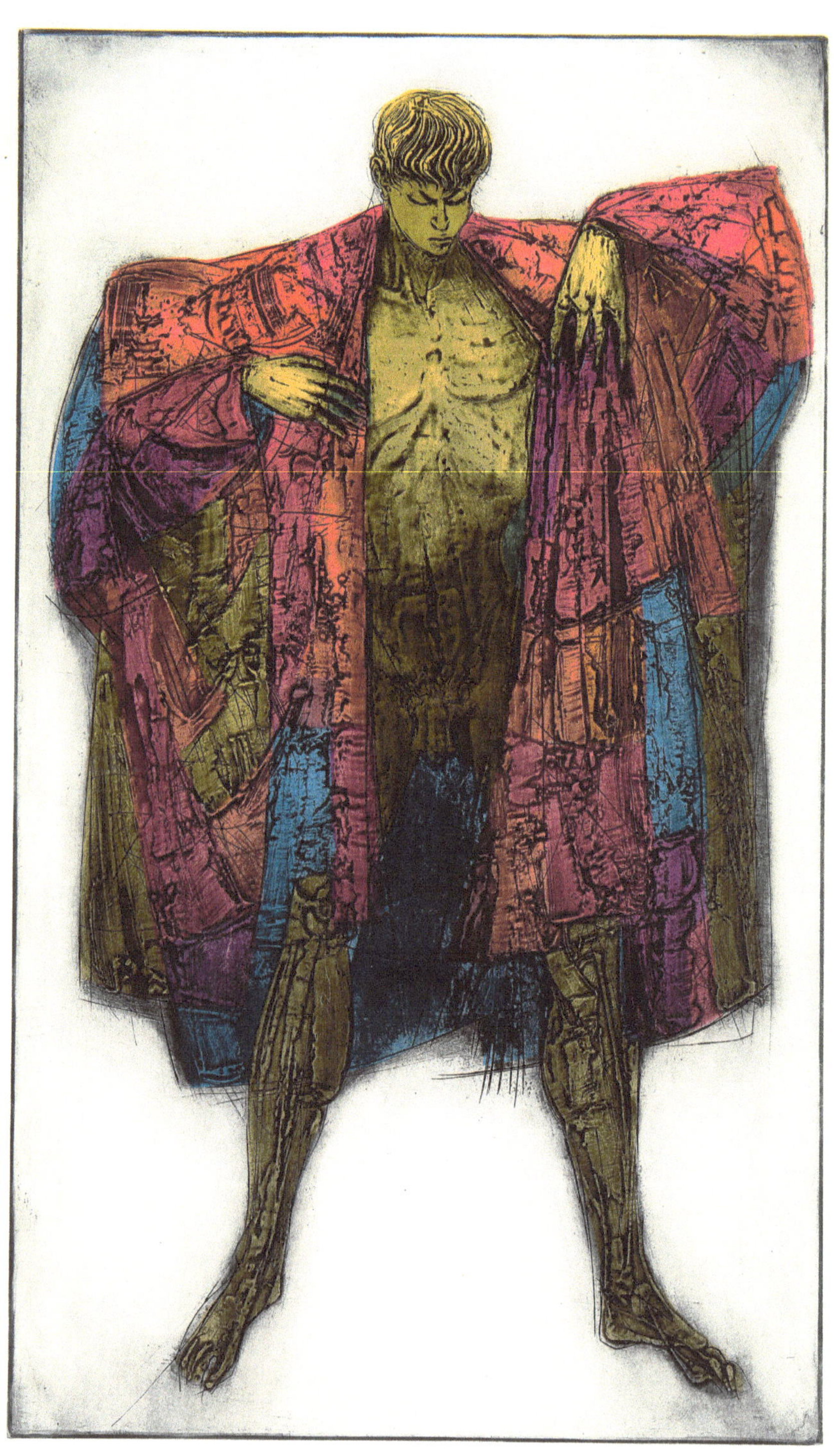

Dean Meeker "Joseph's Coat" Intaglio 20 x 34

Introduction

The following pages define the recent fine arts *Print Renaissance* that exploded onto the art scene in 1944 and continues today. I feel fortunate to have lived during this period of historical change in the fine arts, and to have had personal contact with many of the artists included on these pages. In addition, as an artist/printmaker myself, I was an active, though small part of this historical event. As such, I felt a responsibility to put my first hand thoughts of these significant times in writing, and to share with you some of the wonderful works from my collection of a few of the artists who made it happen. What follows is both educational and enjoyable, a nice mix for a light read and for viewing pleasure.

This book is not a comprehensive historical document, nor was it meant to be, cluttered by footnotes and details suited for textbooks. That information can be gained through other sources. I am not presumptuous enough to think that my modest collection represents the total picture of what occurred during this resurgence, or that the works represented on these pages are a comprehensive view of the many artists who were involved in the *Print Renaissance*. These pages contain merely a snapshot of a few of the notables who took part in this phenomenon. I realize that many fine printmakers and administrators who are noteworthy for their contributions to this occurrence are missing. Any omissions are the result of my own lack of personal exposure and awareness of the printmaking field, plus my limitation in the knowledge of what was occurring in pockets of regional activity throughout the country. Also, due to financial resources, certain works by printmakers of note were not within my reach.

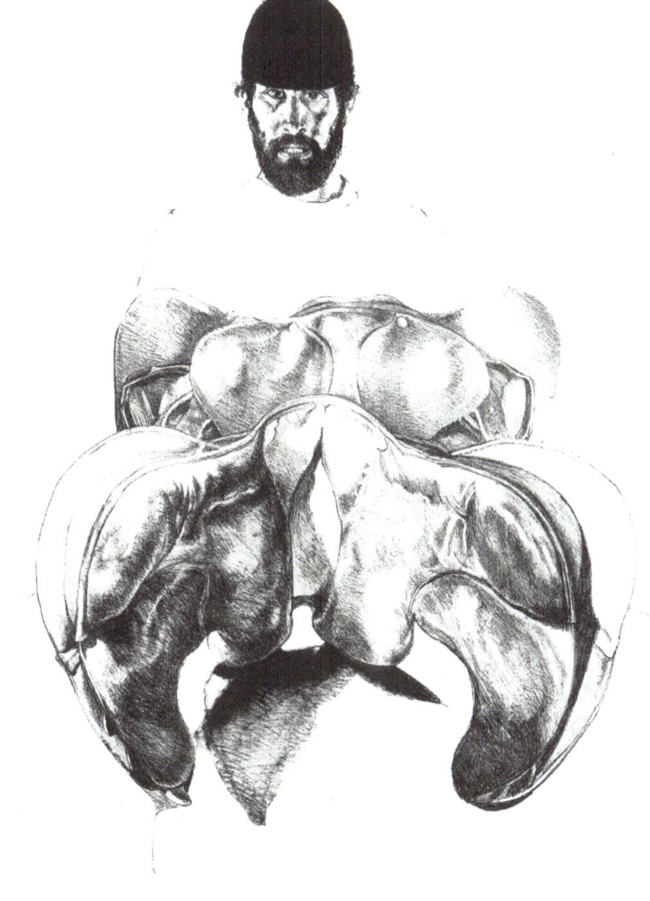

Sigmund Abeles "Self Portrait with Saddles"
Lithograph 30 x 22

Though somewhat confined within these parameters, the collection represents a cross section of the work of many of the creative and dedicated printmakers who were able to establish themselves and their work within the realm of this chapter in art history. It is my story, and as such, is a personal look at some of the prints and printmakers that I was fortunate enough to come in contact with, both personally and also through my exposure to the subject, over the past fifty-some years. My main purpose of this documentation is not specifically the artists, though they were key players, but the happening itself, and its art historical significance. It is the recognition of the event that I want to highlight, and secondarily a few notables who made it happen.

I leave it up to you the reader, to fill in the blanks with other noteworthy artist/printmakers that I did not have the pleasure of knowing, who were also contributors to this significant happening. There were many who played an important role in this phenomenon, and were instrumental in establishing printmaking as it is today, a widely accepted medium throughout the world.

I would like to persuade others to be keenly aware of how this recent change in the graphic arts occurred. It has more or less been somewhat taken for granted by present day practitioners of the medium as having always been a part of every artist's choice for expression. This is not so. Not long ago, printmaking was a sleeping giant, all but forgotten. But through the efforts of many selfless individuals, the giant no longer lays in slumber. It has awakened and has had a dramatic impact throughout the world in a very short period of time. Art history has been changed forever, and we are all enjoying the benefits. That has been, and continues to be, a notable feat indeed. Anyone practicing in the field of printmaking should be knowledgeable as to how this process arrived to where it is today

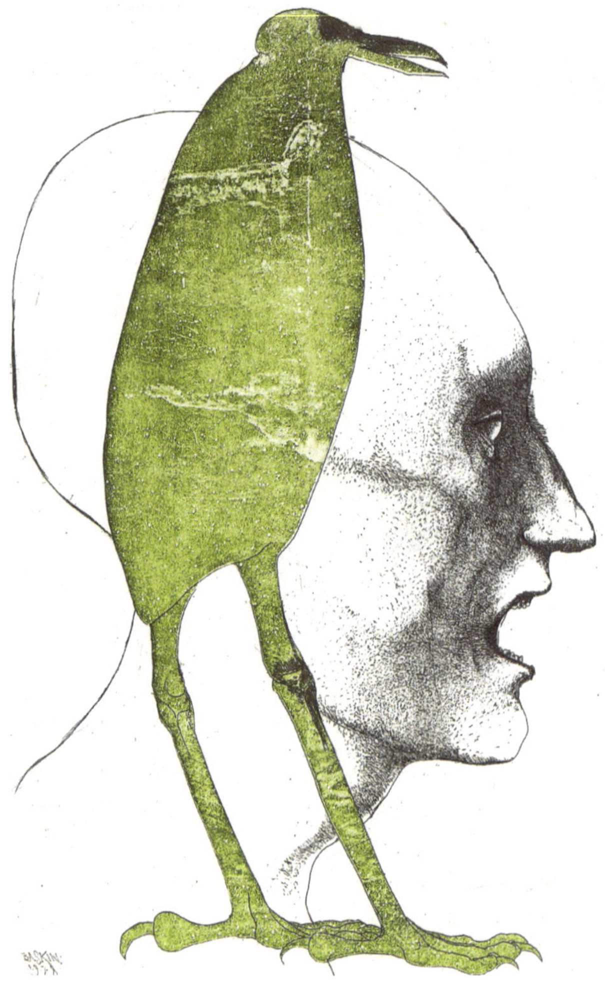

Leonard Baskin "Oracular Sybil" Etching 15 x 19 ½

Foreword

Warrington Colescott is an artist-printmaker of considerable accomplishment who lived, worked and became an important factor in the resurgence of printmaking following World War II, and continues today. He was an active participant as a student, an artist, and finally as an educator. As an educator, Colescott was instrumental along with Alfred Sessler, in developing the graphic art program at the University of Wisconsin-Madison into one of the largest and most dominant programs in the country. It was described as "world class" and as "number one in the nation" during his tenure. He was personally involved and was influential during the massive change that took place in the graphic arts during this time period. Warrington Colescott, along with a handful of others, helped to alter art history, and we owe them all a debt of gratitude.

Colescott has also been a strong supporter in encouraging me to write this book. That has been my good fortune. Following is an edited synopsis of some of the thoughts that he expressed to me in correspondence pertaining to that historical time period. These musings offer a brief look at his first hand experiences which contributed to the change in the graphic arts that we all enjoy today.

A Look Back

"I have been reading at your essay. You have covered a lot of ground and it makes a fascinating story – one we have all participated in with various intimate roles; as artists, teachers, critics, leaders and followers. Your history of this period is very complete and accurate. Looking back, we graduated from school into a gigantic war where we learned trades that had nothing to do with what the schools taught us."

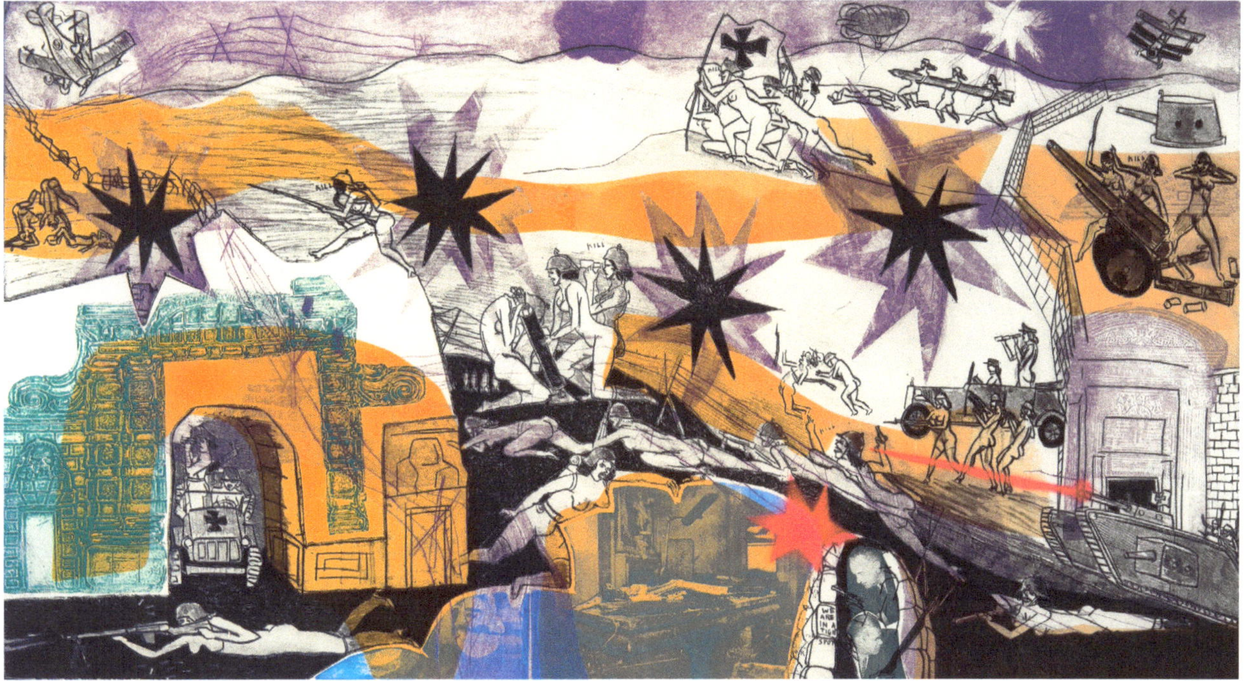

Warrington Colescott "Verdun: Attack" Intaglio Etching 17 ¾ x 33 ½

The War Years

"I had a bachelor's degree in art, but war became everything. In my four years of service, my subject was primarily the Bofors 40 mm automatic cannon. The Army had turned me into a very good teacher; studying the brochures that came with each new weapon, making it understandable to a battery of young men, talking the sergeants through their demos, and then going out to the range and shooting the damn thing. By comparison, art was simple."

University Time

"Following the war, I got a job at the University of Wisconsin, and found a compatible department and talented students that had come out of the same expanded focus that I had experienced. In this period, while trying to find painting again, I stumbled into the wonderful world of making prints. Prints and printmaking began to dominate my life. My prints, first screen prints, then etchings in combination with screens, then off into experimental combining of the two, and pushing into new vistas."

Brushes with Hayter

"We had some good times with Hayter. Went to his birthday party in New York. Visited his studio in Paris, somewhere or other on the Left Bank. While he was in America, he was a busy visitor, lecturing at many schools all over the country."

Other Developments

"It is good that you concentrate on American prints as the line of artists is definable and generational. The European developments were huge, led by the printing/publishing centers in Paris, that drew major graphic artists from Germany and Scandinavia, Spain, and eventually after the war, the world. Today the action is truly worldwide, and American print activity and publishing is correctly the central importance in the worldwide market.

The one unique influence of print art on American production is from the Mexicans. The artists of Mexico City were a strong element to Midwestern print sensibilities, particularly in their social and political ideas. The murals of Rivera and Orozko come to mind. It was in Frida Kahlo's studio that Trotsky was killed. There was regular traffic of American printmakers and painters to Mexico City to make prints in Mexican ateliers, where social and political concerns in cultural issues found an echo."

On Political and Social Issues

"The Works Progress Administration of Roosevelt's pre-war era was a political first, and the general political climate resulting from Viet Nam, as the American army entered the University world of art and politics. The Rivera mural in New York that Rockefeller destroyed can be mentioned also. Mauricio Lasansky was heavily influenced by the political graphic work of Picasso that morphed into the Antonio Frasconi woodcuts. It became America's turn, by artists who had a realization that the actions of war and politics had always drawn on the graphic arts to speak on elements of the human condition."

Summation

"We are in a period of sweetness and light in general, but the bones of graphic art still have things to say.

My best to you and your book."

Warrington

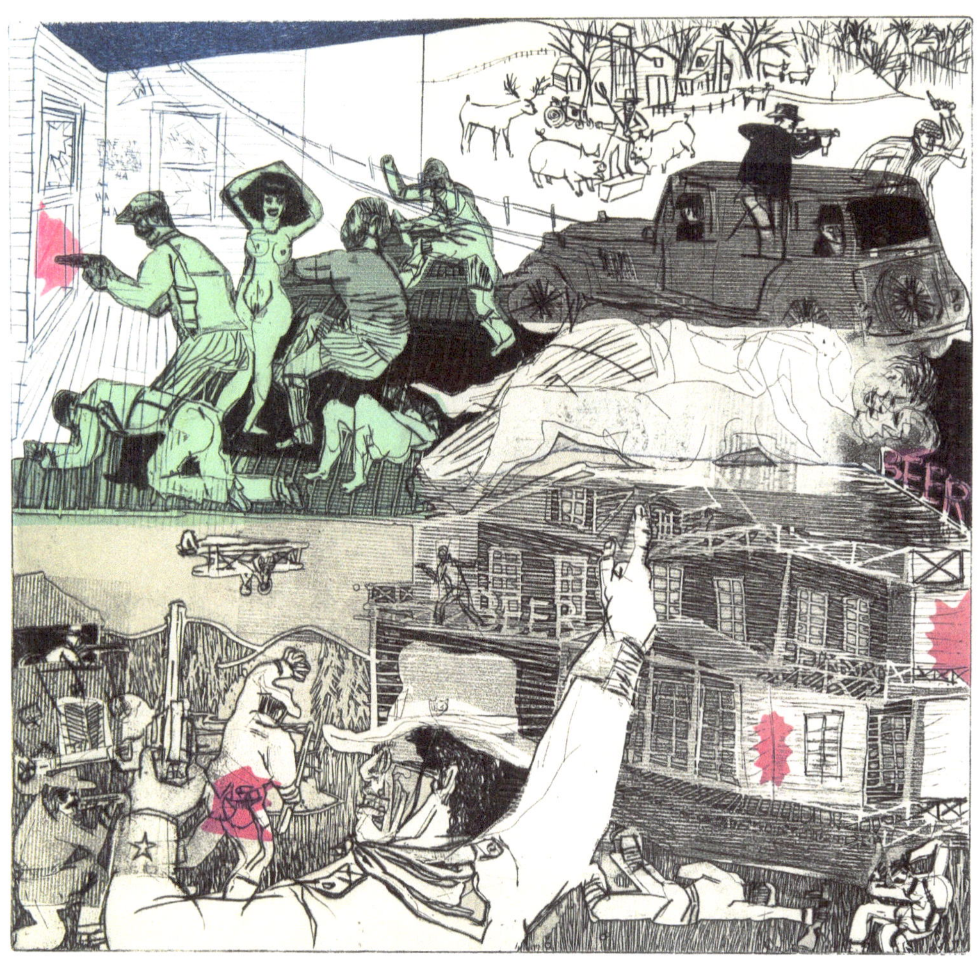

Warrington Colescott "Attack and Defense of Little Bohemia" Intaglio 20 ½ x 21 ¾

HISTORICAL BACKGROUND

"The seeds were sown…"

H I S T O R I C A L B A C K G R O U N D

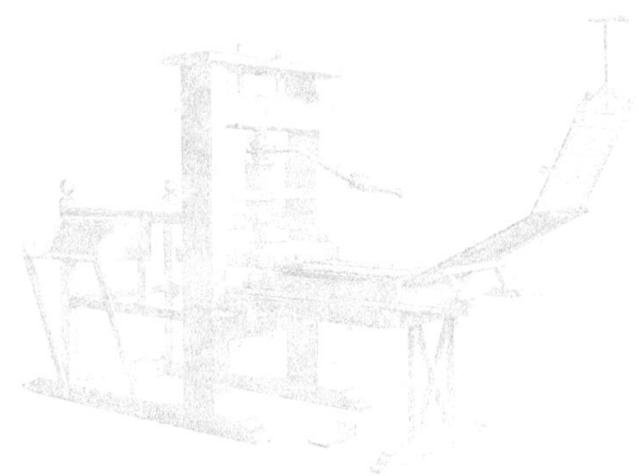

"The social climate of the nation following World War II, had a boom town atmosphere, and was ripe for the changes that were beginning to occur."

Historical Background

History is an account of past events, and as such, it requires time, distance and perspective to determine what has lasting importance. Whether as individuals or as part of a group, we are usually not conscious of the long term significance of our accomplishments or efforts. Change is often incremental, building and gathering momentum until it grows into something that is eventually identified and recognized as being historic.

One such occurrence was the renaissance and rebirth that occurred in the graphic arts beginning in the 1940's. This revival has been referred to as an explosion of sorts, as it had such an instant impact on the art community, and it would change forever the way the world would view the graphic work of art. The catalyst was Stanley William Hayter.

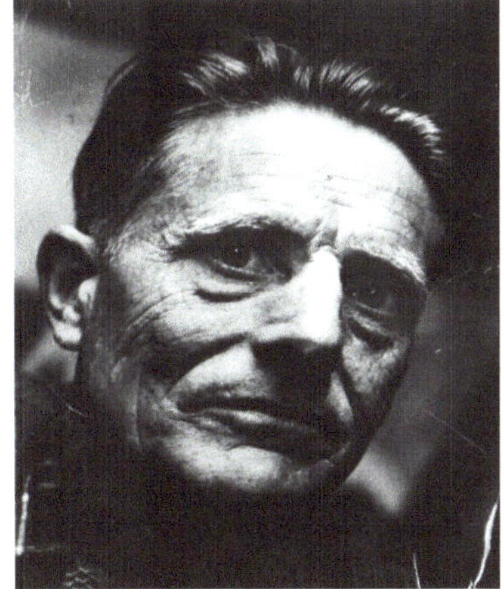
Stanley William Hayter

Beginning in 1927, Hayter had an experimental workshop in Paris named after the street address, No. 17, Rue Campagne-Premiere. It was to become the famous Atelier 17. In 1940, seeking refuge from the harsh realities of war, Hayter crossed the Atlantic and the Atelier 17 was recreated in New York. He was immediately surrounded by students and mature artists, some with printmaking backgrounds while others were novices in the medium, but they were all curious and ready to try their hand with this new method of making images. The Atelier blossomed under Hayter's direction, as he created an atmosphere of innovation and experimentation, plus a spirited work ethic.

In 1944, the printmakers at the Atelier, along with Hayter, presented a show of their work at the Museum of Modern Art. The resulting response to this exhibit by the critics and the art world in general, was one of instant awakening, creating a sudden awareness of the possibilities inherent to the medium. Attitudes abruptly changed regarding the graphic arts. The news of this new thinking and appreciation for the medium spread rapidly, reverberating across the nation, and ultimately the entire world. The show had transformed a medium valued for its reproductive capabilities, to a medium capable of fostering innovative artistic expression. Hayter's inclusion in art history, along with many of his followers, was assured with this single exhibit.

In retrospect, the *Printmaking Renaissance in America* was more of a happening than a planned event. Though some artists had tinkered with the graphic image as art over the course of many centuries, the medium itself was largely ignored, and looked upon by most of the art world as a lesser craft. Printmaking wasn't always as we see it now, as today we have a heightened receptivity to the graphic work of art. In a very short period of time, it is now practiced by most artists, and has become a specialty for many. It has indeed "exploded" onto the art scene and has become part of our daily lives, both as practitioners and devotees to the medium.

Besides Hayter's timely show, other factors were in simultaneous play to boost this sudden change in thinking. The years immediately following World War II were a time of change and innovation in America. Service men and women turned in their uniforms and looked to become contributing members in a new society, much more focused and worldly in their outlook. The GI Bill was a significant factor in the altering of many facets

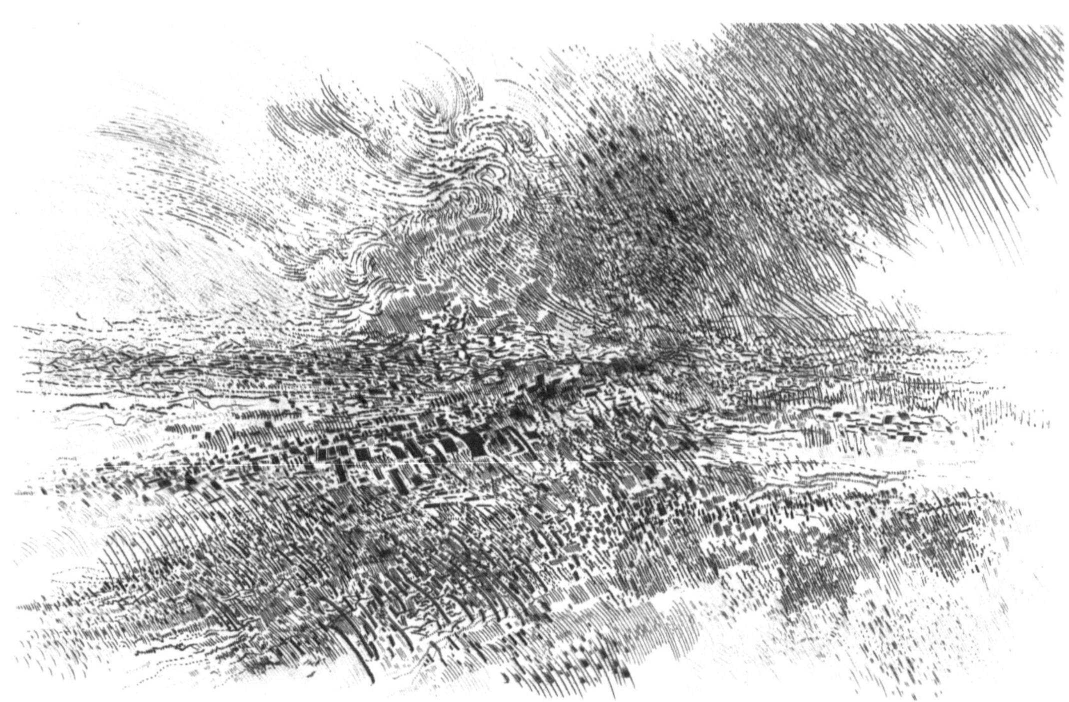

Gabor Peterdi "Rolling Sea" Etching/Engraving 15 ½ x 23 ½

in this new era as thousands of veterans flooded our Universities, curious to learn more about what they had seen and experienced in foreign lands. Their scope had broadened with this exposure, and the graphic arts were no exception. In Europe and Asia, American soldiers were exposed to hundreds of museums, filled with years of graphic history. Their visits to these museums introduced them to prime examples of graphic works by Rembrandt, Durer and Japanese Ukiyo-e colored woodcuts. Many were fascinated with what they saw, and upon their return home looked to their Universities for further knowledge and education, which resulted in a major change from the accepted curriculum of yesterday.

The Universities were initially caught off guard, and were ill equipped to handle this influx of students and their demands. Certain artist/instructors accepted the challenge, and stepped forward to address the issue and ease the pressures. They were not aware that they were teaching and breaking ground in a period of time that would change art history forever.

The arts were not alone in their lack of preparedness following the war. The sudden change from being a nation at war to one of peaceful abundance happened virtually overnight. The onslaught of returning veterans sent the country scrambling to fulfill their basic needs. The entire country was lacking in skilled workers in many different fields, and various industries felt the enormous pressure of the urgent demands of this new consumer population. A good example was the housing market and its related industries that struggled to meet the overwhelming requirements of these returning veterans. Quonset huts sprang up across University campuses in response to the flood of students taking advantage of the GI Bill. These students had a thirst for knowledge and a desire to make up for lost time. It was a new world order, and they wanted to secure their position in it.

Simultaneously, Kline, DeKooning, Pollack and other artists were fanning the fire, introducing and enjoying the new freedom of abstract expressionism. This movement, with its new innovations in painting, soon made

America the center of the art world. We saw ourselves as leaders of change in the arts, and we thrived on our own image. It was a time of independence and exuberance, and artists reflected the mood of the period. With the advent of the new avant-garde of abstraction, drawing was deemed all but dead, or at the very least, it lay in a coma.

But it was only a short time before the pendulum swung in the other direction. Drawing once again gained popularity, and as one result, the discipline and unique qualities of the printmaking media captured the curiosity of artists. The *Print Revolution* had begun.

Culture in America became a hot commodity in the '50s and '60s. The art market boomed like a frontier town leading the world in innovation. Demand for paintings far exceeded supply, and prices escalated. The climate was indeed ripe for the fine arts multiple. The few who were able to recognize this stepped forward and seized the moment.

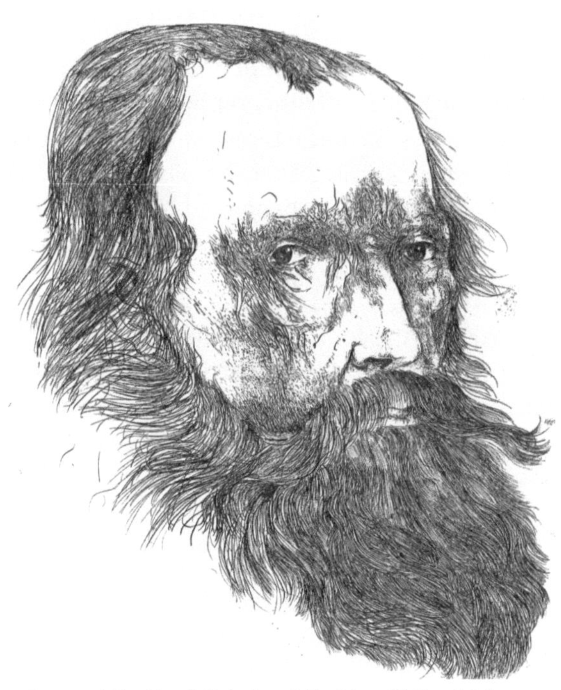

Leonard Baskin "Goltzious" Etching 17 ¾ x 14 ½

Meanwhile, Universities and art schools were developing printmaking courses in response to student demand. For the first time it became possible for students of fine arts to major in printmaking. Many teachers, including Gabor Peterdi, whose book on printmaking processes became the "bible" for most, along with Leonard Baskin, and Mauricio Lasansky, had studied with Hayter at Atelier 17. They and their peers, Will Barnet, Karl Schrag and Antonio Frasconi, changed the blueprint of art curriculum in American universities. These were among the first generation pioneers following Hayter's success. The nation's learning centers were soon in tune with one another, and successful University programs were shared, and set in motion across the country.

Many facets of change for the development of the graphic media were happening simultaneously, and each piece was falling into place to form a cohesive whole. One such innovation outside the realm of academics was the concept of workshops. It was one of the key factors in the acceptance of the printed image by the skeptical art purchasing public.

Tatyana Grossman founded Universal Limited Art Editions, (ULAE), in 1957, and convinced "name" artists to involve themselves in the medium of lithography. At first, these artists resisted, but Grossman prevailed and their first efforts produced a joint venture, a collaboration in book form, with Larry Rivers, the painter, and Frank O'Hara, the poet. Robert Blackburn was the shops first master printer, and the results proved highly successful. With this first successful venture, one artist followed another to Grossman's studio, and as a group, they soon became the country's preeminent painter-printmakers.

Their first ventures were in lithography, but that would soon change as artists became more familiar with the various print mediums available to express themselves. Artists such as Jasper Johns, Robert Rauschenberg, and Jim Dine, among others, became interested in intaglio etching and ULAE expanded their facilities to meet their needs. Helen Frankenthaler, influenced by the Japanese masters of Ukiyo-e prints, followed, and ULAE produced her first woodcuts, masterful works that inspired many others to try their hand with the medium.

In 1960 June Wayne co-founded the Tamarind Lithography Workshop, and as Director her aim was to rescue the fine art of lithography. She, along with co-founder Clinton Adams as Associate Director, and Garo Antreasian as Technical Director, trained a work force of printers who in turn set up lithography workshops across America. This was accomplished at a time when the prevailing attitude was, "real artists don't draw on rocks". This quote has been credited to Robert Rauschenberg, who went on to become one of the greatest printmakers of our time. But Wayne persisted in her goal, and she is credited with single handedly reviving the medium of lithography.

Following in the footsteps of Ulae and Tamarind, other notable print shops joined forces with the concept, and opened their doors to artists. Soon workshops sprang up all across the country. In 1962, Crown Point Press was started by Kathan Brown in her Berkely basement; in 1966, Ken Tyler, Sidney Felson and Stanley Grinstein began Gemini GEL in Los Angeles; in 1968, Donald J. Saff opened Graphicstudio at the University of South Florida; and in 1970, Jack Lemon began Landfall Press in Chicago. Initially, these shops specialized in specific media, but most would diversify to offer artists a range of processes with which to experiment. The idea came to fruition, and the workshop artist/printer collaboration was in full forward motion.

It was only a matter of time before the commercial aspects of the multiple image and the resulting benefits caught the interest of art dealers. Once that occurred, demand for the printed image came into full play. It was an obvious business innovation. The product of print editions offered affordable works of art, in new mediums, by noted artists, to a wider range of collectors. The fine arts print was a natural for the commercial marketplace. The stamp of approval of established painters and now their galleries, coupled with a booming economy and the bountiful spirit which prevailed, created a charged atmosphere for the art of printmaking. The multiple became like a snowball, rolling rapidly down a mountainside, gathering momentum.

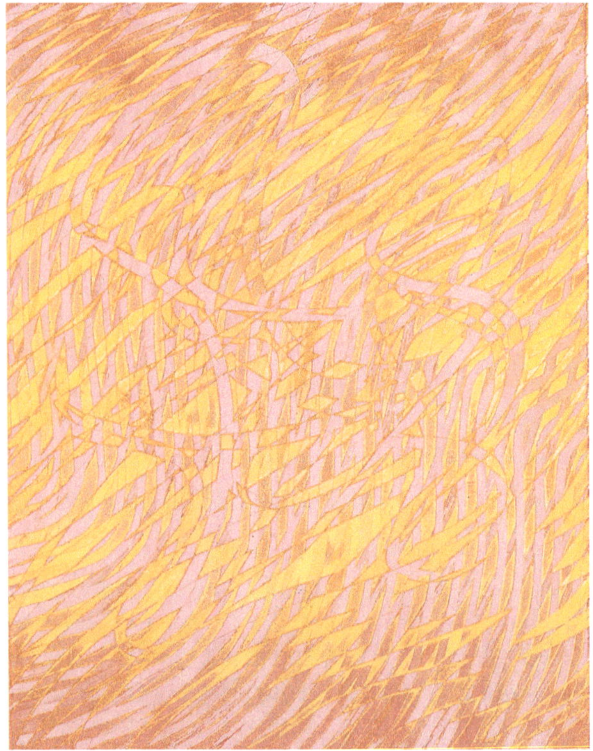

Stanley William Hayter "Flux"
Viscosity Etching 21 ½ x 17

THE SECOND WAVE

"A time to nurture…"

T H E S E C O N D W A V E

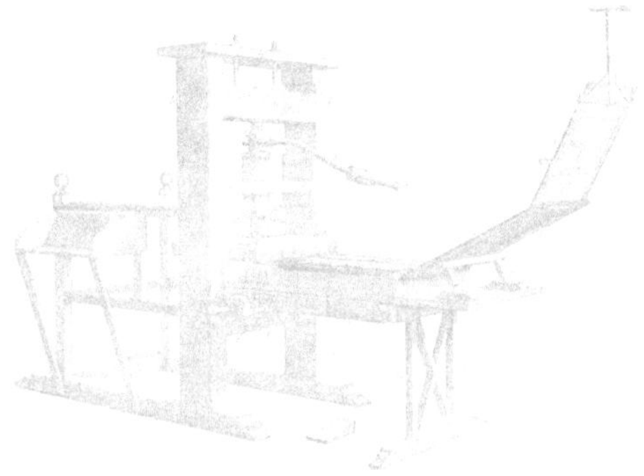

"The seeds had been sown, and the '50s and '60s were a time for nurturing, taking the fine arts print to another level."

The Second Wave

The late 1950s and '60s were a time of awakening and participation. By this time printmaking had gained a foothold in the art world. Artist-printmakers were still looked upon by the few purists in the art community as a step child, but the initial thrust toward universal acceptance had been made, and those who doubted this new order were being left on the sidelines to sit and wonder. They were soon overwhelmed by the rapid changes occurring around them. Printmaking was fully recognized and moving ahead with innovational opportunities unheard of in other art disciplines. The artists became opportunists, as almost everyone wanted to get involved with prints. With that newfound acceptance, the graphic image flourished. Printmaking was no longer an explosion, but rather a series of aftershocks occurring around the globe. Through the efforts of Hayter, a giant was born that even he had not dreamed of.

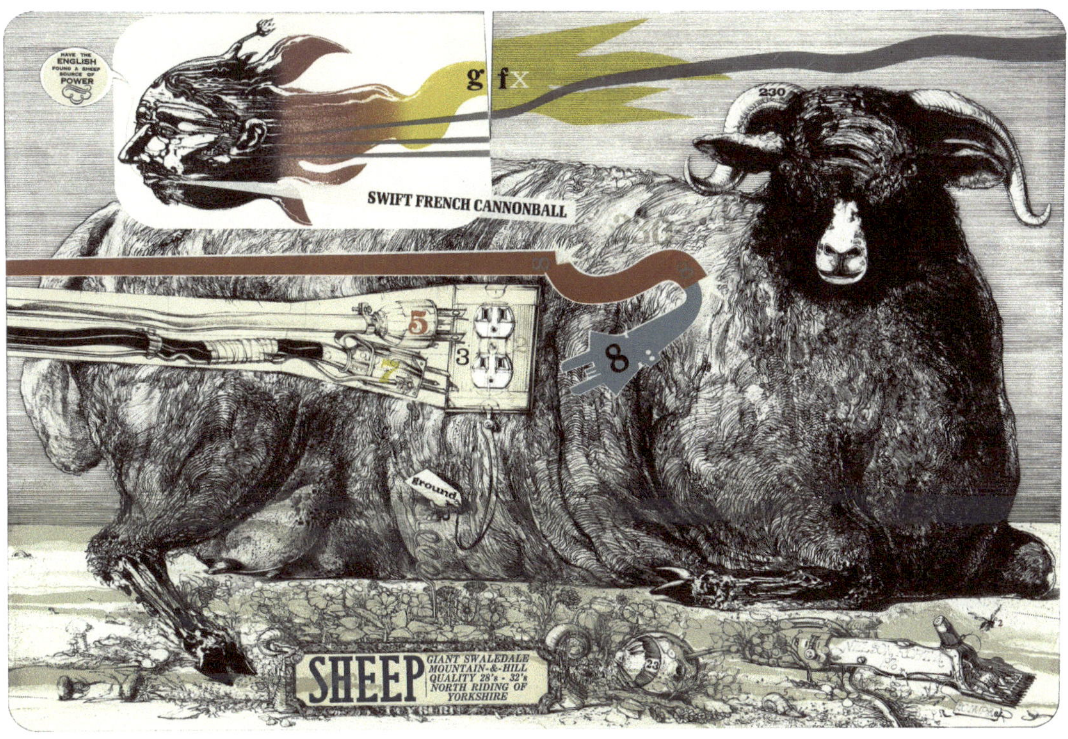

Robert A. Nelson "Sheep" Lithograph/Collage 25 ½ x 36 ½

The pioneers, Baskin, Peterdi, Lasansky, and others such as Barnet, Shrag, and Frasconi were now well established and enjoying the fruits of recognition by a growing cadre of artists, both established and of the student variety. They, along with a handful of others, were also enjoying the new benefits of wide commercial success. These printmaking pioneers, who only a short time before were working in relative obscurity, had already become "Old Masters", and as a result were being paid homage befitting their new status. Their tenacious dedication and meaningful contributions to this major change in the field of art had taken on historical significance.

At the time, it was difficult to pull together the various fragments which were occurring independent of one another to form a complete picture of these rapid changes in mindset towards the graphic arts. The rotation from the wings to center stage still had gaps to fill. The second generation of printmakers that came into play in the late '50s and '60s still had much to offer, and much to gain. The seed had been cast, but now it had to be nurtured. The new wave of printmakers carried the torch well, and progressed the medium in giant steps. No sooner would one technique be mastered, than a new concept would present itself. The sixties

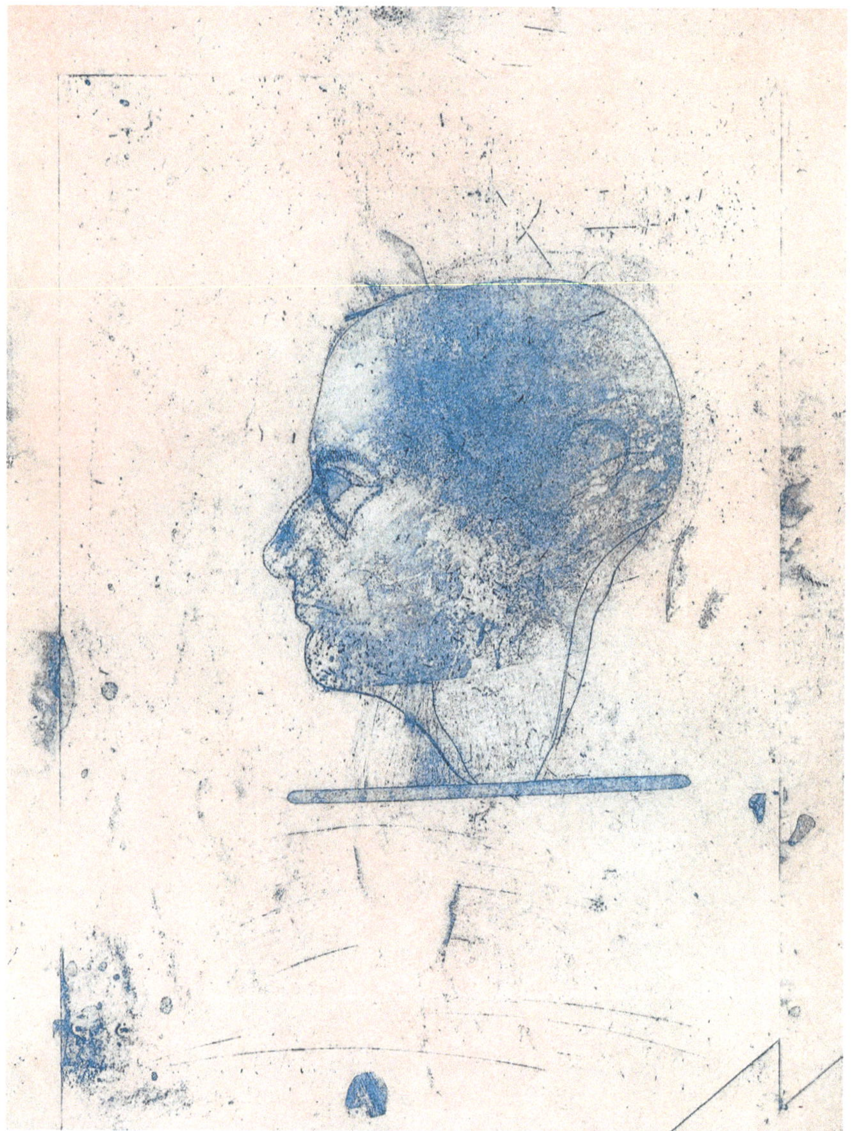

John Paul Jones "Blue Head" Etching 16 x 12

introduced new technical innovations into the mix: offset lithographs, silkscreens, and collagraphs, to name a few. These techniques, along with others, were often combined into a single print to make exciting new imagery. These new methods were initiated, developed and further refined by these second generation printmakers, who were of a more adventurous nature than their predecessors. They were influenced by the day to day environment of abstract expressionism, which was still riding a tidal wave of popularity in the field of painting. They also benefitted from the success of the original pioneers, and coupled with the surrounding conditions of their time, sprinted forward. Any surface was fair game. As long as it could be printed, it found its way into a print workshop and onto a press bed. It was a time of discovery and freedom of expression.

In tandem, teaching institutions were developing key changes in their art departments with the addition of instructors specializing in individual mediums. They were no longer playing catch-up as they had in the years following World War II, but instead they were carving out their own agenda. The student demand continued to grow, but now it was being met head-on, the Universities now equipped to handle this influx of expanded growth. Printmaking had become a high priority, and high quality instructors with excellent printmaking backgrounds and experience were now available. The art schools, colleges and universities with administrative visionaries were among those to prosper as they filled their faculty with notable printmakers. Students wanted to follow and study with these name artists.

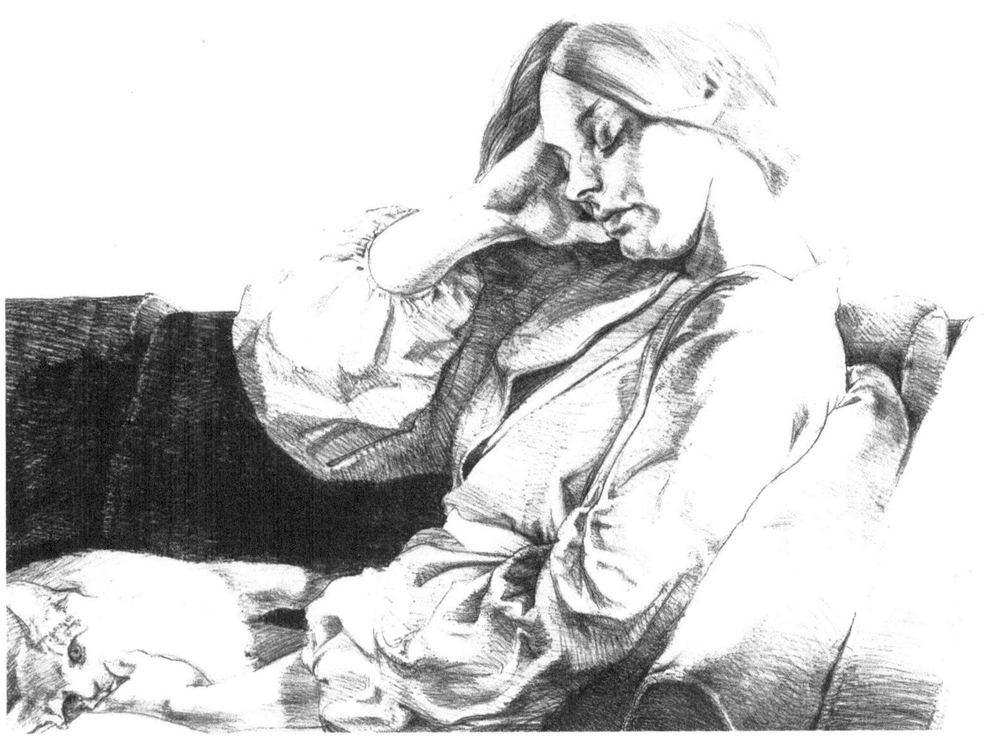

Sigmund Abeles "Woman with Cat" Lithograph 19 ¾ x 29 ½

Simultaneously, national shows were organized for printmakers, usurping what was once the domain of the painters. Exhibitions were initiated by colleges, commercial galleries and museums across the country. Awards for significant work were given and certain artists repeatedly won prizes, establishing themselves as leaders among their peers. Reputations were built as commercial galleries and museums began to recognize those leaders, the galleries exhibiting them and the museums collecting their works. Again, the cream rose to the top.

To single out even a few of the printmakers who rose to prominence during this era would open the subject to much discussion and debate. There were many outstanding printmakers who took advantage of the favorable circumstances available, and made a reputation for themselves as well as the institutions they represented. National exhibitions could not accommodate the growing ranks of printmakers. The void was filled by regional exhibitions, which provided another venue for artists to achieve notoriety. The entire printmaking community benefitted and thrived in this atmosphere, and technical breakthroughs were shared within the field of printmaking, as within a close knit family.

The 60's catapulted seamlessly into the '70s. It was now time for the third generation to take its turn at the helm, and guide the ship along the rapidly flowing current. These printmakers readily accepted the baton, and sprinted into the era referred to as the "Golden '70s"*.

*A comment made by artist/printmaker David H. Becker

THE GOLDEN '70s

"A time to harvest..."

T
H
E

G
O
L
D
E
N

'
7
0
s

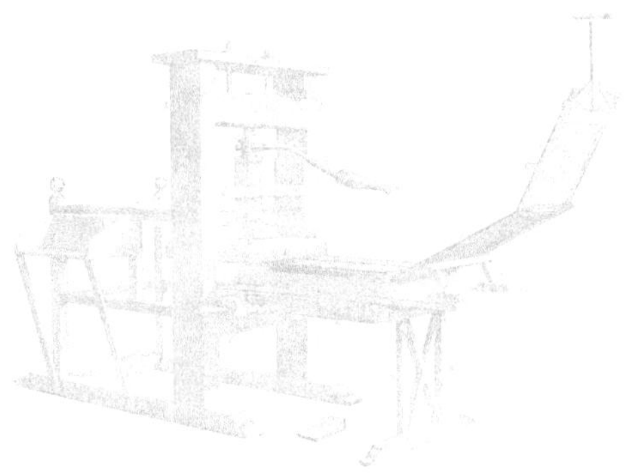

"Printmaking was fully revived and building on its rapid growth as the Universities flourished, and the few practitioners had become many."

The Golden '70s

A full generation had not yet passed, but a new influx of artist/printmakers was waiting their turn. For this new group, the '70s were a time of greater opportunities. Printmaking was well established in the college curriculum, and in some cases had spread further, being introduced in some of the more progressive high schools. The battle had been fought and won. Printmakers had risen to importance in the arts and were now busily occupied, adding significantly to their own history.

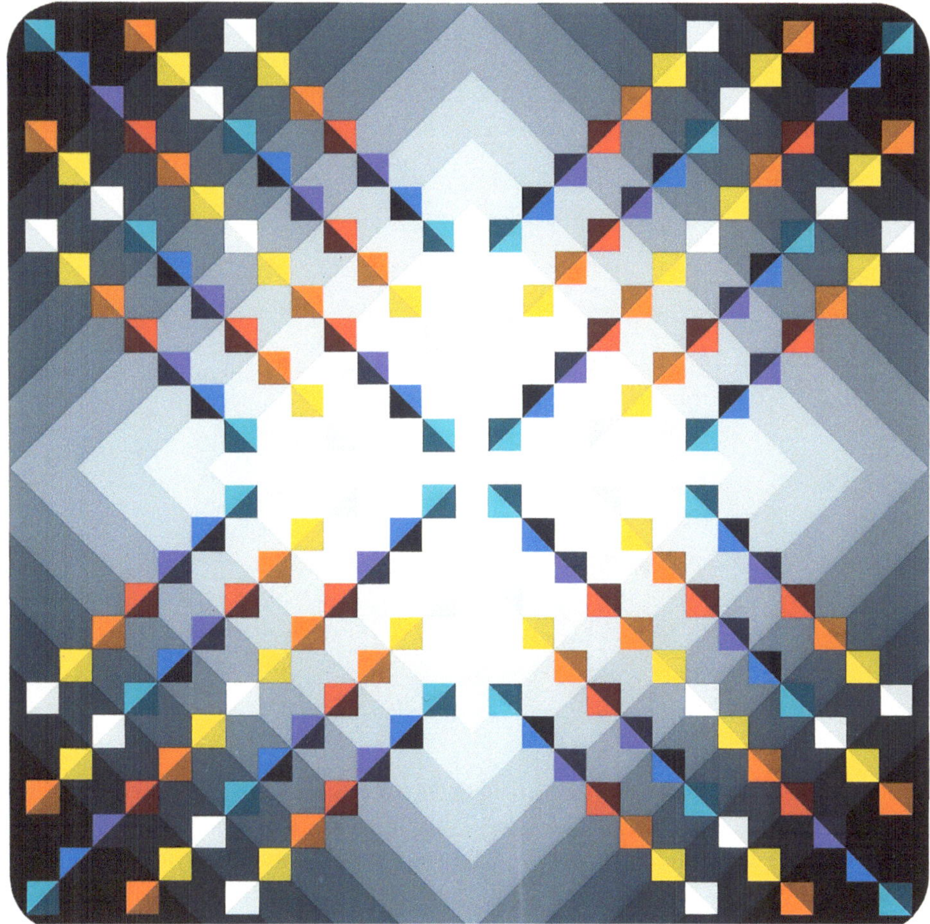

Marko Spalatin "Pulsar II" Silkscreen 20 ½ x 20 ½

Universities, galleries, museums, collectors, and the printmaker's peers, the painters and sculptors, were among the converts. The public had also hitched a ride, and was enjoying the benefits of the fine arts print. It had been twenty-six years since Hayter and his disciples had sent their message that changed the art world. Just a blink of the eye in the history of art, but for printmaking the changes that took place during that period could not be measured by a timepiece. Printmaking had progressed with lightning speed. The universe had expanded for the arts and the choices for the fledgling artist were never better. In printmaking it was time to harvest the proceeds from the investment made by those who had opened the door to this revised medium, and there were many new artists who were ready to add their names to the annals of printmaking history.

The '70s were a close duplication of the '60s, except for sheer numbers of participants and momentum. There were many more active printmakers seeking to make their mark. With increased public awareness, it was a time of abundance. Exhibition opportunities had multiplied, and had now become international in scope, with entire countries vying for a slice of the pie. It was a welcome mat for the artist, increasing their reach worldwide. The commercial galleries blossomed as there were more high quality artworks, modestly priced and readily

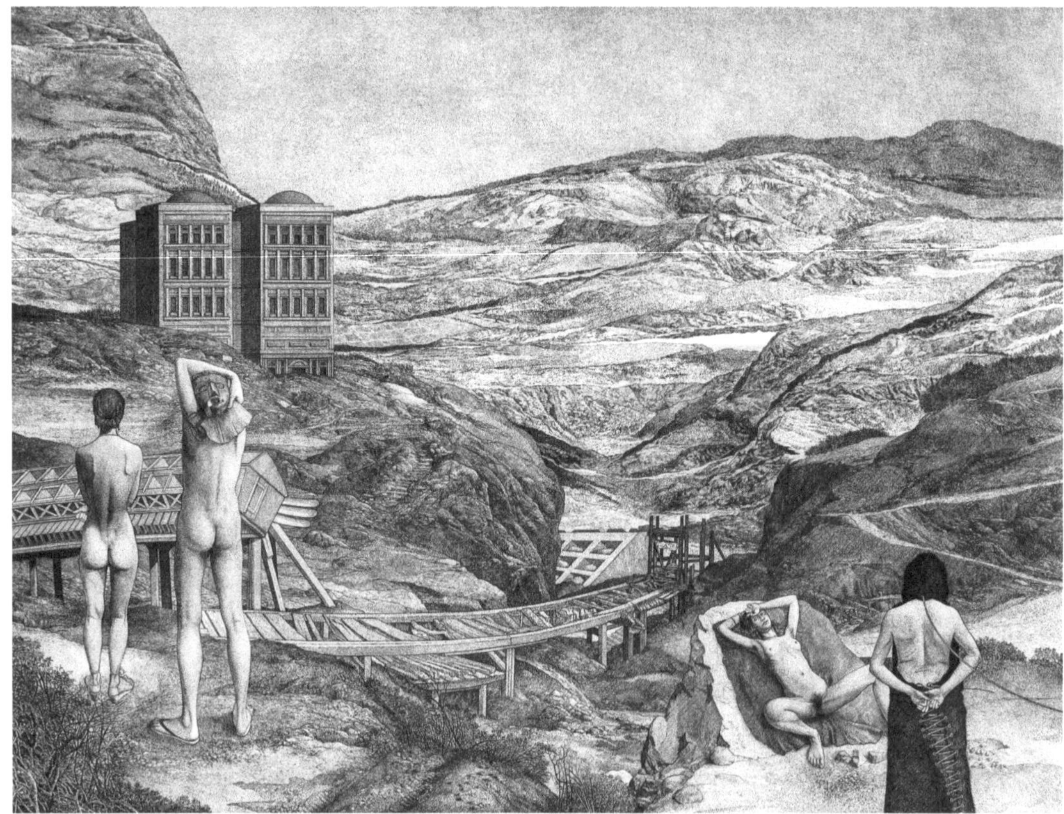

David Becker "A Foregone Conclusion" Etching/Engraving 16 ¾ x 22 ¾

available from this new wave of artist/printmakers. Many galleries began to specialize in fine art prints. The medium lent itself to minimal storage, and maximum artist exposure, thereby allowing for a larger range of choice for their consumer clients. In addition, museums with limited budgets could now bring big name and high quality art works to their communities, while also beginning or adding to their own modest permanent collections. The smallest institutions, and collectors with modest means, were able to become players. It was a time of grass roots expansion. Printmaking was changing the nature of public acceptance of art, and the byproduct was education through exposure. The knowledge gained would eventually become the key to the present and future relevance of the fine arts print.

Art competitions continued to offer an important means to establish an artist's reputation in this new decade. The exhibitions also provided Universities the means to bring current trends in printmaking from across the nation to their students on their own turf. These shows were an important teaching aid, in many cases planned, developed and carried to completion by the students themselves. This hands-on experience was a valuable teaching tool. It created among the students an awareness of the importance of the medium, and as a result, the field continued to attract followers in droves. The spark that had once struggled for its very existence was turning into a full-fledged bonfire.

At this point printmaking was universally accepted and treated as though it had always been here. The attitude among artists and their supporters was becoming matter of fact. The struggles of the many pioneers and their accomplishments were taken for granted to some degree. Their accomplishments were not necessarily diminished, but rather put on temporary hold while the art world attended to the business of the present. No one cared at the time to read much about this phenomenon in the field of printmaking as they were fully involved in the process of doing it. Within a few short years these artists had taken traditional printmaking from hundreds of years of quiet hibernation to a period of explosive growth and change. The significant changes in the medium had occurred so rapidly that historians hadn't the time to thoroughly reflect on and document this extraordinary episode in the field of art.

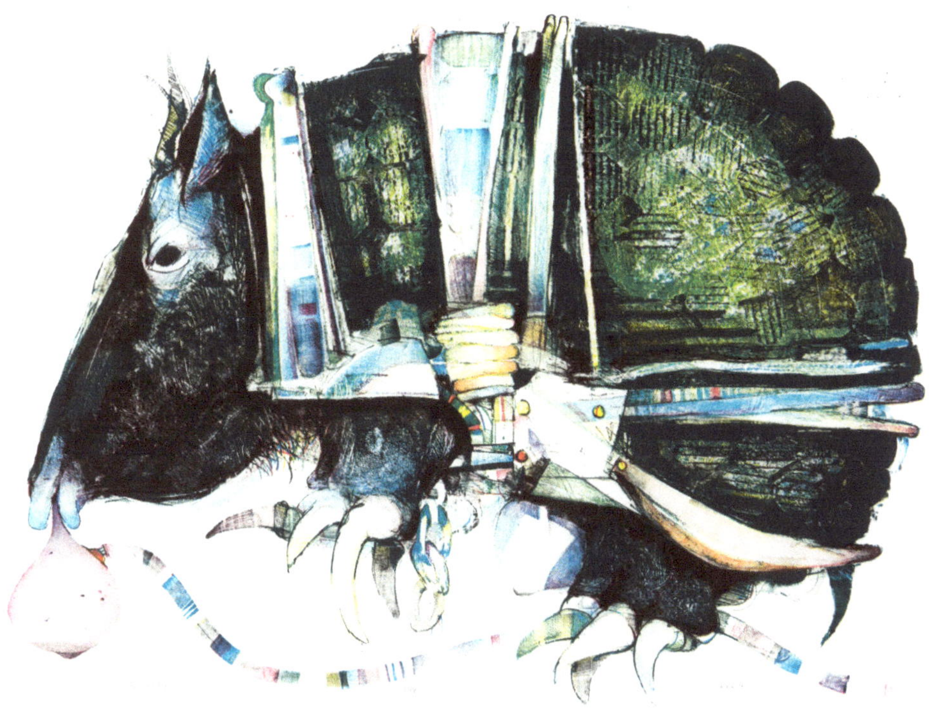

John Doyle "Armadillo" Lithograph 30 x 40

Printmaking had become a dominant force in the '70s and early '80s. It had come full circle from an also ran to take its place on a level with the other art media. Documentation of its revival would have to wait for another day.

That day is now. We owe it to history and to the key players involved to sit back and think about where we have been, where we are today, and what could be possible for tomorrow. It has truly been an era of accomplishment and progress, one that boggles the mind with its rapid transition from mediocrity to dominance. It is a wonder that the many autonomous factors could somehow mesh together to make the whole. But it was meant to be, this rebirth of a medium that has risen to dominance like the flash of a lightning bolt, to make art history. It has been an awesome accomplishment indeed, unsurpassed in the art world.

We are now living in an era of rapid change, and one of abundance. Printmakers no longer have to accept leftovers, or use the broom closets in universities to house our presses. They now have first class facilities, first class teachers, and are producing first class art work. The world has changed for the better. The title of printmaker is now acknowledged with pride and universal admiration.

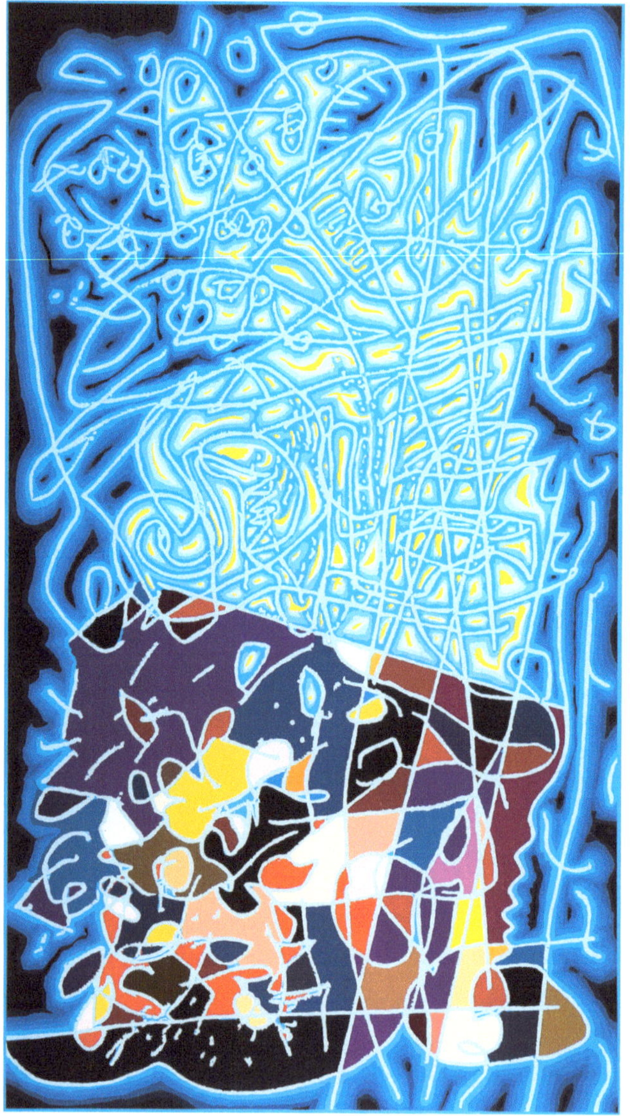

Arthur Secunda "Metamorphosis des Fleurs" Silkscreen 47 x 29

TOMORROW

"All we have to do is listen"

T
O
M
O
R
R
O
W

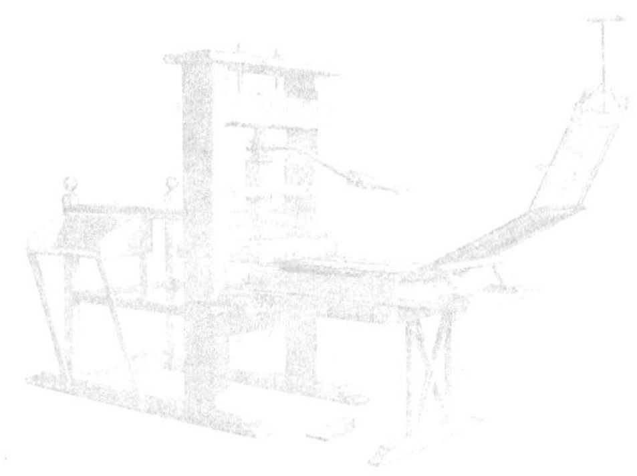

"The graphic media continues to grow, attacking our senses, rapidly becoming the dominant force in our lives."

Tomorrow

No other media in the field of the fine arts promises more to the artist in the future than the graphic arts. Commercial innovations in printmaking processes are driving changes in fine arts in a manner undreamed of just a short while ago. It seems that each day we are faced with new tools and new challenges to explore. The digital process is the most recent new technology to revolutionize the world of graphics. The possibilities of the digital image appear boundless, and it is innovations such as this that point to the unlimited opportunities within the graphic media.

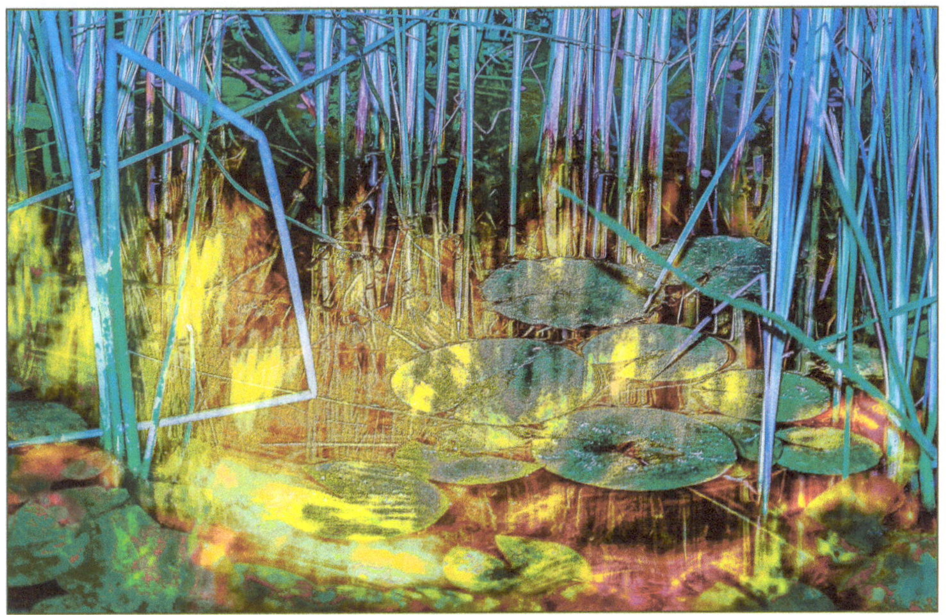

Steven Agard "manifestation II 2186" Archival Ink Jet Print 30 x 40

Not unlike the introduction of offset lithography and silk screen printing in the past, the entry of digital into the mix of tools for the artist has its detractors. However, the incorporation of digital processes into the field of printmaking is unstoppable. The youth of today are surrounded by digital technology, in a world where vintage processes have been supplanted by new technologies and electronics. This creates an atmosphere of excitement for seasoned printmakers as well as students, and offers additional challenges to instructors, who must keep abreast of these changes. The purists in our midst may ignore the signs, and malign the process, preferring to fight change rather than venture far from their comfort zone. Others will seize the moment and embrace this new technology, becoming pioneers in this new territory.

The secret is to keep an open mind and welcome the opportunity to seek a compatible marriage, combining the new with the old. As with any tool, there is the danger of overplaying its use. But to sit by and not explore these innovations would be a major error. For a creative mind, new tools create new avenues for personal artistic expression.

The history of the print is rooted deeply in the past, but in its rebirth, it has proven to be well suited to the present. No other media offers artists such an engaging and fluctuating bag of possibilities to express themselves. Printmaking fits the time, and is continually reinventing itself to be an exciting prospect for the future.

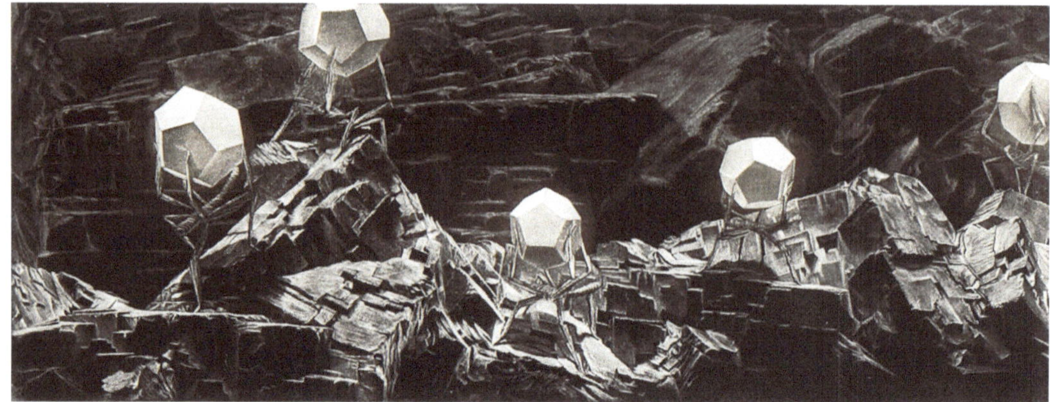

Douglas Bosley "LD 4334_4366" Mezzotint 6 x 16

The basis of art is communication. Graphics define communication. Printmaking utilizes graphics. Printed media, photography, the written word, three dimensional objects, and even music are being combined to create new imagery in printmaking that literally defies the imagination. Those who are willing to incorporate what is going on around them are integrating mind boggling technical innovations into their finished product. Common subject matter and everyday objects are being inserted in new combinations each day, presenting a new perception and scope to the artist's imagery. We now have the means to do that, and much more. Just the thought ignites a fire in the creative spirit.

The graphic arts, along with all artistic endeavors, recognize no boundaries, and have no limitations. It is a medium of transfer, an evolving species that invites new methods. It beckons to the adventuresome among us to take the processes further, faster.

No one can know the future, but I see a future filled with graphics. We are surrounded daily with billboards, signs, books, magazines and newspapers, all communicating messages to us. We were born with graphics, and they have been a part of our daily visual experiences since birth. Graphics are the great communicator, and a major influence in our lives. We cannot escape the message. It is talking to us; almost shouting.

All we have to do is listen.

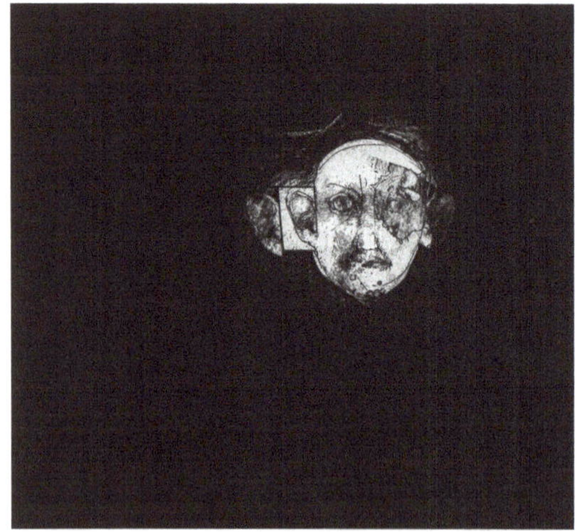

Robert Marx "Rogue"
Etching 12 x 12

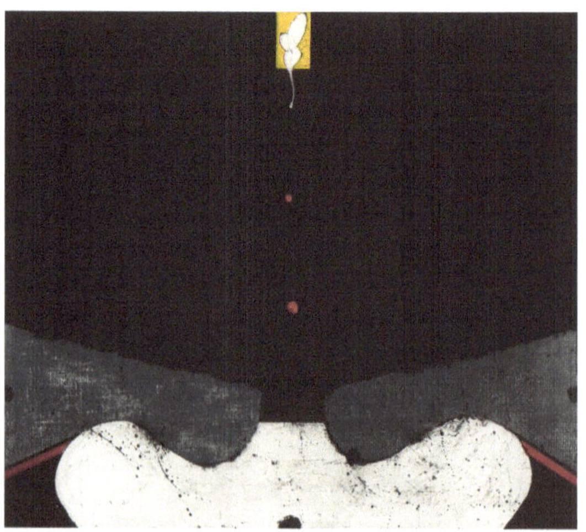

Tetsuo Araki "Space Series"
Intaglio 16 ¾ x 20 ¾

ARTISTS SHOWCASE AND BIOGRAPHIES

"National Treasures"

A R T I S T S S H O W C A S E

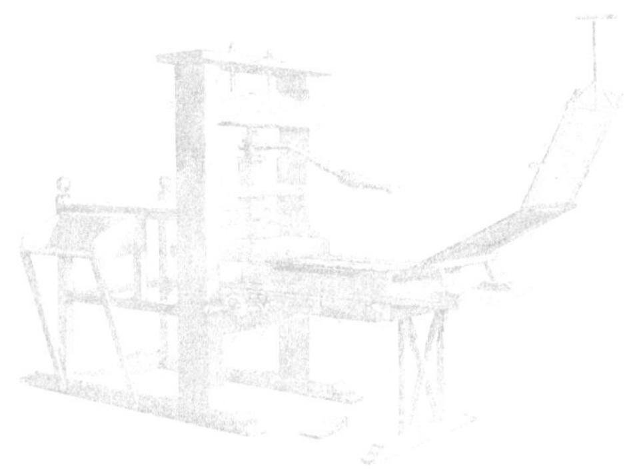

"A few of the notable key players and their role in the historical Print Renaissance in America - A Revolution."

Artist Showcase and Biographies

The following pages contain images of prints that are part of the Ronald L. Ruble Collection and feature some of the artists who were involved in the defining of *The Print Renaissance in America– A Revolution.* Each work is associated with a short biography of the artist and also alludes to a general time period of their contribution.

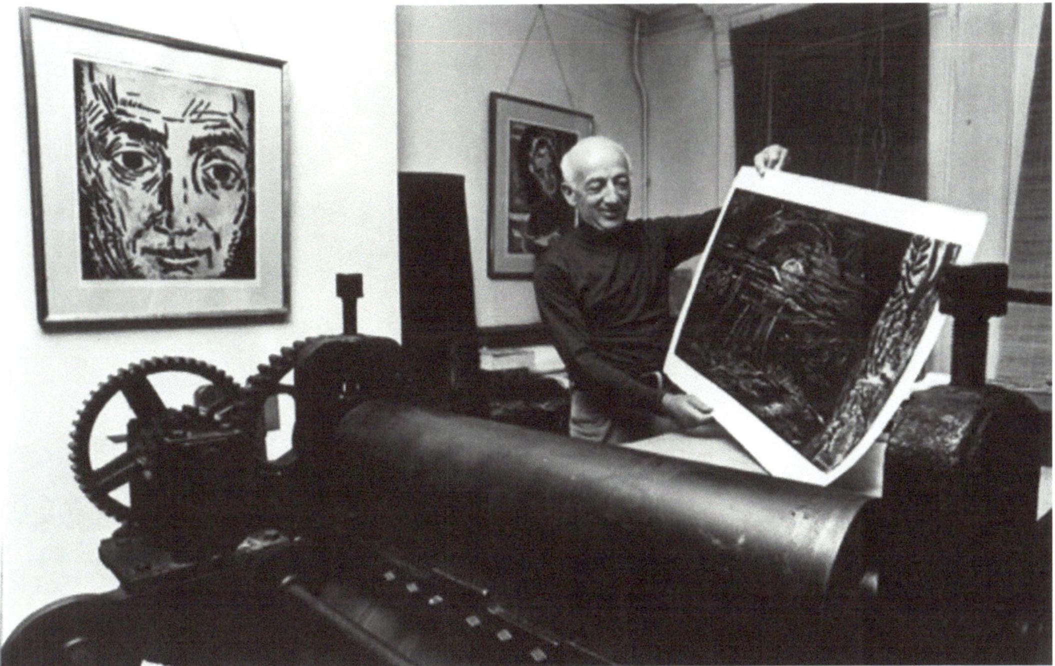

Karl Schrag pulling a print at Atelier 17

My research has shown that each of these artists have exhibited in important exhibitions, won significant awards and most have received academic honors and degrees as educators. As a result, I have purposefully kept this type of information to a minimum, so that the reader would not be burdened by similarities that could become repetitious. What you will find is concise information which highlights each artist's contribution to the printmaking field, and personal data to help define their uniqueness. If the reader wishes to seek additional specifics regarding any of the artists featured here, that information is as close as your computer. There is a wealth of information on the internet concerning these individuals, and it can be easily found using a search engine, gallery promotions pertaining to the artist, or the artist's personal website.

The showcase is an impressive display of creative images, with examples of every printmaking medium and process: etching, woodcuts, photography, silkscreen, digital imagery, lithography, etc. Today, many of these artists do not limit themselves to a single medium, but use a combination of these processes to achieve their final result. They have at their disposal a tool box of technical support not dreamed of just a few short years ago. This new freedom of choice has given printmakers new ways to view their subject matter and present their ideas. The prints being done today are vibrant works of art, full of texture, color and forms that rival, and in many ways surpass, other art mediums. Printmaking is the only medium that offers such choices, and such an abundance of ways to present creative thought. We are in an era that is refreshing in spirit, and one that provides us with great promise for the future.

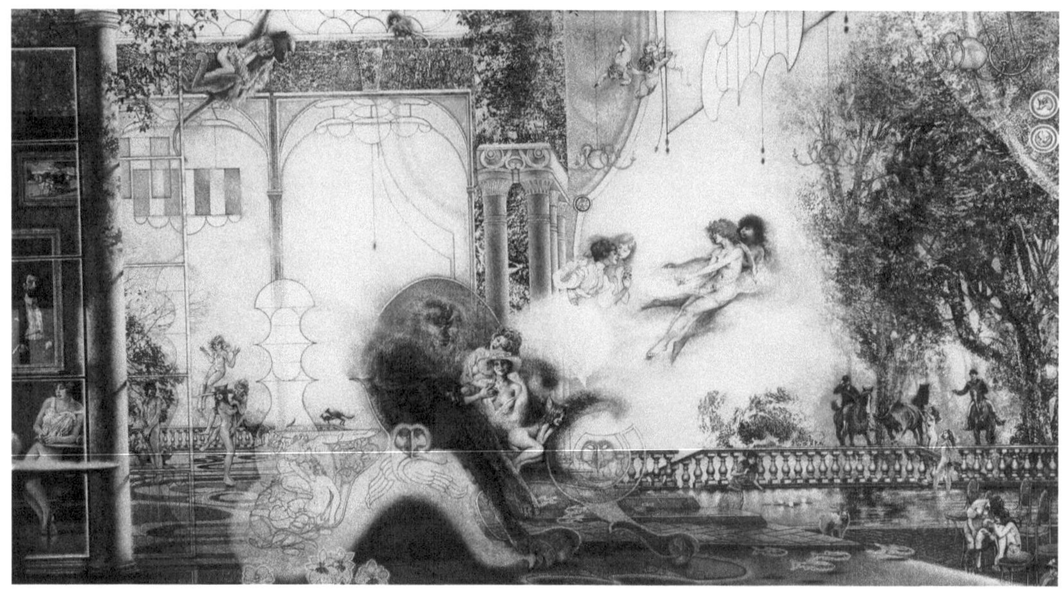

Peter Milton "Les Belles et La Bete II: Before the Hunt" Etching/Engraving 24 x 36

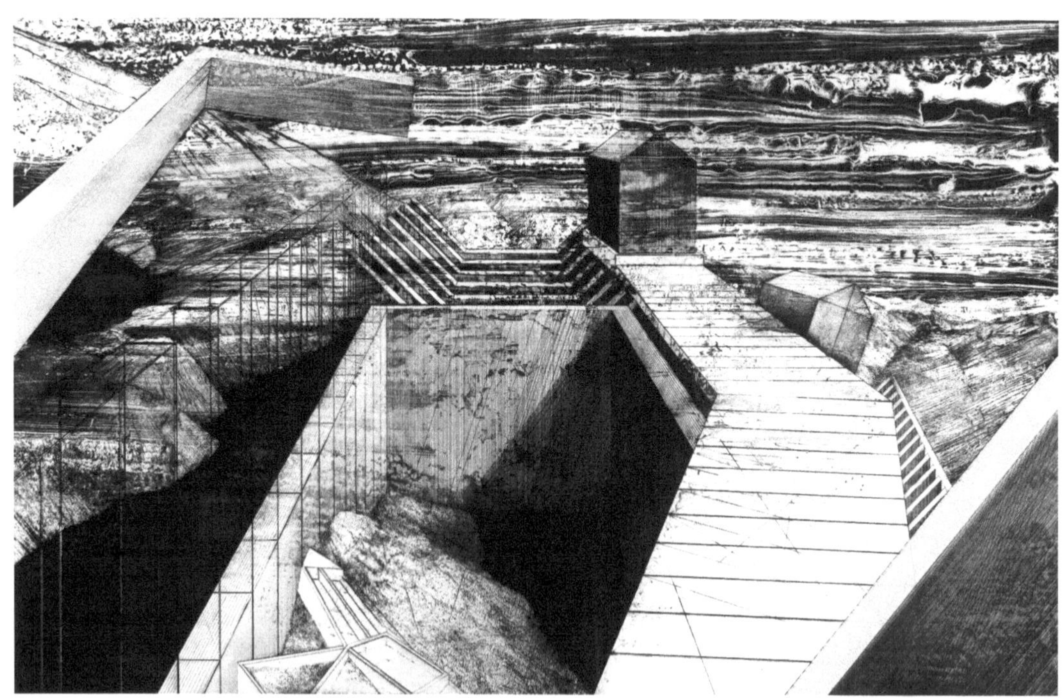

Evan Summer "Northern Sky" Etching/Drypoint 23 ½ x 35 ¾

Michael Aakhus
"The Healing Formula" Etching 20 x 16

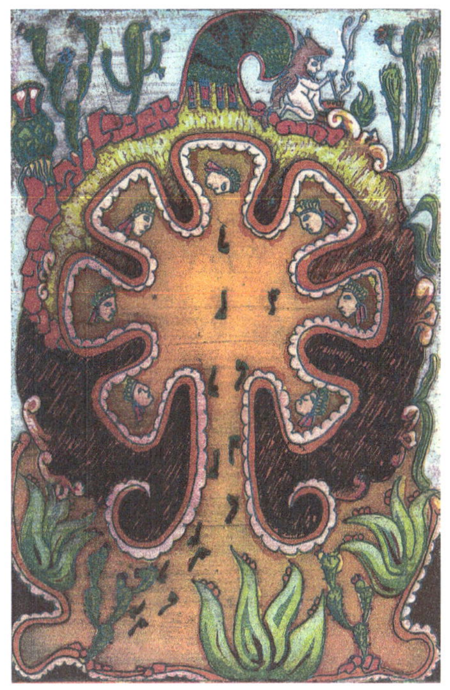

Michael Aakhus has taught at the University of Southern Indiana at Evansville since 1977 as Professor of printmaking and painting. He is presently the Dean of the College of Liberal Arts. His current prints and large canvases are based on images from his travels in Latin America, and touch on themes related to their indigenous cultures. His prints are strong in color and bold in line and structure. They have a sophisticated, yet primitive quality, relating well to his subject matter. Working in series, Aakhus has developed handmade books in collaboration with other writers and poets. These books allow him to fully develop his vision and aggregate thinking on a subject. They are creative jewels, and masterfully rendered. His interests are large in scope, as is his influence on his students.

Sigmund Abeles
"Experiment #1" Etching 21 ½ x 17 ½

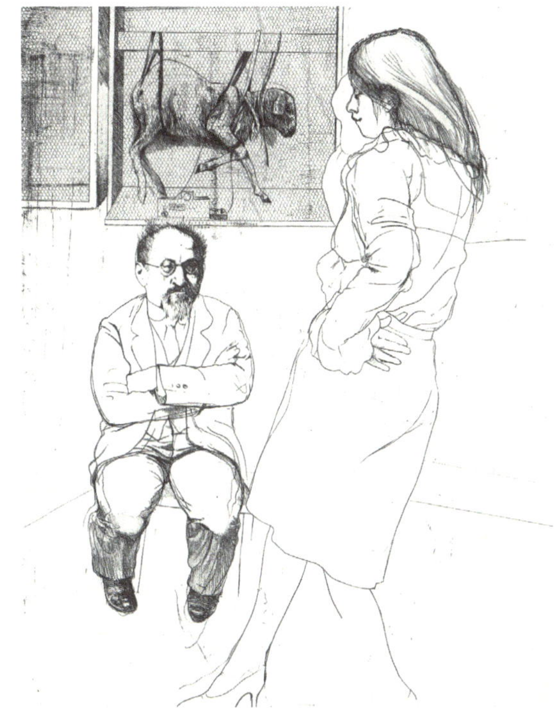

Sigmund Abeles is the consummate draftsman. A master of the drawn line, the artist provides us with insights into the human condition with his narrative portraits and figurative works. Abeles is true to his beliefs, forgoing trends to make significant imagery his way. His beliefs are solidly grounded in the fact that he believes an artist needs to draw well to communicate what he sees, senses and dreams about, in order to create visual expression. Abeles walks the walk. His images are a soul searching, psychological journey into his subject matter. Drawing informs all of his work. After 27 years of teaching, countless lectures and residencies, Abeles has made a profound footprint on the printmaking field.

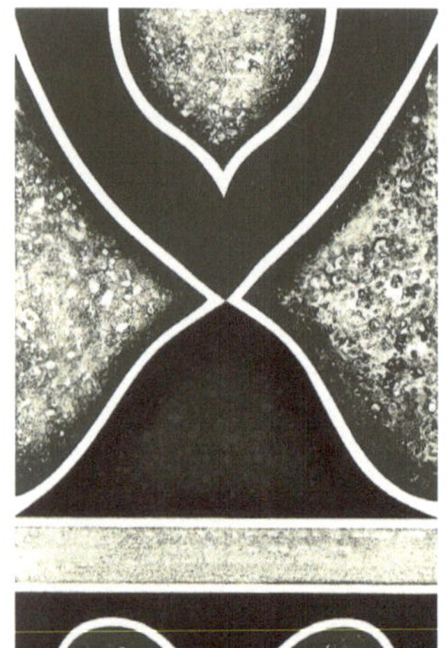

Clinton Adams
"Arabesque I" Lithograph 26 x 13

Clinton Adams was a co-founder, along with June Wayne, of the Tamarind Lithography Workshop in 1960, an historic event in American printmaking. Adams subsequently co-authored with Garo Antreasian, the Tamarind Book of Lithography. He became the director of Tamarind in 1970 when the workshop moved to the University of New Mexico in Albuquerque. It was renamed the Tamarind Institute, and made a division of the University. Clinton's prints were a low key mix of traditional realism and Modernist abstraction. His influence has been a major factor in the printmaking field. Adams died in 2002.

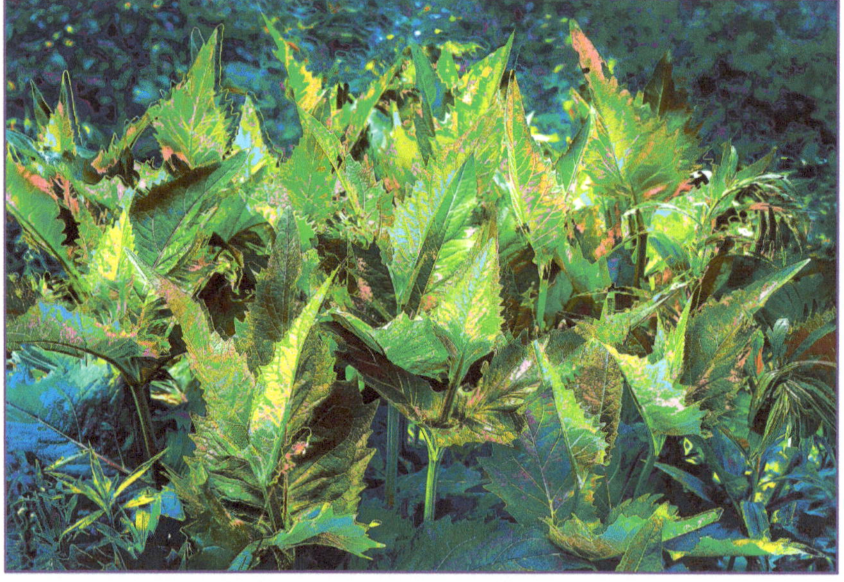

Steven Agard
"shimmer 1674"
Archival Pigment Print 30 x 40

Steven Agard is a photographer who has taken his craft to a high level of fine art. His subject matter is in his own back yard; his koi pond, wooded areas, and along the lake shore near his home. Like a modern Monet, he works in series, allowing himself to study and thoroughly research his subject matter. At first glance, his work appears as realistic renderings of his chosen subject, but he has transformed the ordinary into abstracted three dimensional details. Layers of contrasting color, offer a complex realism to the viewer. The results are beautiful floating vistas of dappled texture and brightly colored forms as they work their magic across the picture plane. They are an allusion of reality. Agard knows his medium well. He has stated of his work, "These are pictures of a time and place that has never been". His are extraordinary images. Agard lives and works in his studio in Madison, Wisconsin.

Roy Ahlgren
"Oscillation" Silkscreen 18 x 24

Roy Ahlgren was a teacher and designer as well as an outstanding self-taught printmaker. Ahlgren was intrigued by hard edge Optical art. A "basement printmaker", he exhibited widely in national juried shows in the Golden '70s. Commercially viable, his work can be found in more than 100 public collections, as well as innumerable private collections. His compositions depict motion, and modulated linear striations of color. They remind one of rhythmic pulsations of sound. Ahlgren passed away in 2011.

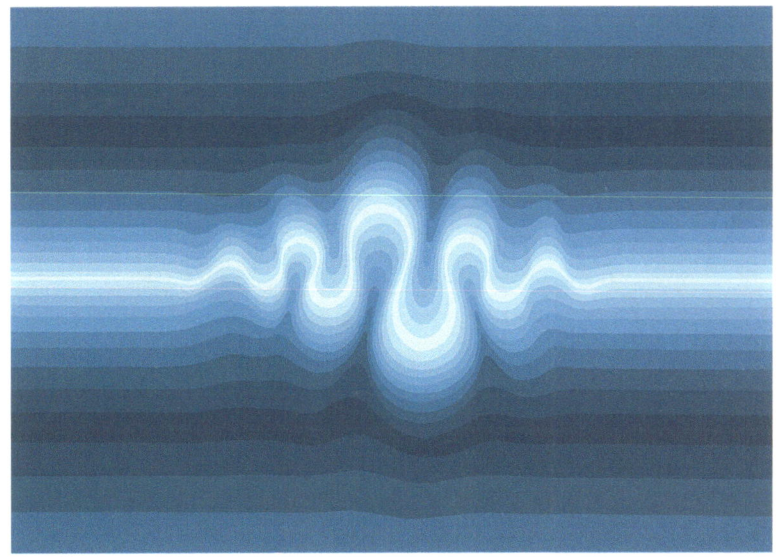

Glen Alps
"Untitled" Collograph 23 ¼ x 17

A first generation pioneer of the Print Renaissance, Glen Alps made several important contributions to the field of printmaking. Chief among these was the development of the collograph process. Alps was the first to exhibit this innovation at the Brooklyn Museum in 1957. Since that time, the technique has been absorbed into the mainstream of the printmaking processes, extending throughout the US and around the world. Alps was also a major influence on several generations of art students through his teaching at the University of Washington in Seattle from 1945 to 1984. The artist passed away in 1996.

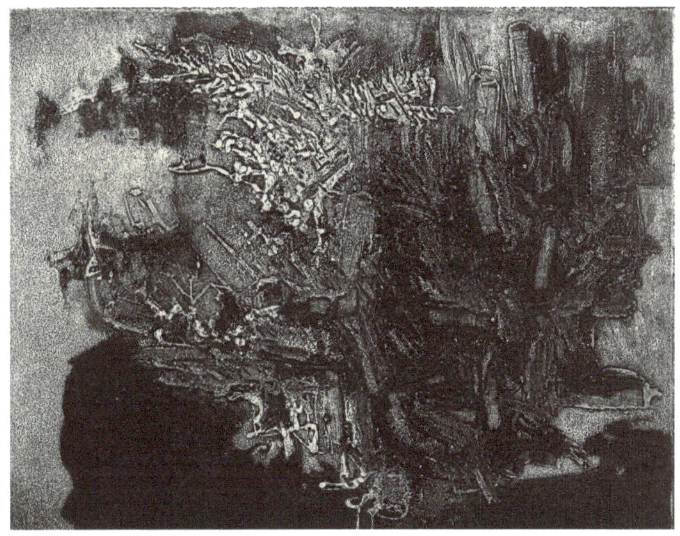

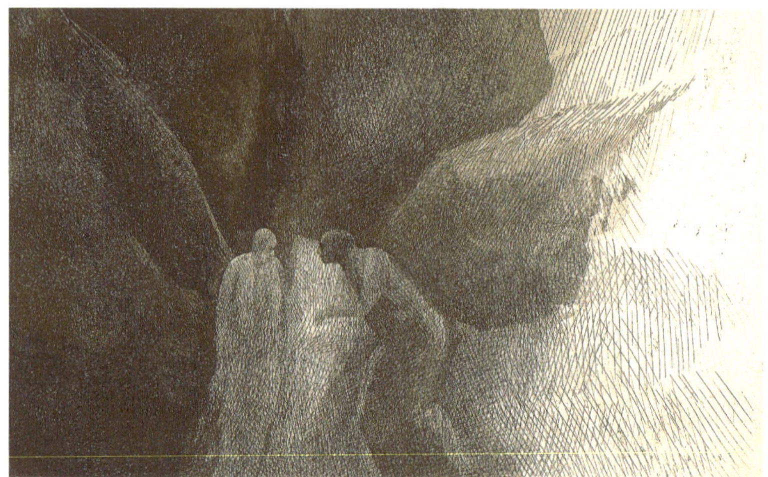

Harold Altman
"Angels II" Etching/Aquatint 9 ¾ x 16

Harold Altman is one of the most successful commercially viable printmakers of our era. His work is in every major museum collection in the world, and he has had a strong influence on his many followers. His early cross-hatch renderings of parks, markets and figures in black and white etchings are some of his strongest imagery. A prime example of this early work is shown here. He later moved on to lithography and full color renderings of a softer, more appealing nature that proved to be highly commercially successful. The artist died in 2003.

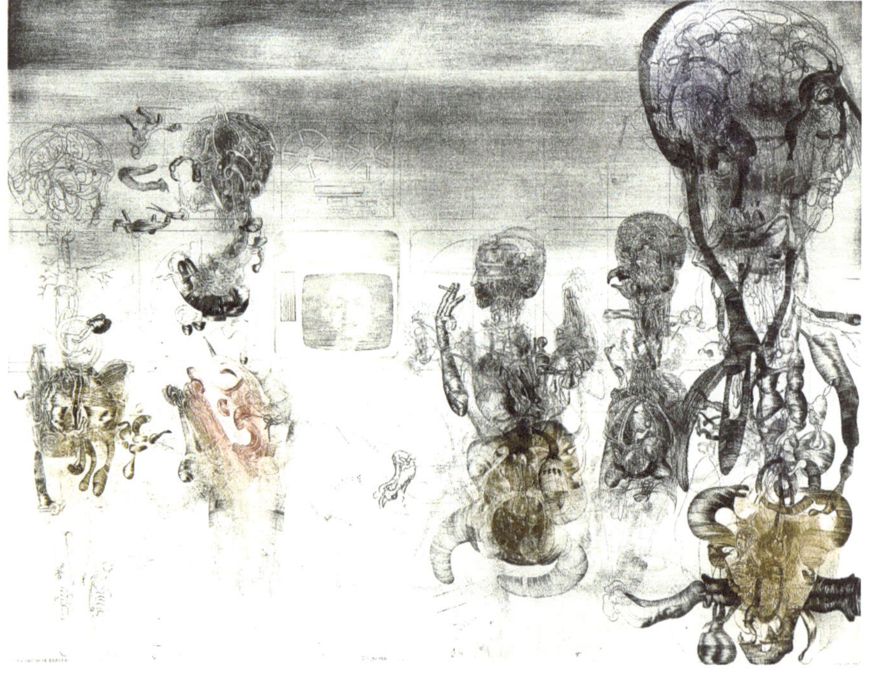

Jiri Anderle
"TV Game"
Drypoint/Mezzotint
19 ¾ x 25 ¾

Jiri Anderle is a Czech painter, illustrator and graphic artist. He is well known for his depictions of powerful surreal expressions of human anxiety and timelessness. His works are unbelievable in their technical virtuosity, and are presented with intense, dark imagery. They are captivating, and so lovely in their rendering that the viewer is easily drawn into his world. His influence is worldwide with solo exhibitions and major awards around the globe.

Garo Antreasian
"Untitled" Lithograph 22 x 30

Garo Antreasian was born in Indianapolis, graduated and then taught at the Herron Art Institute in the same city. He studied with Hayter at the Atelier 17 and with Will Barnet at the Art Students League of New York City in the late '40s. He exhibited widely in the '50s, building a reputation as an artist as well as a master craftsman in lithography. In 1960 the Tamarind Lithography Workshop was founded in Los Angeles by June Wayne and Clinton Adams. Antreasian took over the role of Technical Director and Master Printer. By 1970 they had hosted more than 200 artists at Tamarind and had spawned Gemini G.E.L., a workshop also in Los Angeles. He played an important role in the field of lithography, and his influence has been far reaching.

Shusaku Arakawa
"Is As It: Blind Intentions" Etching/ Aquatint 17 ½ x 23 ½

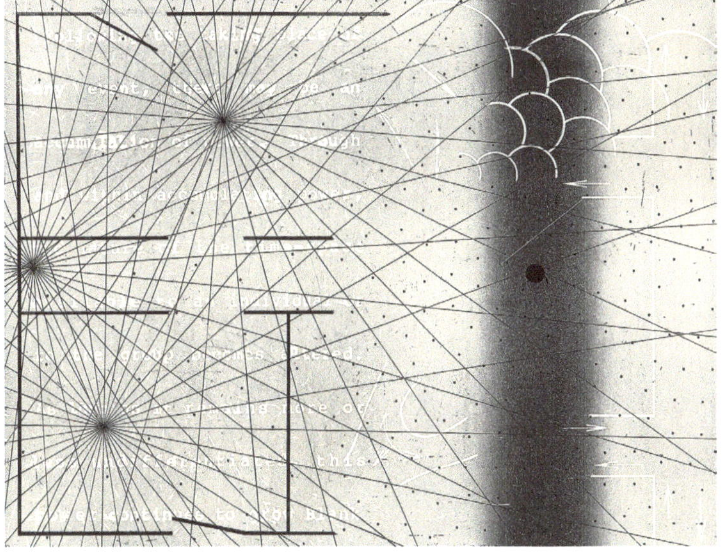

Shusaku Arakawa was an architect and a poet, as well as a significant printmaker. He was one of the most philosophical artists of our times. Marcel Duchamp was his friend and mentor. Along with Madeline Gins, he co-founded the Reversible Destiny Foundation, dedicated to extending the human life span. They stated that it was immoral that people had to die. Arakawa's prints use layers of diagrams and writings that add more questions than answers to his works. They are captivating statements of thoughts that lay just beyond our reach and comprehension. Labeled a conceptualist, he personally referred to himself as an "abstractionist of the distant future". Arakawa passed away in 2010 at the age of 75.

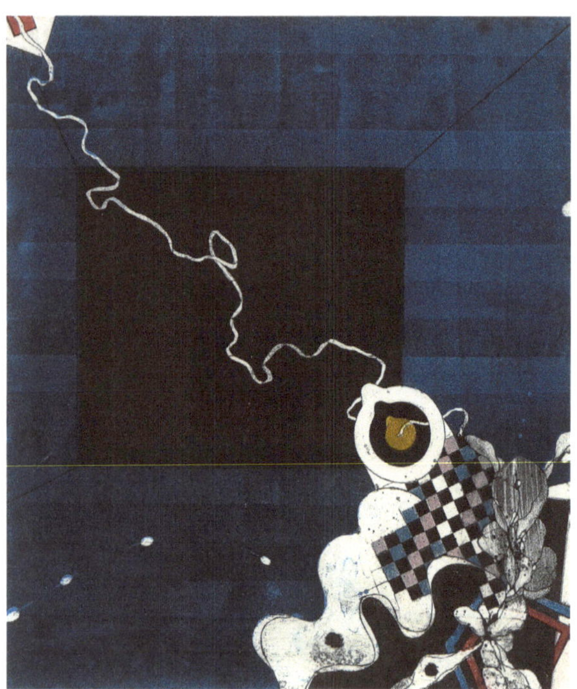

Tetsuo Araki
"Space Kite" Etching/Aquatint 23 x 18

Tetsuo Araki was born in Tokyo, Japan in 1937. Early in his career as an artist, he went to Paris to study with the famed printmaker Johnny Friedlander. He was marketed in the United States by the Collectors Guild, and his prints gained notice in the Golden '70s. Araki was represented by major print galleries in the US and is still a popular choice of collectors. He died in 1984.

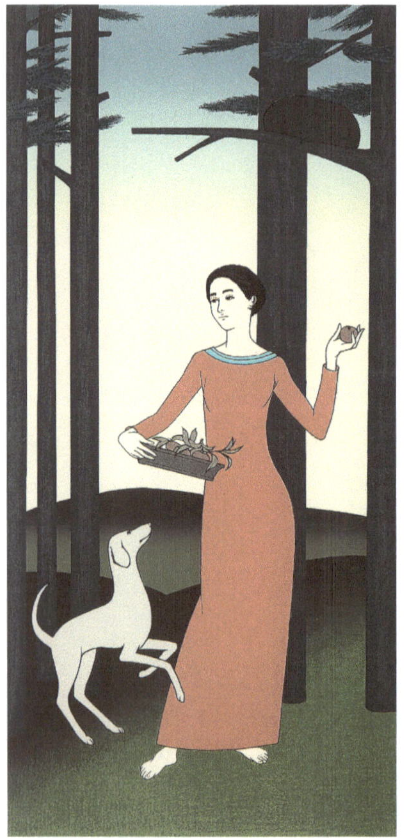

Will Barnet
"Persephone" Silkscreen 34 x 16 ½

Will Barnet was another first generation pioneer of the Print Renaissance, and as such, was an important influence in the printmaking field. As an educator, he was the head of the graphic arts department at the Art Students League of New York, and had a significant effect on an entire generation of artists. His works are poetic figurative renditions that exude a simple elegance. They are representational, yet push to explore the abstract with their large flat surface areas. Strong in color, they are stylized and classical visions of symbolism, and have substantial commercial appeal. He is best known for his enigmatic portraits of his family and pets. Barnet died at the age of 101 in 2011.

Leonard Baskin
"Children and Still Life" Wood Engraving 12 x 12

Sculptor, printmaker, illustrator and bookmaker, Baskin was one of the giants of a handful of first generation artists of the Print Renaissance. He was a superb and prolific artist-printmaker who has had universal influence in the field of the graphic arts. Personifying the human condition, Baskin's work rose to prominence with his monumental woodcuts, the first of their size executed by any modern artist. He also founded the Gehenna Press, a fine arts book publishing entity, promoting collaboration between art disciplines. Baskin did major sculpture commissions for the Franklin Delano Roosevelt Memorial in Washington, DC, and for the Holocaust Memorial in Ann Arbor, Michigan. Baskin passed away in the year 2000.

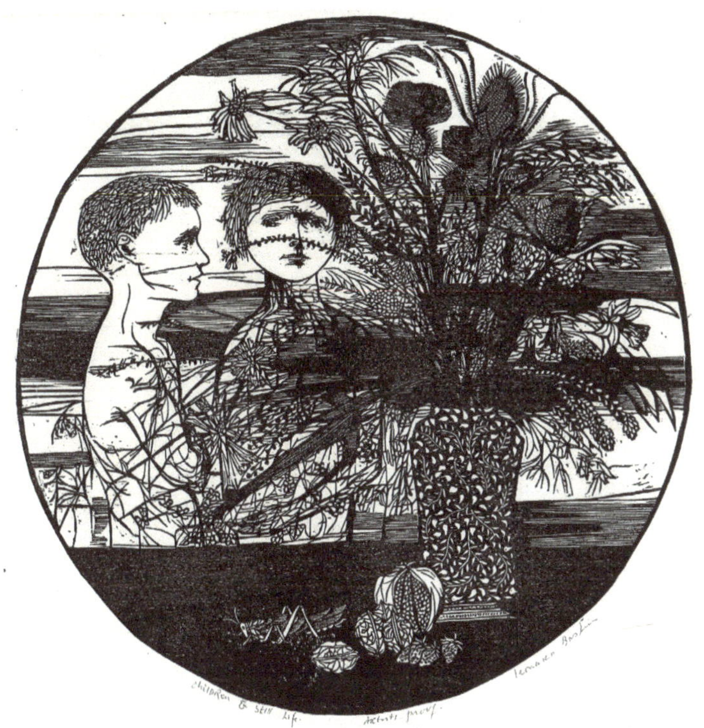

Walter Darby Bannard
"Jacaranda" Silkscreen 22 x 30

Walter Darby Bannard is a painter and printmaker. His painting experimentation and exploration crosses over to his silkscreen prints. His is a world of abstraction and crashing color. Bannard is Professor and head of painting at the University of Miami. The renowned critic Clement Greenberg proclaimed him one of the five or six best of the living painters in America. As Bannard has said in his artist statement, "I hope you enjoy the pictures".

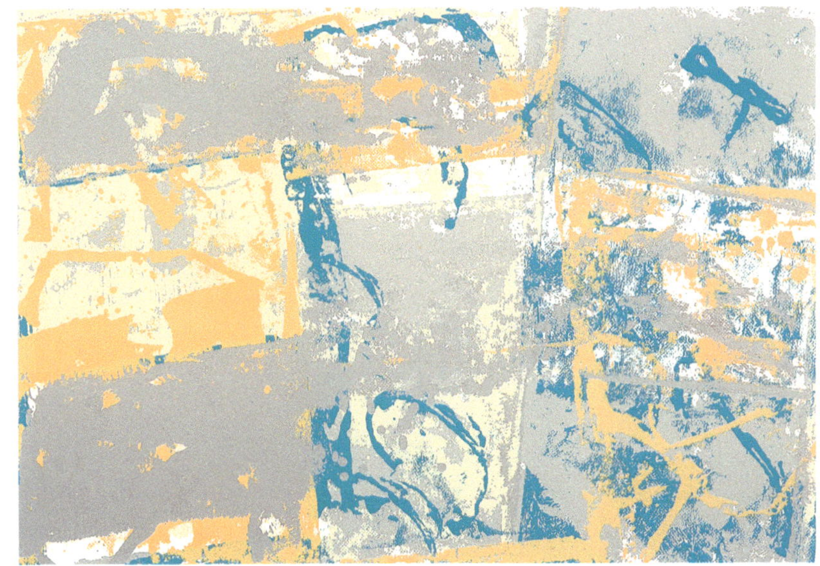

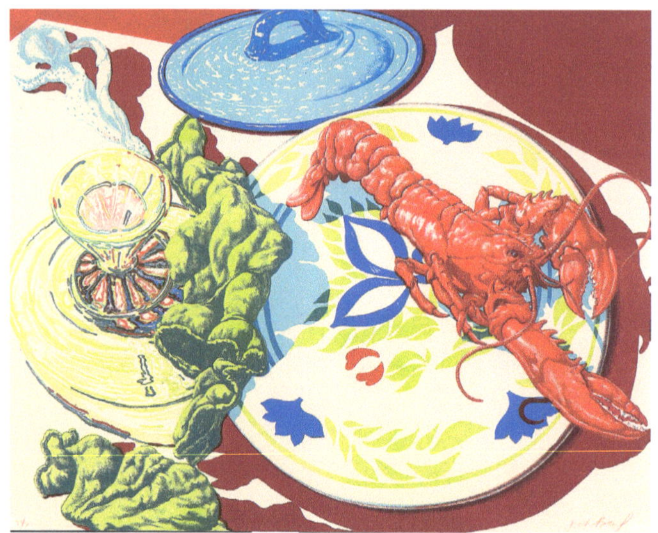

Walter Henry "Jack" Beal, Jr.
"Still Life with Lobster" Lithograph 19 ½ x 25

Jack Beal was a leader in the New York Realist movement as a painter, printmaker and muralist. His subject was the figure, and as one of the dominant forces in the revival of figurative art in the '60s and '70s, he had great influence on others. His four murals, "The History of Labor", installed in the Labor Department in Washington, DC, established Beal as the most important Social Realist to emerge since the 1930's. The overall effect of the finished murals was reported as "breathtaking". Beal was married to the artist Sondra Freckleton. He passed away in 2013.

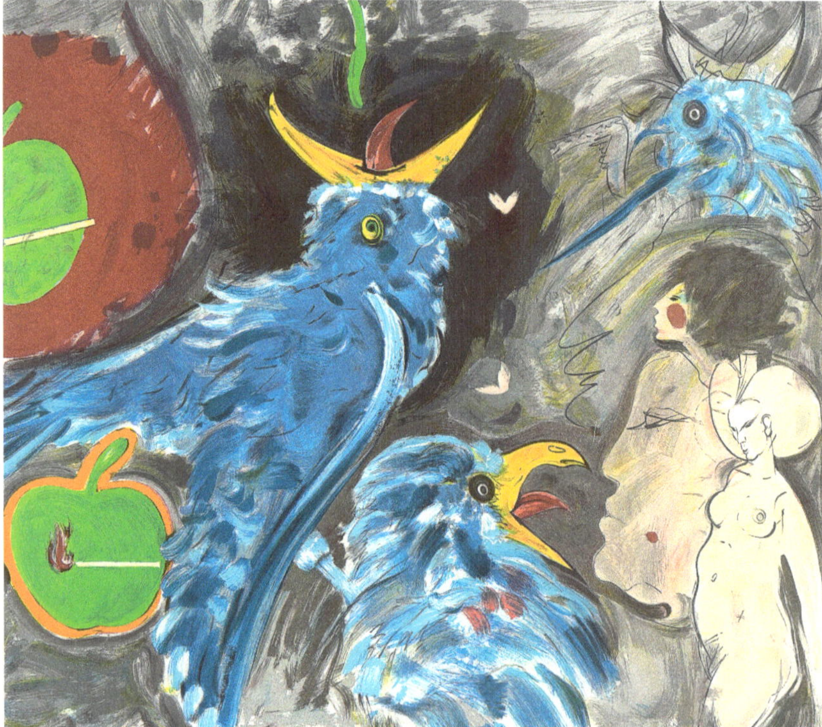

Robert Beauchamp
"Apple Dream" Lithograph 22 x 25

Robert Beauchamp was orphaned by the age of three during the great depression. He and his siblings grew up in a community house with other families, and this experience had a profound effect on his art. Beauchamp studied with Hans Hoffman. He was a figurative painter and arts educator, and his work has been described in the New York Times as "both frightening and amusing". His work is filled with personal symbols: apples, lit matches and wild beasts, which add to the mysterious qualities of their meaning. Beauchamp was not overly concerned with selling his works, being content to enjoy the pure act of creating them. He became involved in the slow and intense experience he received from the process itself. During the last fifteen years of his life, he taught at the Art Students League of New York. He died in 1995.

David H. Becker
"Monuments"
Etching/Engraving 21 x 31

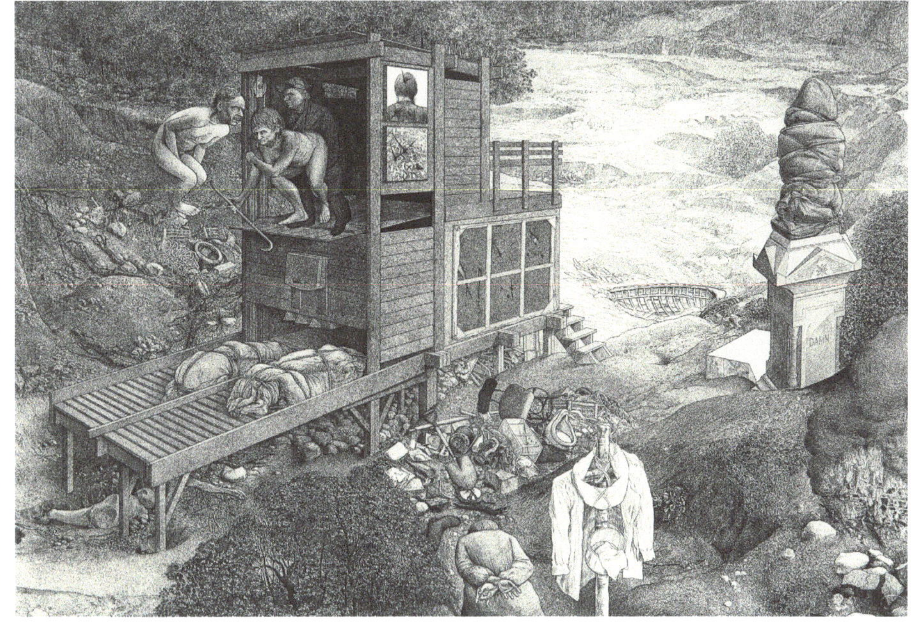

David H. Becker's etchings are masterful renderings of the etching medium that are in a category all their own. Becker's work defined the Golden '70s of printmaking, winning countless awards in national and international juried exhibitions. His work stood apart from the best printmakers of that era, and they continue to hold their own today. His subject matter is allegorical drawings that depict human frailty. The images are figurative scenes set amidst a sprawling, complex background; they are separated as groups in the midst of their own personal chaos, some grounded, others floating in their surreal environment. These are statements with ambiguous meanings with only Becker having the key. They are not necessarily for the viewer to solve, but to enjoy as something unique and special to the eye and mind. Becker coined the phrase, "The Golden '70s".

Ed Binkley
"Changeling"
Archival Pigment Print 15 x 21

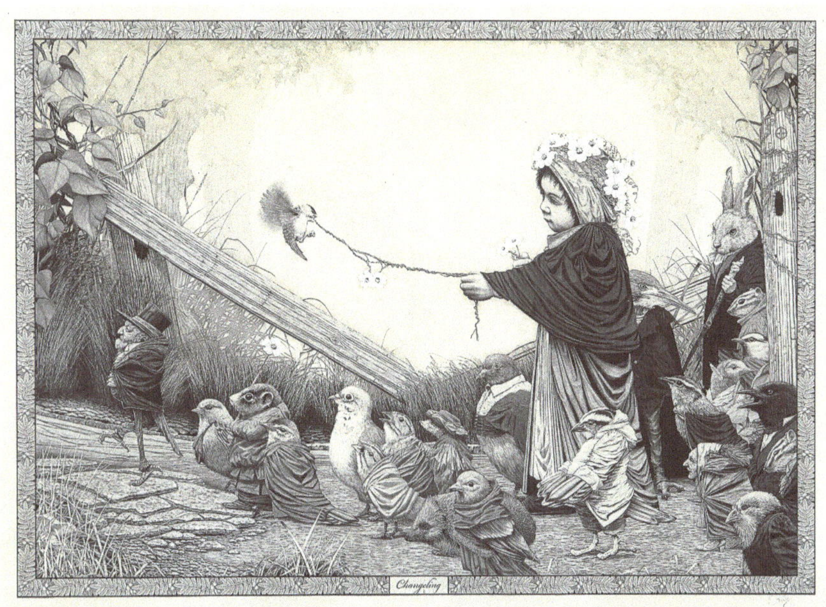

Ed Binkley is an artist and illustrator of high accomplishment. He has been described as one of the "twenty best digital fantasy artists in the world". Binkley's work is a demonstration of the beautiful craftsmanship of the drawn line, combined with narrative mystery and a delightfully unnerving fantasy. He describes his work as "worlds within worlds", and has done personal and commercial commissions for George Lucas of Star Wars fame, the Disney Studios and other notable venues. Binkley has changed the perception of what we used to term "illustration", and has brought his imagery into the realm of fine art. His work is best termed "fantastic". He lives and works in Madison, Wisconsin.

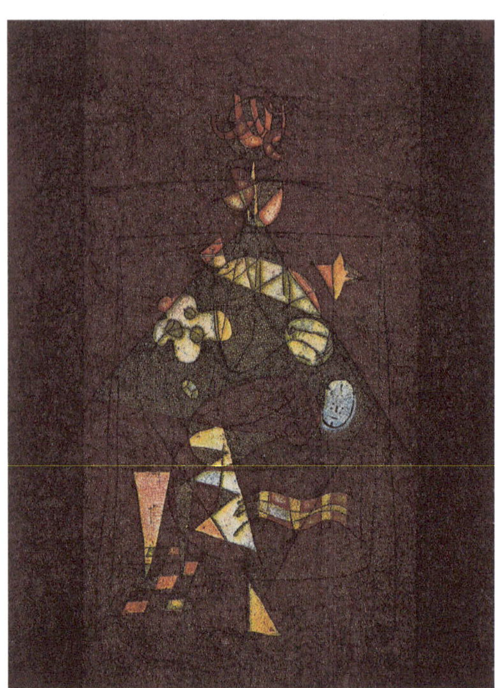

Richard Black
"Quantum II" Etching 11 1/2 x 9.

Richard Black is a highly regarded printmaker who has made a significant contribution over the years to the arts in Iowa. For thirty five years he was professor of art at Drake University where, in addition to his teaching, he founded the Drake University Biennial Print Symposium, influencing student and journeyman printmakers alike. His work is exquisite, and they have a playful, collage like appearance. They are exhibits of technical virtuosity, gemlike journeys into a fun filled world of delight. They are exquisite.

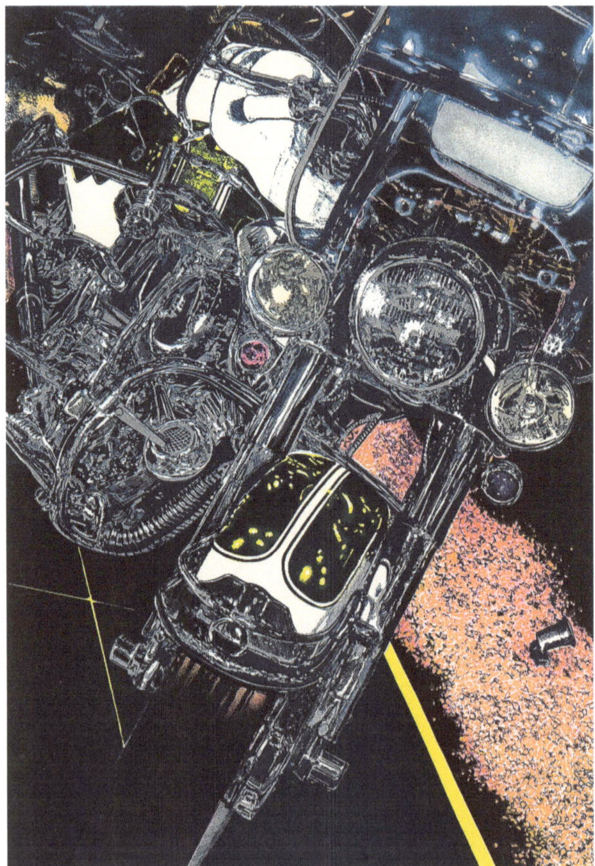

Tom Blackwell
"Harley" Lithograph 33 x 23***

Tom Blackwell is one of the original first generation Photo-realists. He started his career as an Abstract Expressionist. However, under the influence of Pop Art in the 1960's, he realigned himself with photo-realism, producing naturalistic depictions of motorcycles that conveyed the shiny surfaces of modern consumer culture. He has stated, "A common element in all my work is the reflective surface. I have discovered that transferring the subject matter from the photograph requires the most intense discipline, and while working through this translation, the image achieves a reality of its own."

Al Blaustein
"Fiegele" Intaglio Etching 23 ¾ x 17 ¾

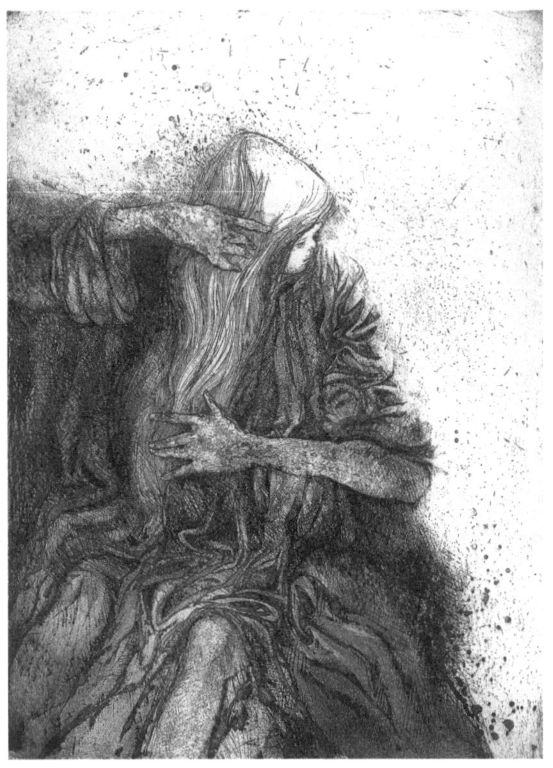

Al Blaustein was Professor of Fine Arts at the Pratt Institute in Brooklyn. He taught from 1949 until his death in 2004, guiding generations of students. In his own work, Blaustein never strayed far from figuration, and "Fiegele", shown here, is a prime example of his oeuvre. Constantly working, he produced a prodigious amount of work in his lifetime. After thirty-five years of teaching, he has had significant influence on both his students and peers. Blaustein died in 2004.

Douglas Bosley
"KO40: 34.09.10.02.10.28"
Mezzotint 6 x 16

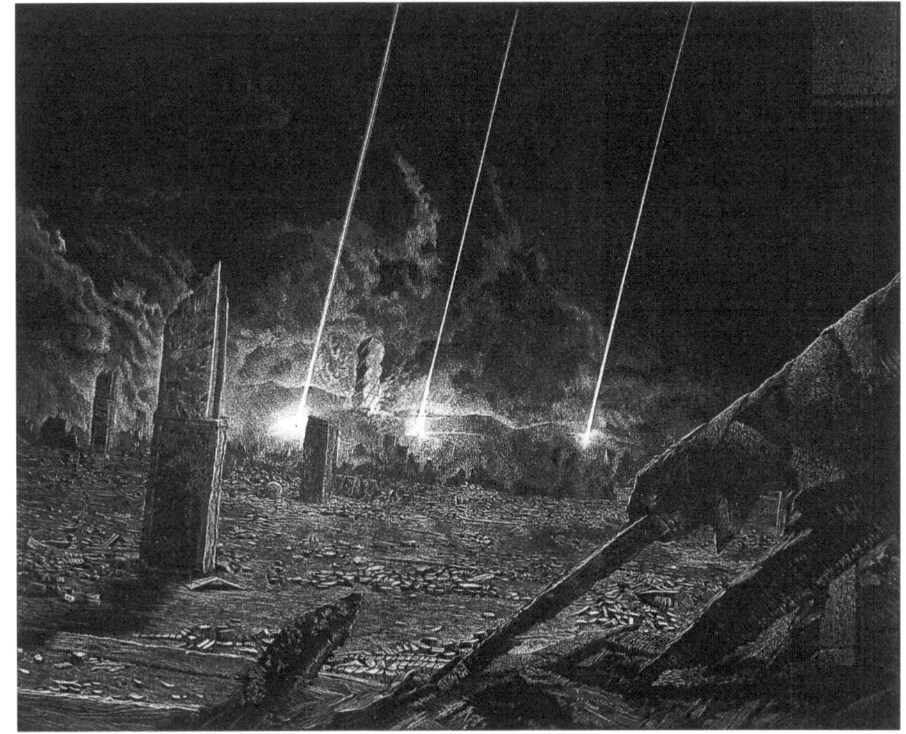

Douglas Bosley is a new face to followers of printmaking, but is already making a strong case for his work. Major awards in national shows are building his biography, and include the first prize award in the National Society of Arts and Letters Competition in Printmaking for 2013. Bosley captures our attention with mezzotint prints so luscious in their surfaces that we are easily seduced. Their surreal presentation in rich blacks with a glowing dollop of butterscotch are desserts to satisfy any appetite. Bosley's prints are extraordinary, and are done in a work intensive medium, as mezzotints offer few shortcuts for the artist to take. Bosley should be on every collectors watch list.

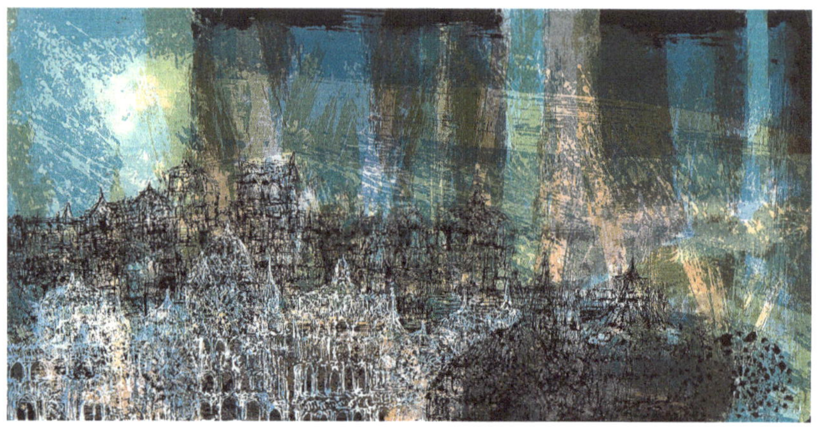

Dorothy Bowman (Bradford)
"San Francisco Moon"
Silkscreen 18 x 36

Rhythm and movement are central to the silkscreen prints of Dorothy Bowman. Her urban subject matter are bejeweled visions of brightly colored radiance. As a child she collected bits of broken glass in the Mojave Desert. Crushing them and putting them into jars, she would hold them up to the sun. Bathed in the brightness, a million tiny surfaces glinted. It was this inspiration that fired her imagination. She states, "That day, the artist in me was born". She was married to artist Howard Bradford, and they enjoyed a personal and artistic relationship.

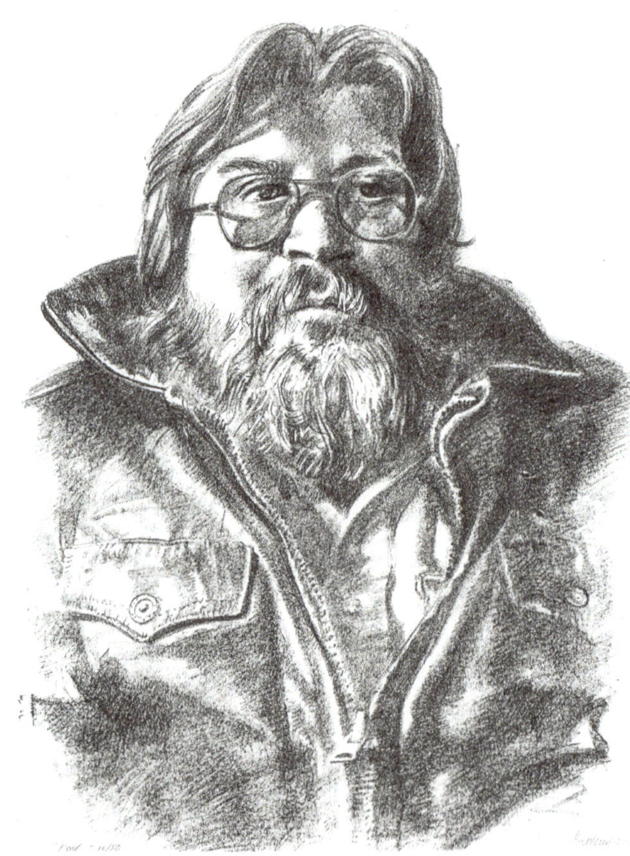

Harvey Breverman
"Paul"
Lithograph 25 x 19 ½

A second generation pioneer in the Print Renaissance, Breverman developed a significant printmaking program at the University of Buffalo in New York state beginning in 1961, retiring after forty-four years of formal teaching there. His influence on his many students is wide spread. Human drama is his primary source for subject matter and his portraits are journeys into his subject's distinctive character. He addressed this by saying of his work, "it is particularized by the figure in all its frailty and grandeur".

David Bumbeck
"The Morning"
Intaglio Etching 17 ½ x 14 ¾

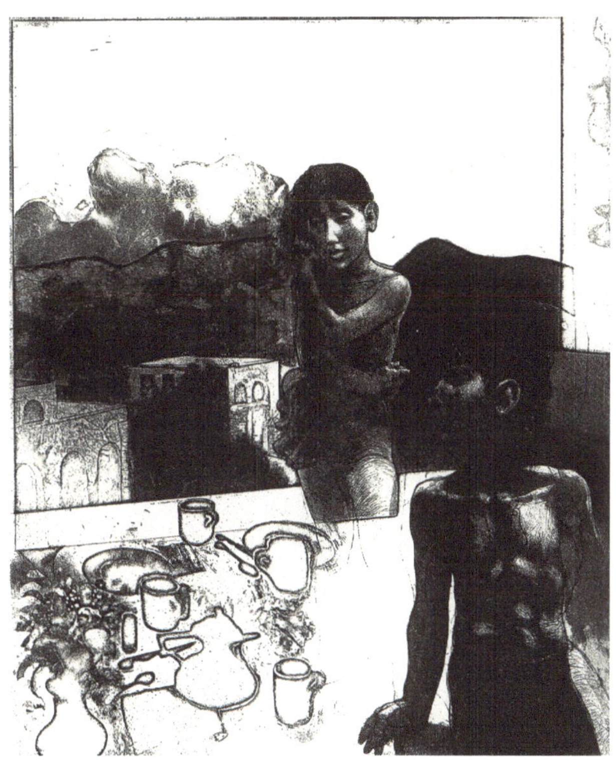

After 36 years of teaching, David Bumbeck retired in 2002 as Professor Emeritus from Middlebury College in Vermont. Bumbeck came to prominence and was a leading figure in national shows in the Golden '70s. The human figure has been the dominant motif in his prints, using multiple techniques such as etching, aquatint, engraving and photo transfer to arrive at a final conclusion of his thoughts. Bumbeck has an interest in the old masters and transfers this interest into his own modernist approach to both the figure and the landscape. The past melds with the present, resulting in a timeless message. His work has been described as "deepening pleasure: the longer you look, the more you see".

James D. Butler "One Dip Please"
Lithograph 22 ¾ x 18 ½

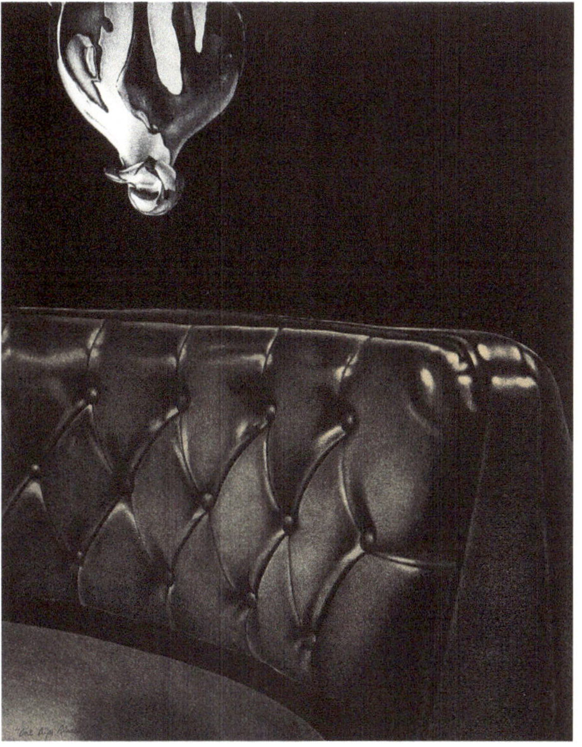

Now retired as Professor Emeritus, James D. Butler was head of the printmaking program at Illinois State University at Normal as an active, practicing printmaker for forty years. An outstanding printmaker and educator, Butler along with his workshop director, Richard Finch, brought in a steady stream of visiting artists to make prints and visit with students. The success of the program is realized with hundreds of graduate printmakers working, teaching and running their own studios and print shops throughout the US and Canada. His lithographs, startling in their presentation, portray surrealistic, ambiguous imagery. An active participant during the Golden '70s, Butler's influence has been ongoing.

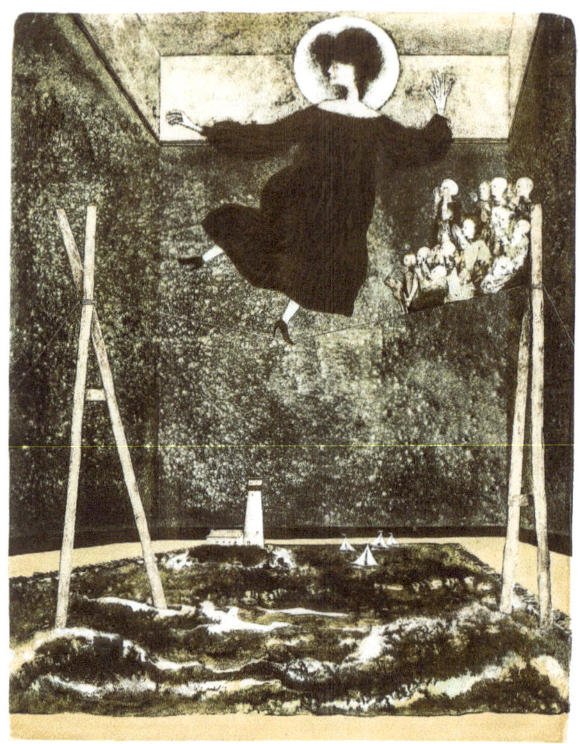

Federico Castellon
"Tightrope Walker" Lithograph 26 x 20 ¾

Federico Castellon was a painter, sculptor, printmaker and illustrator of children's books. He was one of the first Americans to foster Surrealism. His work takes us on a journey into his own personal world of myth and fantasy. His main printmaking medium was lithography and one of his first series of prints was to illustrate Edgar Allen Poe's, "The Masque of the Red Death". Although his formal training ended with high school, Castellon taught at several Universities including Columbia and the Pratt Institute in New York City. "Tightrope Walker" is a wonderful example of his mastery of the lithography medium and his unique imagery. Castellon died in 1971.

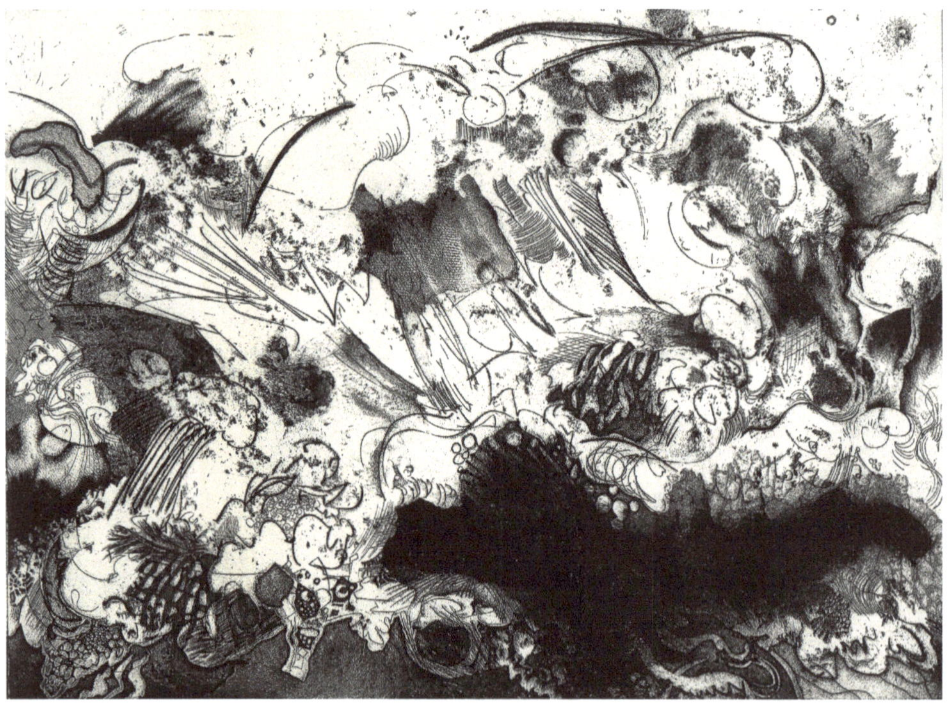

Lee Chesney
"The Wave"
Intaglio Etching 17 x 23 ½

Lee Chesney is a printmaker, painter and educator. He studied at Atelier 17 with Hayter and at the University of Iowa with Mauricio Lasansky. A second generation pioneer in the Print Renaissance, his influence has been far reaching. He taught at several universities as an educator over a thirty-four year period. He lives and works in both Los Angeles and Burgundy, France. Chesney is a recognized master of intaglio processes, and boldly asserts "balanced chaos" in his structured prints. They are filled with seductive nuances and rhythms, and the technical virtuosity is a delight to the eye.

Judy Chicago
"Old"
Lithograph/Etching 22 x 30

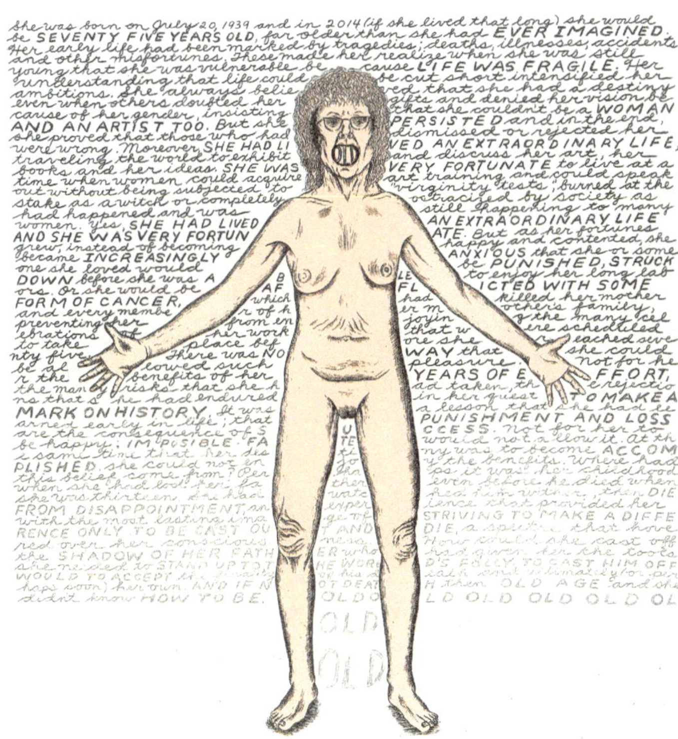

Born in Chicago as Judith Cohen, Chicago changed her name to do away with male dominated naming conventions. She is first and foremost an artist of international influence. She is a renowned feminist as well as an author, educator and intellectual. Judy Chicago is most famous for her multi-media masterpiece, "The Dinner Party", now housed in the permanent collection of the Brooklyn Museum. Created with hundreds of volunteers, this monumental work honors the history of women in Western Civilization and was five years in the making. Judy Chicago founded the first feminist art program in the United States and her work has had a powerful impact on her many followers and admirers, not only in the US, but throughout the world. Her career has spanned over five decades.

Chryssa Vardea-Mavromichali
"Untitled – Classified Ad"
Monoprint 30 x 22

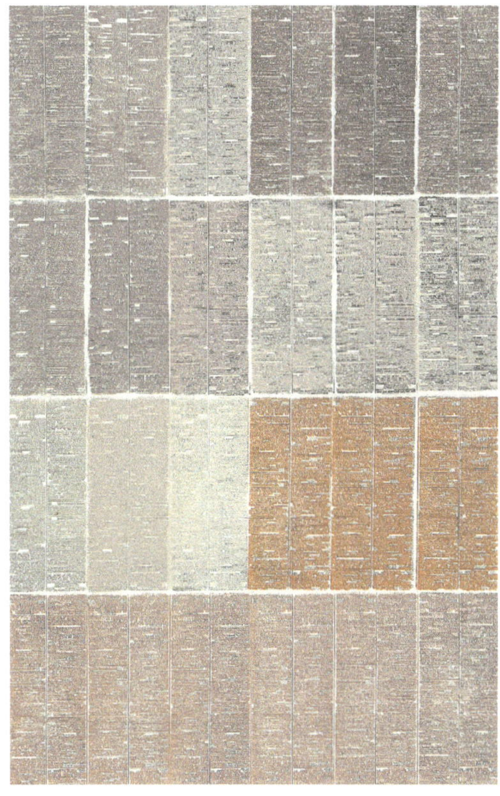

Using the mononym Chryssa, she was a Greek American artist who worked in a variety of media, but was best known for her work as an American pioneer in light art and luminist sculpture. It has been noted that her sculpture piece, "The Gates of Times Square" is regarded as "one of the most important American sculptures of all time". The piece is in the permanent collection of the Albright-Knox Art Gallery in Buffalo, New York. She found inspiration in news media, typography, news print collages, metal molds and alphabetical forms. Chryssa's image pictured here, "Untitled Classified Ad", is a fine example of her news media influence involving works on paper. Chryssa passed away in 2013.

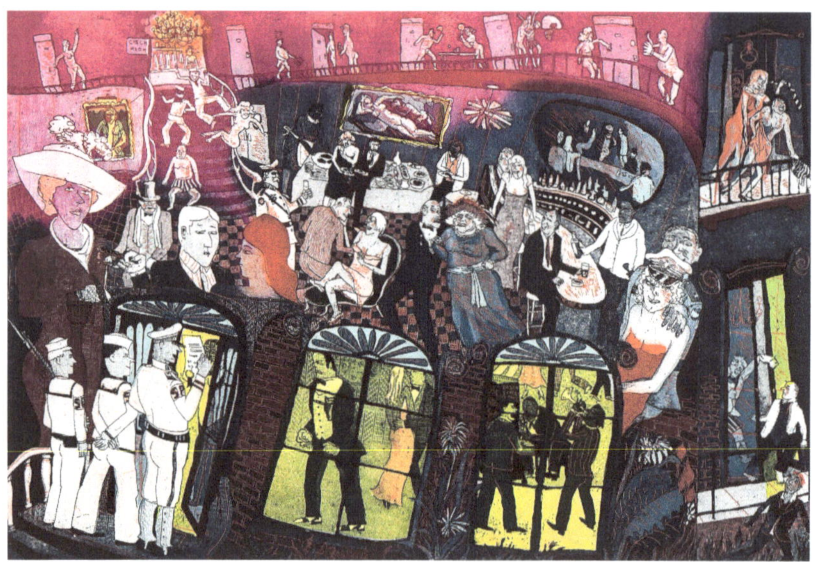

Warrington Colescott
"Suite Louisiana: Storyville-The Last Salon"
Intaglio Etching 23 ½ x 35 ¾

Warrington Colescott is a dynamic and influential second generation pioneer in the Print Renaissance. He is best known for his satirical and biting, fun poking intaglio etchings. His influence has been far reaching, teaching and guiding students for thirty-seven years at the University of Wisconsin – Madison. He played a key part in the success in making the University's graphic department arguably the premier printmaking department in the country. Starting in 1949, he was on the ground floor alongside Alfred Sessler, developing a standard for other print departments across the nation to follow. His intaglio methods include shaped etching plates and incorporated bits of letterpress, forming narrative story lines of historical whimsy. He is a recognized master of the medium and is highly respected by his peers for his contributions to the printmaking field. Colescott lives and works in Hollandale, Wisconsin, and was married to artist Frances Myers who passed in 2014.

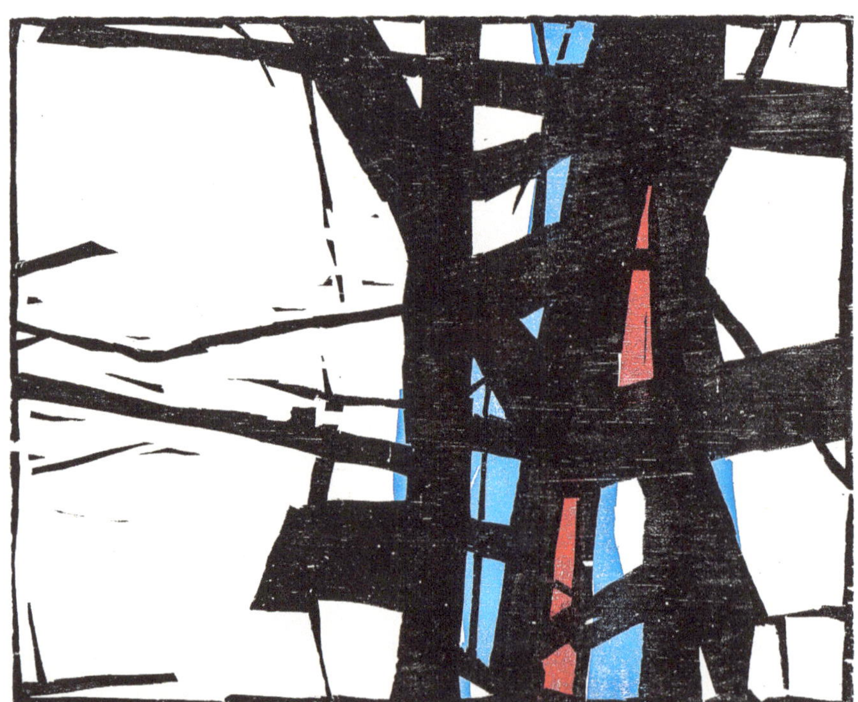

Robert Conover
"Cityscape"
Woodcut 13 x 16 ½

Teacher, printmaker and painter, Robert Conover studied under Will Barnet and Max Beckman before teaching at the New School for Social Research and the Brooklyn Museum Art School for a combined forty years. His influence on so many students who have received his guidance and knowledge in the printmaking field is immeasurable. In the '50s and '60s, Conover was a second generation abstract expressionist whose main medium was woodcut, portraying cityscapes which emphasized strong diagonal movement. His woodcuts were vaguely reminiscent of Franz Kline's gestural abstractions. He has been described as a master of his medium, a printmaker's printmaker, and a very fine artist. Conover passed away in 1998.

Thomas Cornell
"David Berry's Pigs"
Etching 15 ¾ x 19 ¾

Early on in his career, Thomas Cornell was known mainly for his drawings and prints. His art revolves around themes of social justice, and mankind's relationship with nature. His print, pictured here, is a beautifully rendered etching demonstrating his command of the medium. One critic noted, "Cornell puts the idea before the art. Art for him has been a means of giving form to a specific socially significant theme". He taught at Bowdoin College from 1962 until his death in 2012.

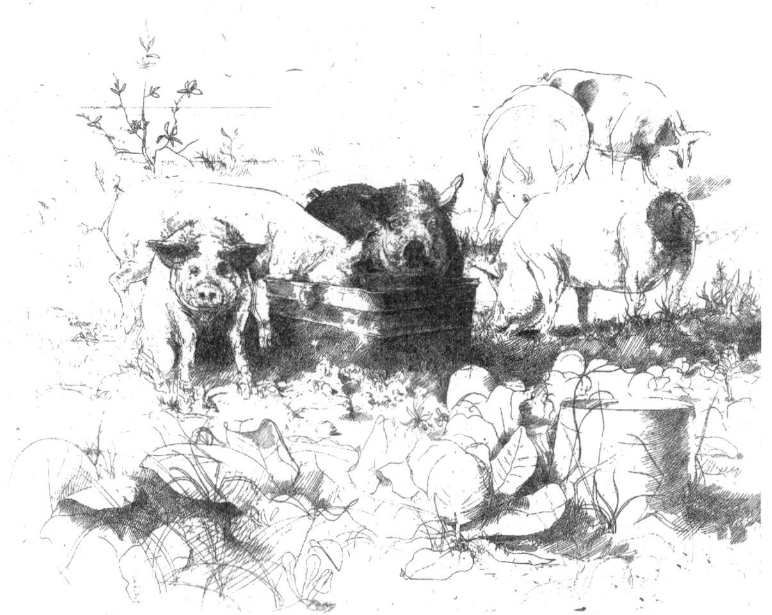

Dennis Corrigan
"Queen Victoria Troubled by Flies"
Lithograph 13 ¼ x 10 ¼

Dennis Corrigan is an illustrator as well as a painter and printmaker who is known for his surrealist drawings and prints. He teaches fine art at Marywood University in Scranton, Pennsylvania. Corrigan was a frequent prize winner in national competitions during the Golden '70s. This image of Queen Victoria offers whimsy, superb draftsmanship, and delightful tongue-in-cheek subject matter. It is pure Corrigan and aptly demonstrates his art.

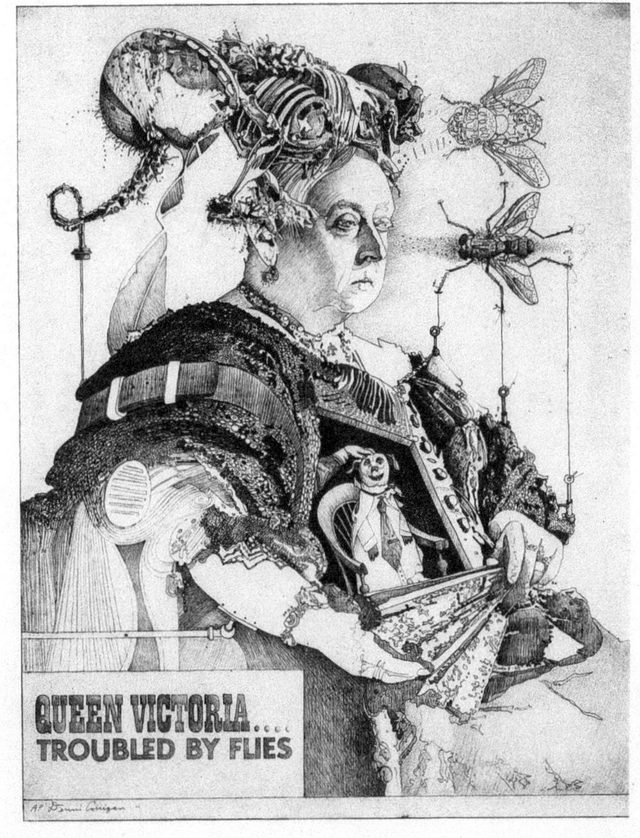

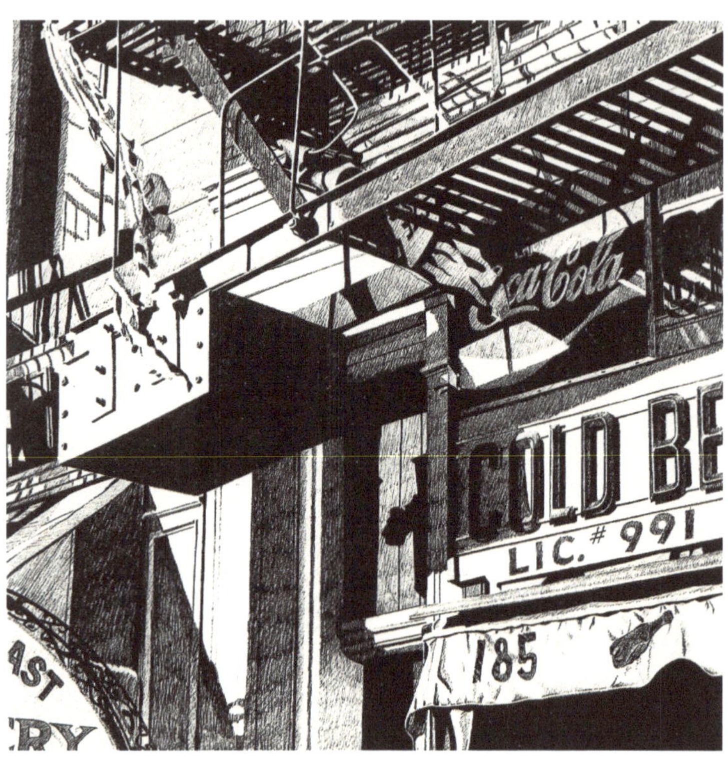

Robert Cottingham
"Cold Beer"
Lithograph 14 x 14

Robert Cottingham does not consider himself a Photo-realist. He states that while his imagery is derived from photographs that he likes, he then expands on the photo image, and does not replicate it. However, the art world sees Cottingham's work in a different light. He is considered to be one of the most important Photo-realist painters and printmakers working today. His subject matter of signs, neon lettering and building fragments are readily identifiable as Cottingham, and have spurred many followers. His prints, using etching and especially lithography, lend themselves to his hard edge style and subject matter. His work has far reaching appeal and influence.

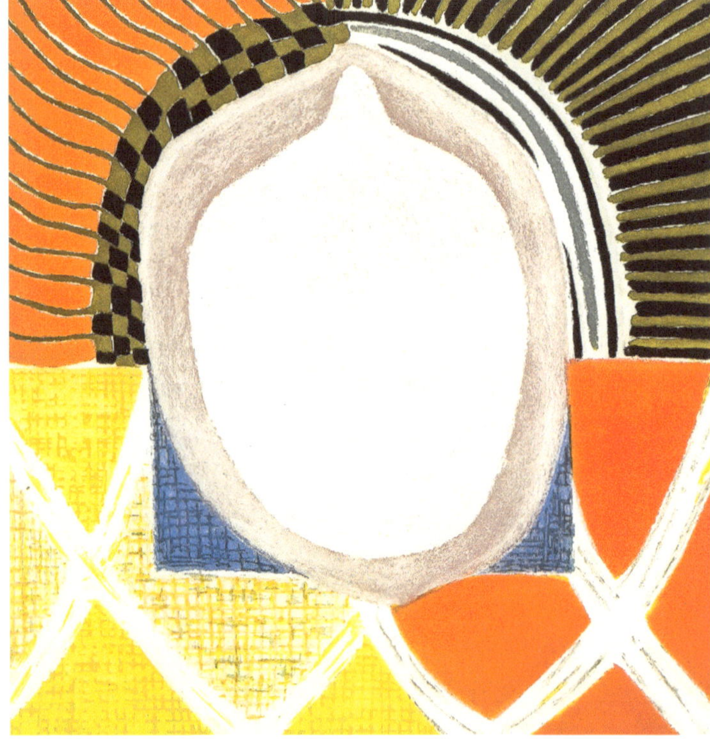

Susan Crile
"Shimmer"
Etching 20 x 20

A painter, printmaker and educator, Susan Crile has been teaching at Hunter College in New York City since 1982. Based on oriental rugs and other patterned textiles, her work somewhat recalls the inspired patterning in the work of Matisse. Geometric evocative abstract shapes and strong purity of color are a hallmark of her images.

Jack Damer
"Driving Wheel"
Etching/Engraving
17 ½ x 22 ½

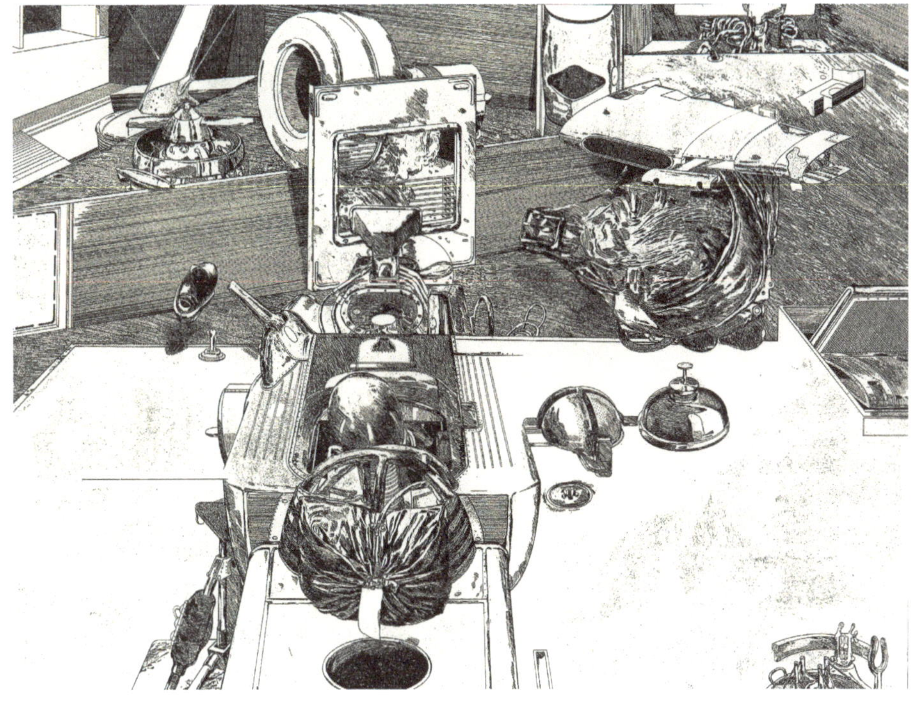

Jack Damer has been with the University of Wisconsin-Madison since 1970, and is presently Professor of Lithography and Drawing. Damer's end product, like many other contemporary artists is hard to categorize. He moves fluidly between representation, abstraction and narrative in his work. Damer is not a traditional artist. In his own words, he plays "fast and loose" with printmaking, readily accepting the introduction of new tools, incorporating photo mechanical and digital processes to enhance his imagery. Damer's contribution has been significant to the University of Wisconsin's reputation as one of the finest graphic programs in the country. After forty-five years of teaching, his influence has been far reaching. Damer is a technical master of the printmaking processes. He has stated, "I categorize my role in creating the images as part investigator, part judge and executioner".

Donald DeMauro
"One Eyed Man"
Lithograph 24 x 19

Donald De Mauro is a painter and printmaker who is totally devoted to the figure in his work. For De Mauro everything evolves around the body. He has stated that "art is language, and the body is the site of language". His search is a personal journey, "seeking to give physical matter its own logic – a voice". De Mauro's figures are bared to their essence, the human condition shed of layers, to get to the inner depth of the soul. They are what they are, no holds barred; powerful, dynamic works that hit you like a thunderbolt. These are masterful works of art that draw you into the artist's world, and lend no soft ground. What you see is a venture into the human spirit.

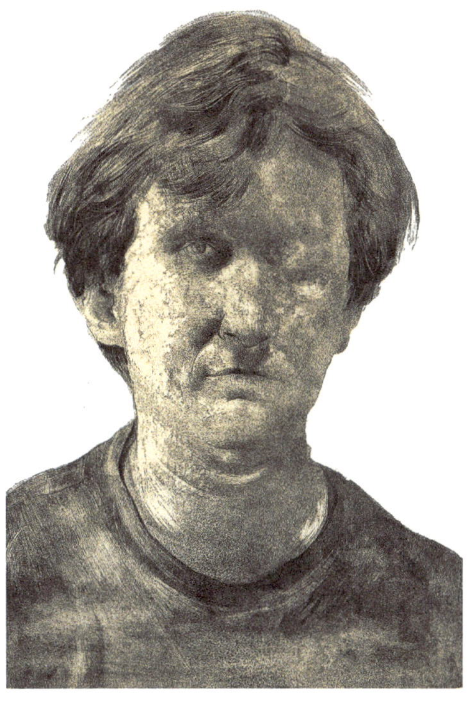

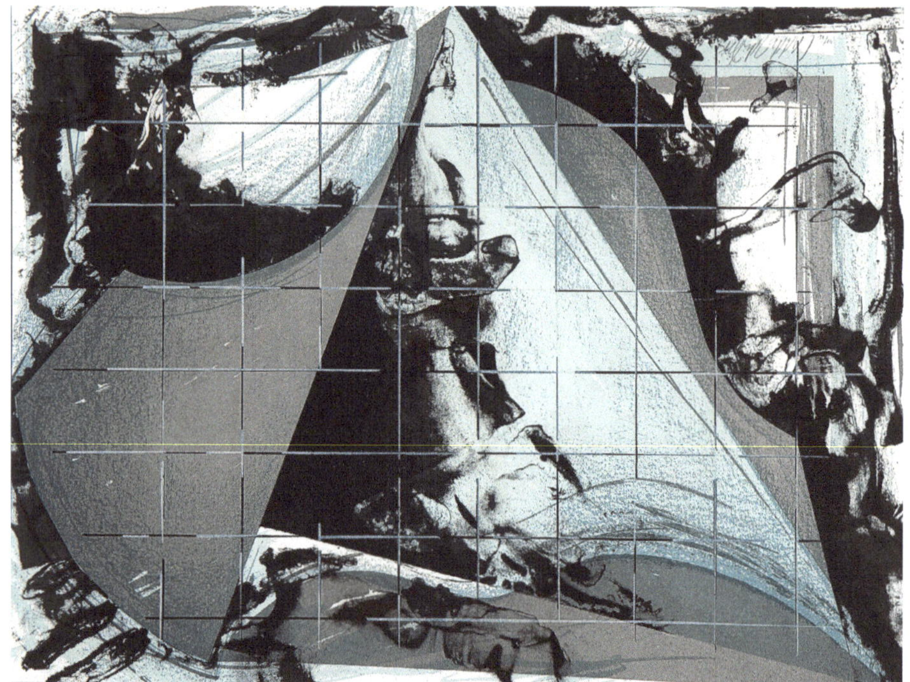

Laddie John Dill
"Untitled"
Lithograph 22 x 30

A painter, sculptor, light artist and printmaker, Laddie John Dill is a highly regarded national and international contemporary artist. Starting as an apprentice printer at Gemini G.E.L. in Los Angeles, Dill had the opportunity to work alongside and be influenced by established well known artists. Gemini also allowed him to experiment with materials not considered traditional art media, including neon, glass and dirt. "It was a good healthy time for experimentation", Dill has said. He currently uses up to sixteen processes in a single work, and has this to say about the finished effort: "there is something magical going on in the ones that work".

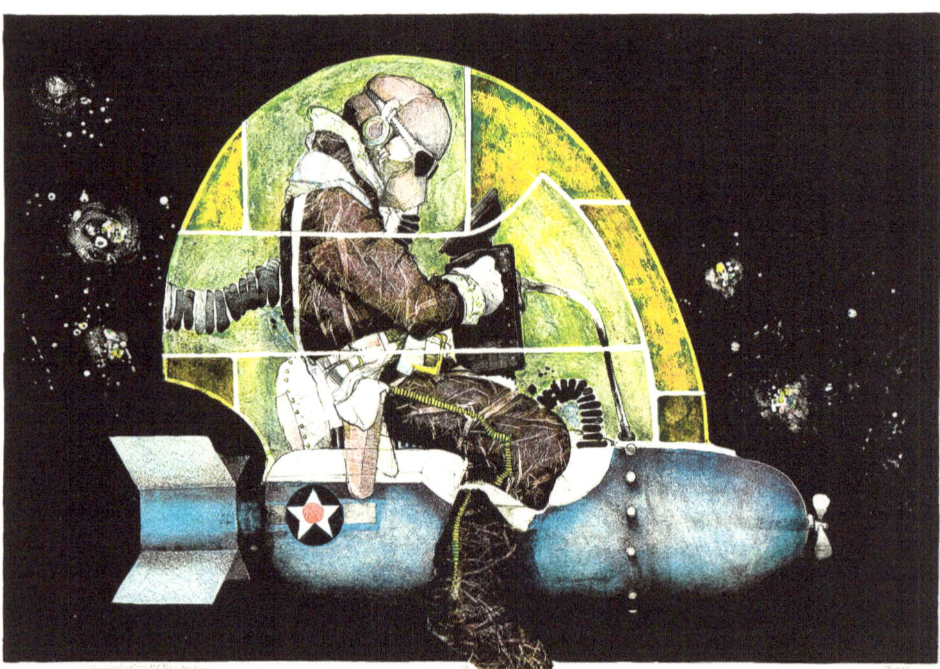

John L. Doyle
"Bombardier"
Lithograph 30 x 40

John L. Doyle was a master of design and pattern. As a printmaker, Doyle worked mainly in lithography. His art reflects his fascination with historical significance and the role of the human element. Collaborating with Roland Poska of the Fishy Whale Press in Rockford, Illinois, the pair produced a series of suites defining "The Great Human Race". The art visually records categorical statements about the development of civilization by racial segregation. Each series touches on the cultural development of particular disciplines such as Medicine, Law, Architecture and Business. They are remarkable, beautifully drawn and printed. They pay tribute to the most profound and spiritual aspirations of humankind. The art project developed into a life's work for both artists. Doyle died in 2010.

David F. Dreisbach

"Albert's Dog" Engraving 23 ¾ x 36

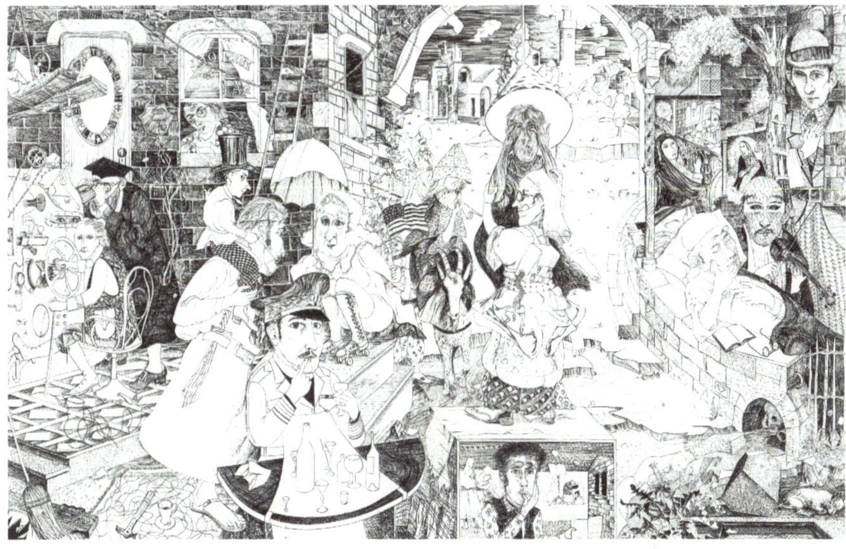

David F. Dreisbach was an educator and is a renowned printmaker. Dreisbach taught at various universities, until finally retiring from Northern Illinois University in 1991 after thirty-nine years of teaching. During his tenure, he instilled strong artistic commitment to a large impressive group of students. With teachers like Mauricio Lasansky and Stanley William Hayter at Atelier 17, he was well grounded in the demands of printmaking. He is an internationally known expert and innovator in the printmaking field, helping to create advances in color viscosity printing. A yen for humor, his collage like images are vivid playgrounds of his own making, using neighbors and family members for inspiration. While working in all processes of printmaking, his large engravings stand out as masterful examples of the medium.

Leonard Edmonson

"Burial Mound"

Intaglio Etching 11 ½ x 18

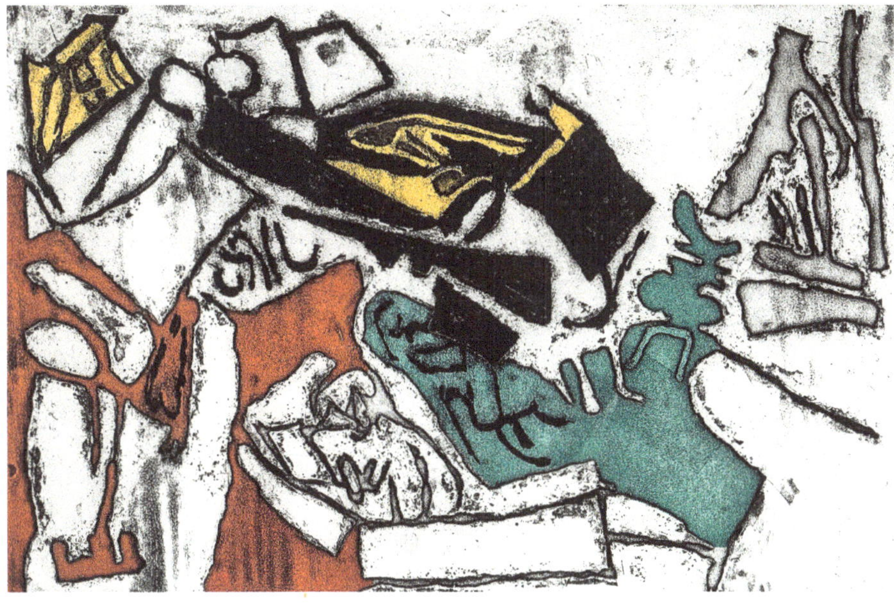

A California native, Edmonson's teaching career spanned five decades, influencing innumerable students. He retired from California State University in Los Angeles in 1986. In 1970, he published his technical treatise, "Etching", which is still a valuable reference book for printmakers. Edmonson has written, "I am equally concerned with what I want to say, and the formal values I use to say it. My art is not one of rebellion, but one of discovery and sharing". His remarkable prints are pure abstractions based on form, texture and shapes. They are a microscopic look into the landscape. His work is highly revered by collectors. Edmonson died in 2002.

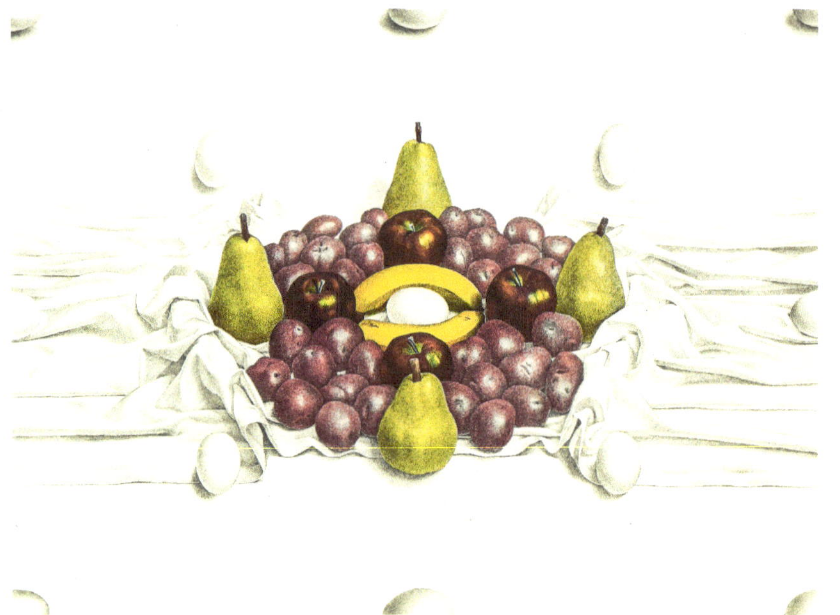

Martha Mayer Erlebacher
"Potatoes and Pears"
Lithograph 22 x 30

Originally trained as an Abstract Expressionist, Erlebacher broke from this school in the late 1960's. Soon afterwards she became recognized as one of the leading representational figurative and still life artists in America. Erlebacher fuses classical techniques with modernist ideals; the results are thought provoking vanitas, sumptuously rendered still life images, and skillfully depicted nudes. Erlebacher's interest was in creating art that is both intellectually insightful and purely beautiful. She was also a gifted printmaker. Erlebacher passed in 2013.

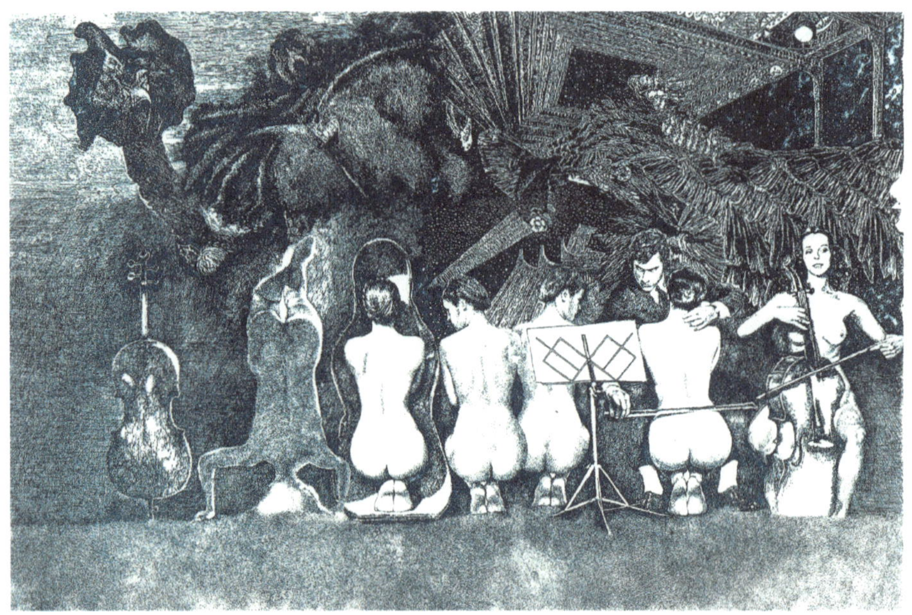

Herbert L. Fink
"Metamorphosis"
Etching 13 x 19 ¾

Herbert Fink had a distinguished career at the School of Fine Arts at Southern Illinois University - Carbondale, spanning the time period 1961 to 1987. It was an exciting time of great changes in the field of printmaking, and Fink was in the midst of it. A painter, printmaker and educator, Fink was best known for his etchings, and through them, he was noted as one of America's great modern masters of the nude. His landscapes and especially his figurative work brought him notoriety, and his influence as a printmaker and educator was significant, with both his students and contemporaries. Herb Fink passed away in 2006.

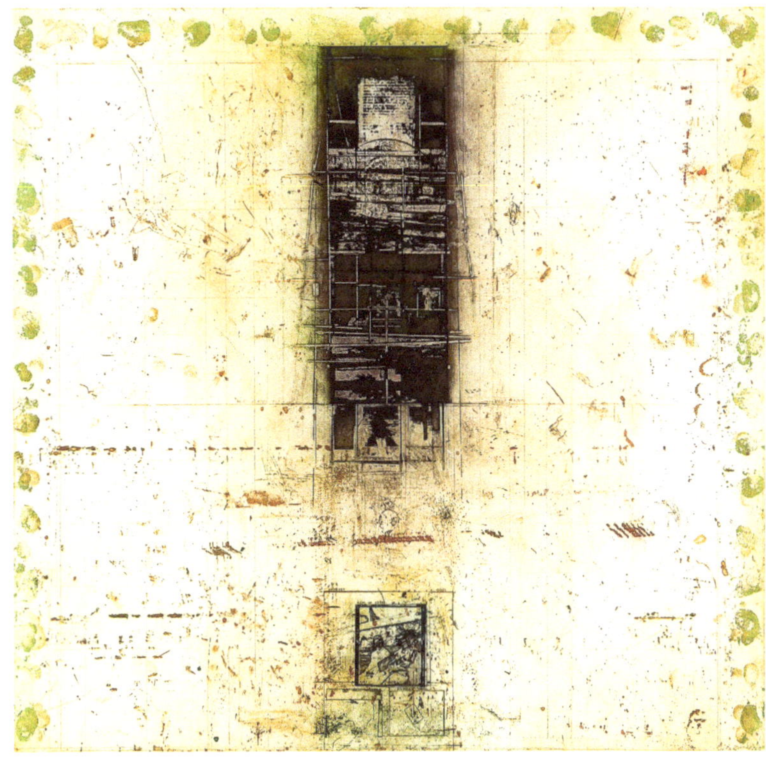

John W. Ford
"Untitled"
Monoprint 23 ½ x 24 ½

John W. Ford is a printmaker and site-based sculptor presently living in Hamilton, Ontario. He has exhibited and lectured throughout the United States and Europe. Ford creates mono-prints that reference, both visually and metaphorically, architectural sites. Imagery, as well as content, is revealed through layer after layer of printing with traditionally etched and photo-polymer plates. The results are compositions representing what Ford describes as "the syntax of residue". Pictured here is a wonderful example of his work. He is currently an Assistant Professor of Art at McMaster University.

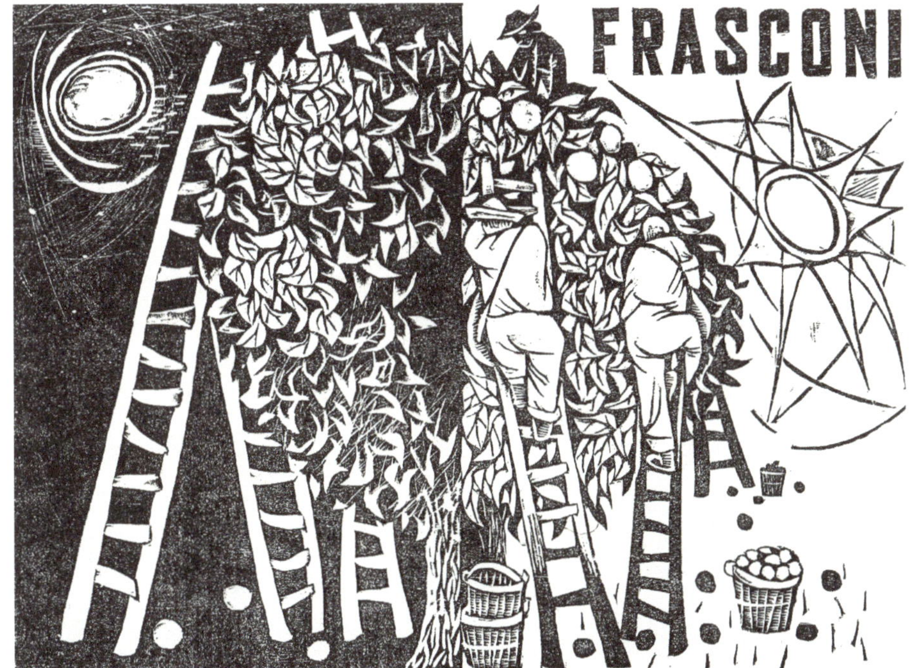

Antonio Frasconi
"Night and Day"
Woodcut 9 ½ x 12 ¾

Uruguayan-American printmaker, Antonio Frasconi, was a first generation pioneer in the Print Renaissance. Frasconi moved to the United States in 1945 at the end of World War II and became an American citizen. He is best known for his woodcuts, and has been called the "best practitioner of that medium of his generation". He was influenced and drawn to the process by an exhibition that he attended of woodcuts by Paul Gauguin. Frasconi was attracted to printmaking by the idea of making multiples, in part so he could offer art to people at reasonable prices. Frasconi was also an illustrator, illustrating more than 100 books, and found inspiration in comic books as well as the old masters. His influence has been and continues to be major in the printmaking field. Frasconi passed away in 2013.

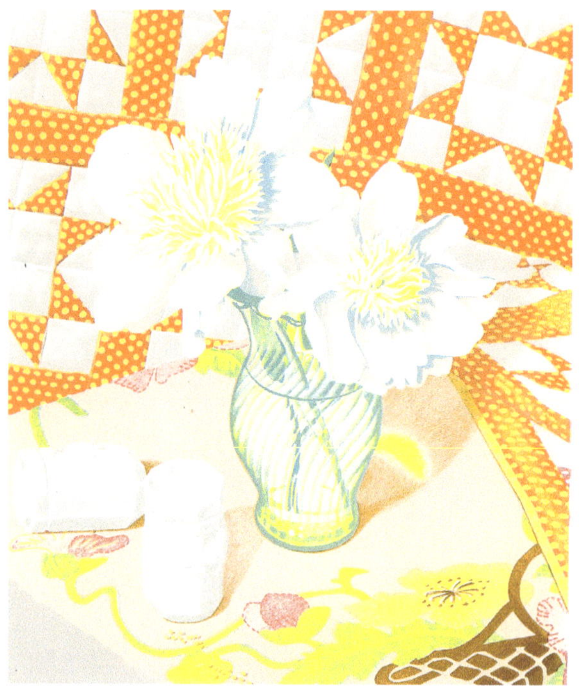

Sondra Freckleton
"Peonies"
Lithograph 20 x 17

During the 1970's, Sondra Freckleton was one of several noted abstract artists who turned to realism in their work. She is mainly known for her expertly crafted watercolors, and her multi-color silkscreen prints. Her subject matter is complex studies of the still life genre using flowers, color and textile patterns to construct her imagery. About her work, she has stated, "I want things to appear more round, more spatial, more full of life than they really are". She was married to the late artist Jack Beal.

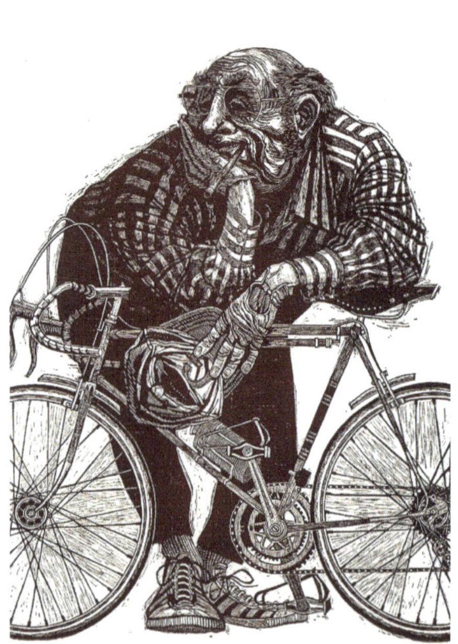

Raymond Gloeckler "Big Biker" Wood Engraving 14 x 9

Raymond Gloeckler began teaching at the University of Wisconsin – Madison in 1961, and retired after thirty-five years of influential teaching. During this time he became known as "one of the world's great masters of wood engraving art". His subject matter was social commentary, whimsical and satirical in nature, poking fun at humanity's follies. His is a sharp eye for the ludicrous in American Society, and Gloeckler creates images that lampoon the inflated and celebrate the everyday people among us. In his unique style, he has followed his own path, defying the art world trendiness surrounding him. He presently resides in Portage, Wisconsin.

John Goray
"Untitled – Maze"
Monoprint 9 ½ x 15 ¾

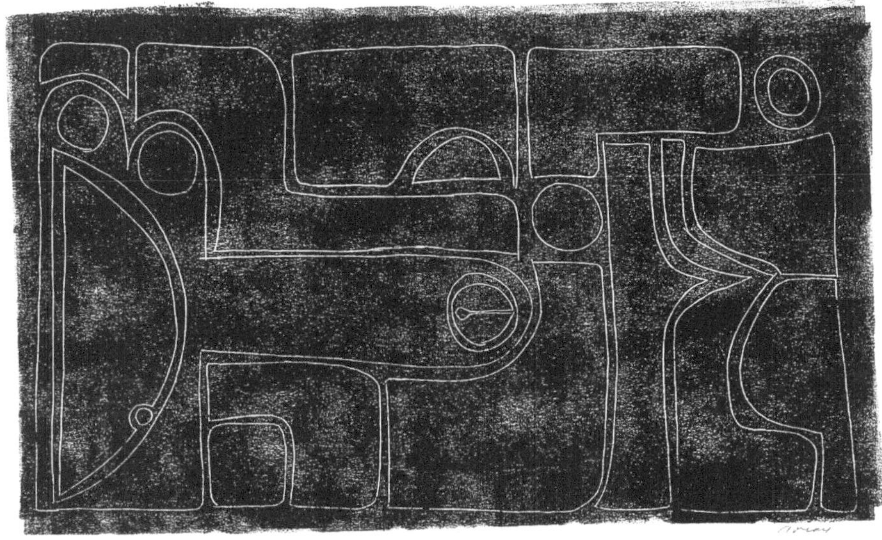

John Goray was born in Marinette, Wisconsin, in 1912 and was known for his work as a painter. He studied at the Minneapolis School of Art, and the Arts Student League in New York. Following that he worked for the Walt Disney Studios where he was assigned to and refined the character of "Thumper". He moved to Kenosha, Wisconsin where he made an impact as a Regional instructor teaching at the Kenosha Public Museum, the Wustum Museum in Racine, and finally the University of Wisconsin – Parkside. He was a strong influence on his students and peers alike. Goray passed away in 1990.

Michael Goro
"Chicago Blues"
Etching 24 x 36

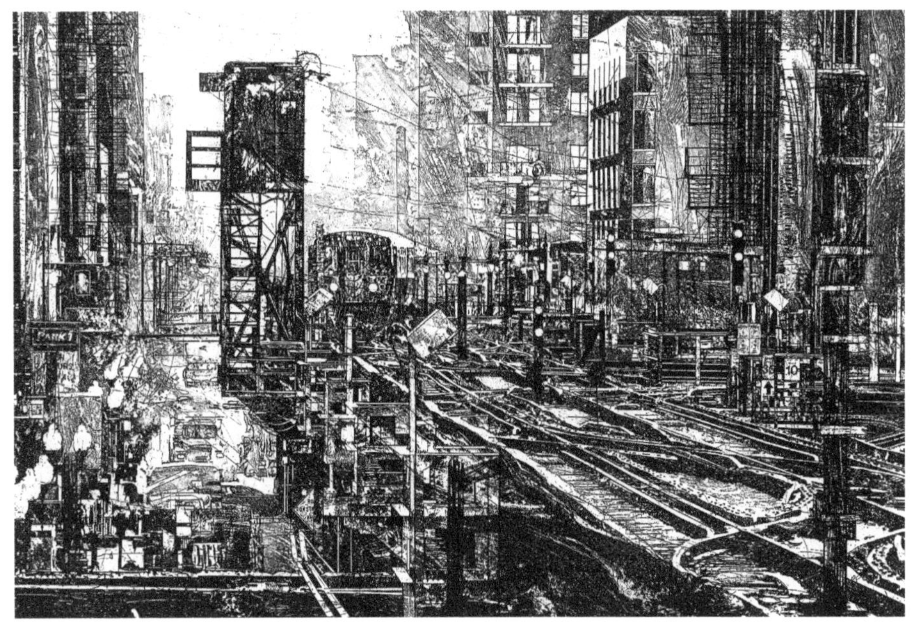

Michael Goro is a unique voice of the new wave of contemporary printmakers. Goro knows Chicago and its distinctive rhythm. His work takes us there, as he hosts an enjoyable visit, using his mastery of printmaking skills. His etchings reverberate with an excitement that packages the dirt and the grease, the screech of metal on metal sounds of the raised L, and the controlled chaos that simultaneously occurs beneath the two tiered city. Goro and his subject matter are one, and his work takes the viewer to another level of experience. His art is exceptional.

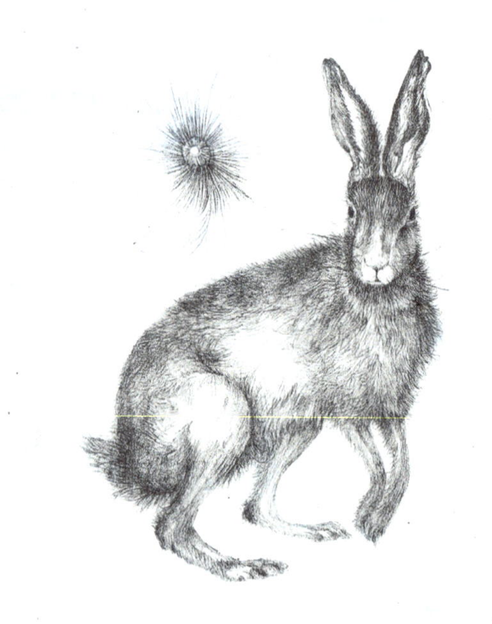

Valerie Hammond
"Untitled – Hare"
Lithograph 13 ½ x 12

Born in Santa Maria, Caifornia, Valerie Hammond lives in New York City. Hammond is a prolific sculptor and printmaker, drawing from places and objects that are full of mystery and superstition. This image of a hare was one of a series made from drawings while in Ballinskelligs, Ireland. It resonates an Irish belief that upon death, one's soul resides in the body of a hare so that it can attend to unfinished business or visit loved ones. Her art is one of symbolism. She has stated; "I am interested in evoking sensation and making work which is corporeal in nature. It is important to me that the work is not sentimental, but experiential".

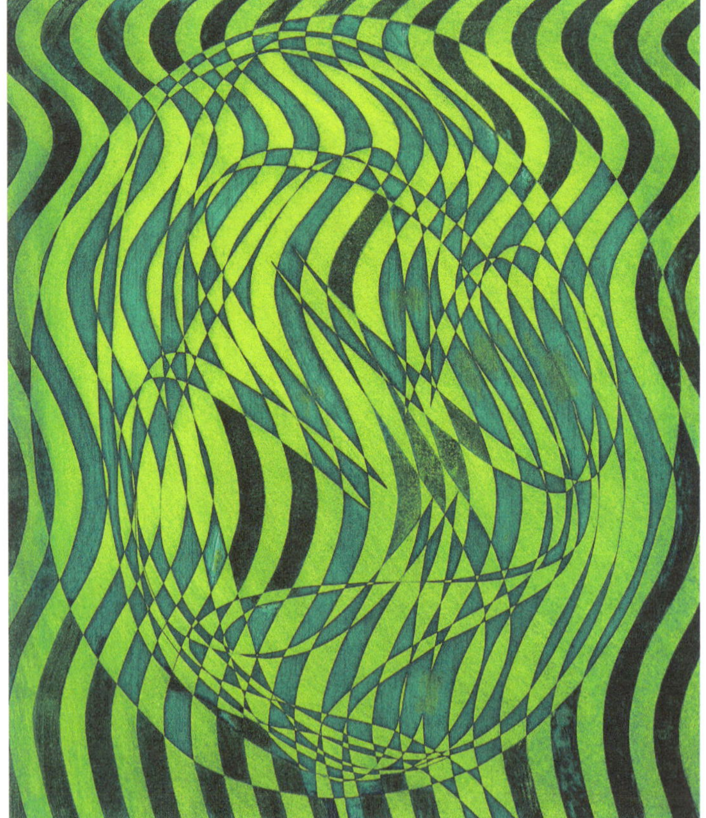

Stanley William Hayter
"Mere"
Viscosity Etching 21 ¼ x 18 ½

Stanley William Hayter is aptly referred to as the founding father of modern printmaking. His work at Atelier 17 made a significant contribution to the medium, and he was the main impetus behind the Print Renaissance in the graphic arts that we enjoy today. He is also credited for the innovation of viscosity printing, a multi-color process produced in a single pass of the inked plate through the press. He referred to it as "simultaneous colour printing". Hayter is known, and has received recognition as one of the outstanding graphic artists of our time. He died in 1988, having made an indelible mark in art history.

Nona Hershey

"Wires II: Running Figure" Etching 18 x 11 ½

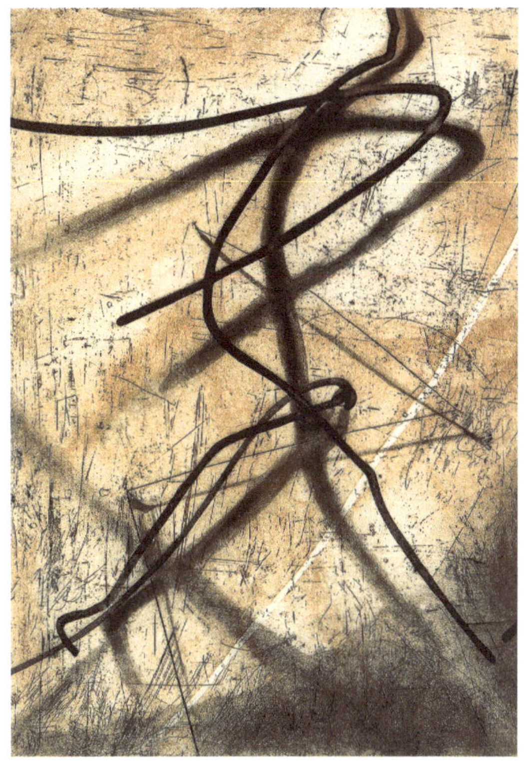

Nona Hershey is a noted printmaker and educator, presently a professor at the Massachusetts College of Art and Design. Hershey has been an active participant in national juried exhibitions since the late 1970's when her detailed landscapes first brought her acclaim as a printmaker. She has stated; "I want to evoke a sense of wonder" and "to measure and control forces larger than ourselves". Her works are lyrical images of intimate dreams that fringe on the outer edge of the surreal. Her work pictured here is a figurative shaped piece of rusted wire that virtually dances across the façade of what could be an aging building. It is a masterful handling of the understated. Her influence extends to her students and peers alike.

John Hultberg

"Witness" Silkscreen 28 x 24

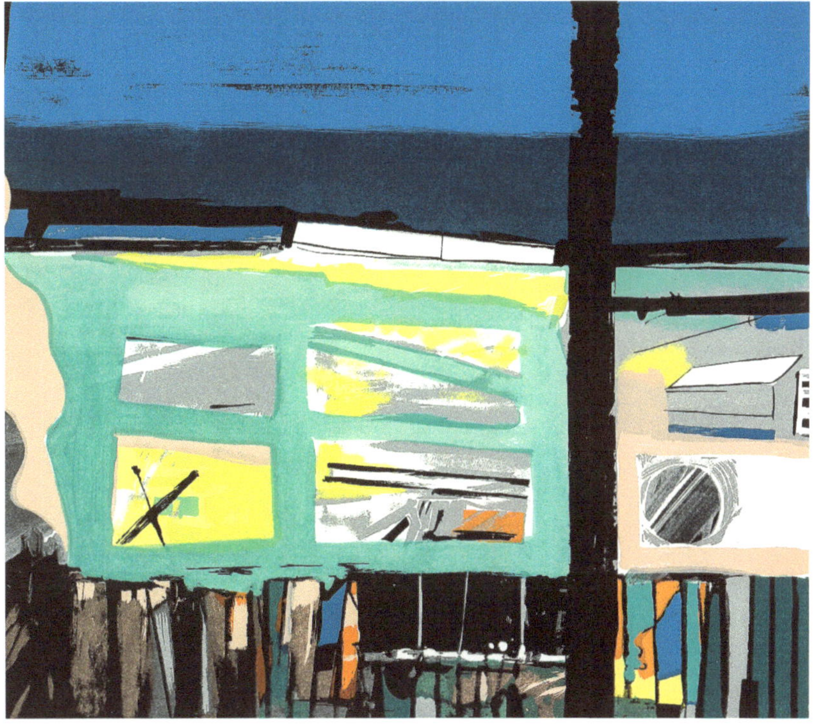

Born in 1922, John Hultberg is a printmaker and painter of note, whose works possess the dreamlike quality that is associated with Surrealism. Distorted dark urban landscapes, apocalyptic and alien, take the viewer into the world of Hultberg. Ships and shores, peopled landscapes and deteriorating architecture are snapshots into the unknown. His works are very prophetic, with pollution and environment issues as their theme. Reminiscent of Abstract Expressionism, the artist has created a style all his own, and is considered an abstract realist. Hultberg articulates strong forms and design, balanced by a forceful use of color. He has stated, "When I walk back and forth in this small room, this cellar which is my studio, a dream state takes over". John Hultberg passed away in 2005.

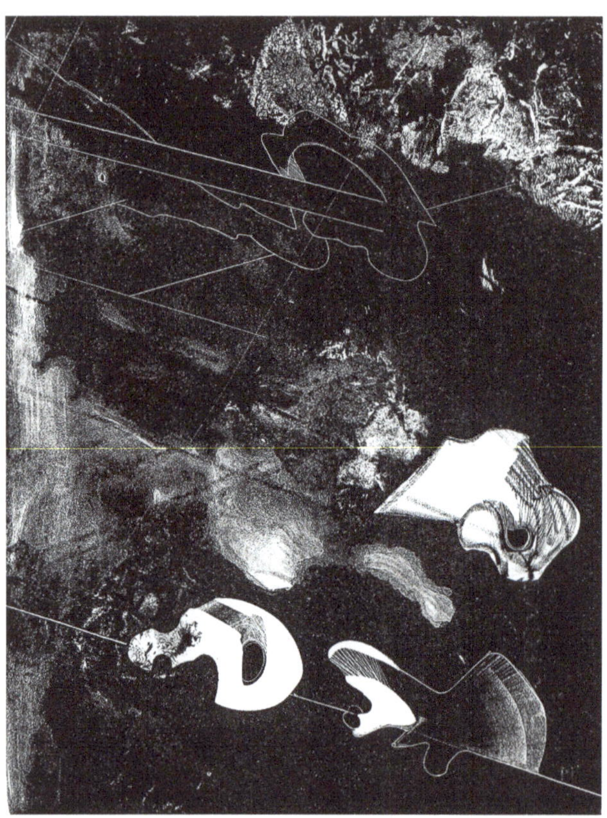

Richard Howard Hunt
"RH224LS" Lithograph 14 x 11

Richard Hunt was born in Chicago in 1935, and prefers to be called a "Midwestern sculptor". Hunt uses automobile junk yards as his quarries, and transforms cast off automobile bumpers and fenders into elegant abstract welded sculptures. Hunt is also an accomplished printmaker who works in the medium of lithography. His print imagery reflects the same elegant forms that you see in his sculpture, and some of his lithographs have been studies for his outdoor sculptures. He has stated: "In some works, it is my intention to develop the kind of forms that Nature might create if only heat and steel were available to her."

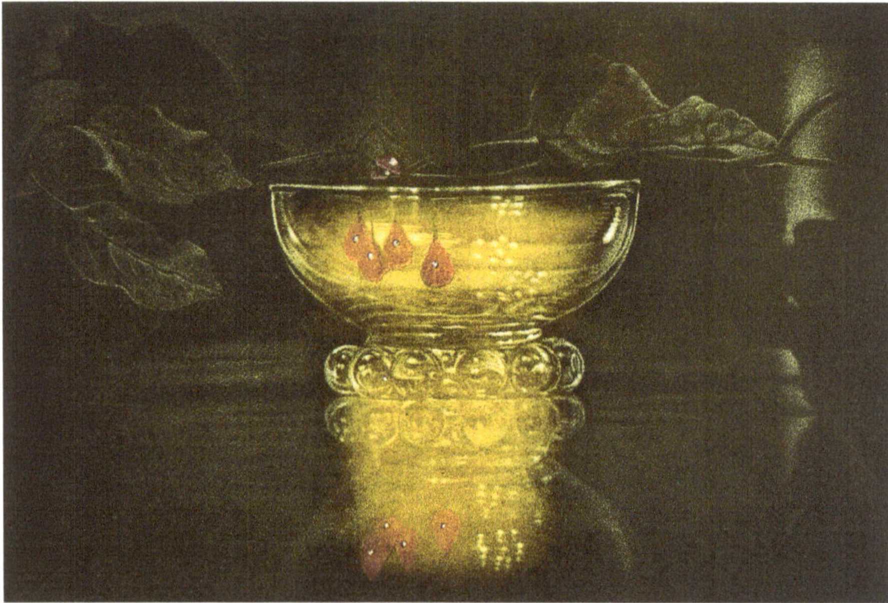

Jayne Reid Jackson
"Bittersweet" Mezzotint 6 x 9

A contemporary "basement printmaker" of exceptional abilities, Jayne Reid Jackson is internationally known for her still life mezzotint prints. A full time printmaker, she uses everyday objects as her subject matter which are imbued with a timeless and classical feel. She states, "As someone whose artistic expression is firmly based in drawing, I find that printmaking, especially intaglio, provides me with the widest range of tools for my needs". The image "Bittersweet", pictured here, is a prime example of her use of the mezzotint medium to fulfill her vision. It is a beautifully rendered and flawlessly composed still life.

John Paul Jones
"Annunciation" Intaglio Etching 27 ¾ x 21 ¾

John Paul Jones was a West Coast printmaker, painter, sculptor, author, educator and lecturer and was widely revered among his students and peers. A multi-faceted artist, Jones first gained recognition and was described as "one of America's foremost printmakers" in the '50s and '60s with his figurative prints. His imagery has been described as announcing itself "in a whisper, having taut understatement, laconic calm, and thoughtful refinement of form". As an educator, he established the printmaking program at the University of California – Los Angeles in 1953, and retired after thirty-seven years of teaching in 1990 from the University of California – Irvine. Jones ignored fashion and did not seek notoriety in favor of pursuing the intrinsic demands of art. Jones passed away in 1999, and in his own words, he has left his many students and colleagues "to do good work".

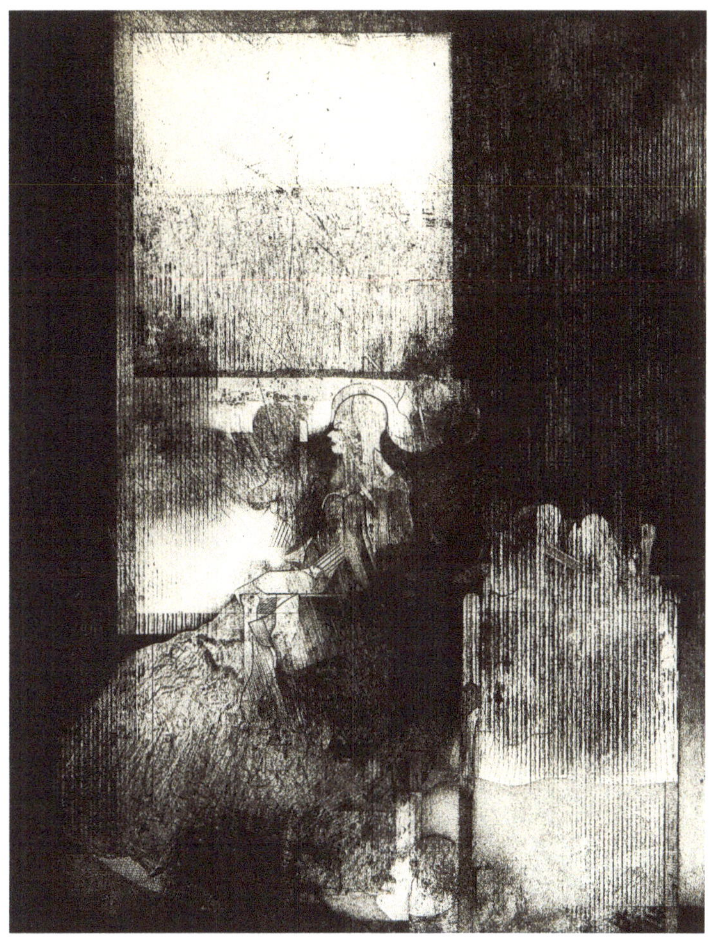

Jacob Kainen
"Bright Afternoon" Etching 20 x 16

Jacob Kainen was a Renaissance man, highly skilled on many levels. A painter, printmaker, curator, scholar, educator and patron, Kainen was for decades a beloved and highly respected figure in the art world. A major force in the Washington, DC art scene, Kainen helped to build and manage the print collection at the Smithsonian Institution. He was a fascinating person and a force behind contemporary printmaking. His influence has been felt by many and will continue for generations to come. His work and accomplishments in the printmaking field have not yet received their just due. Kainen died in 2001.

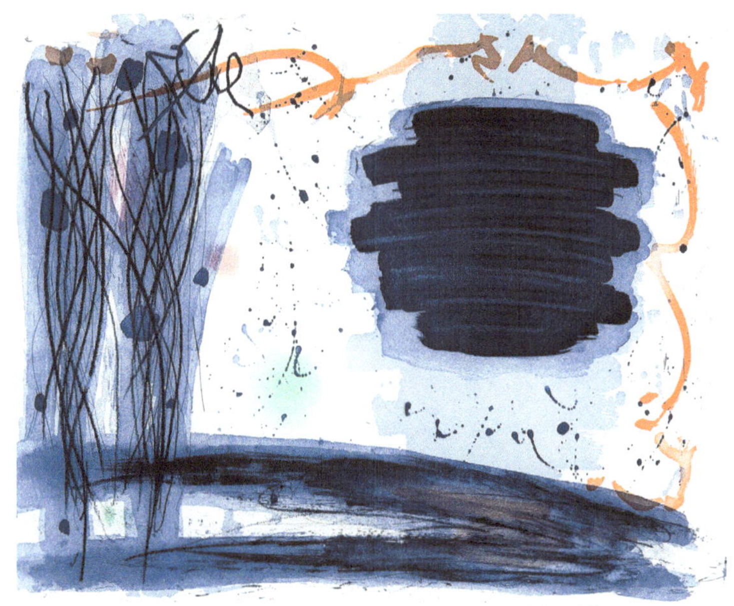

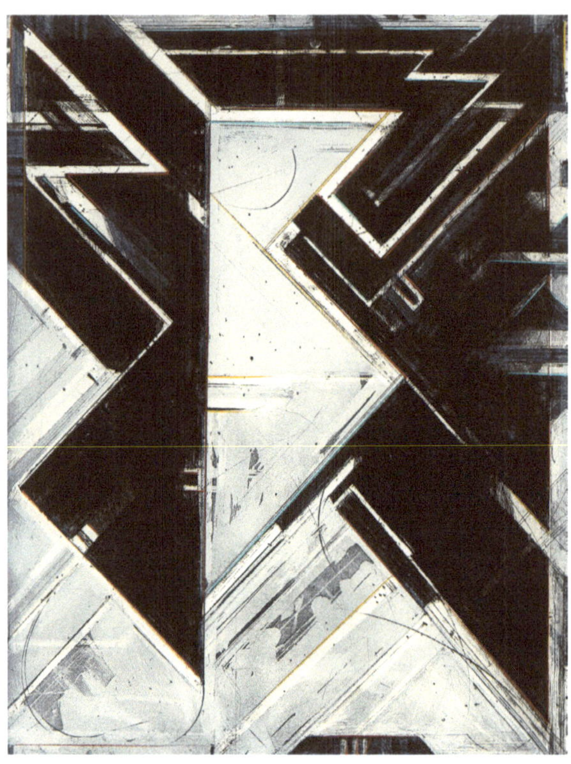

Robert Kelly
"Alma IV" Etching 20 x 16

Born in 1956, Robert Kelly is an American artist based in New York City. He is a full time artist and has produced prints of extraordinary skill and technical expertise. His abstract etchings have a remarkable elegance and a beauty of process that is masterful and visually exciting. His compositions and color harmonies are held in perfect moments of balance. His work is fascinating and exemplary.

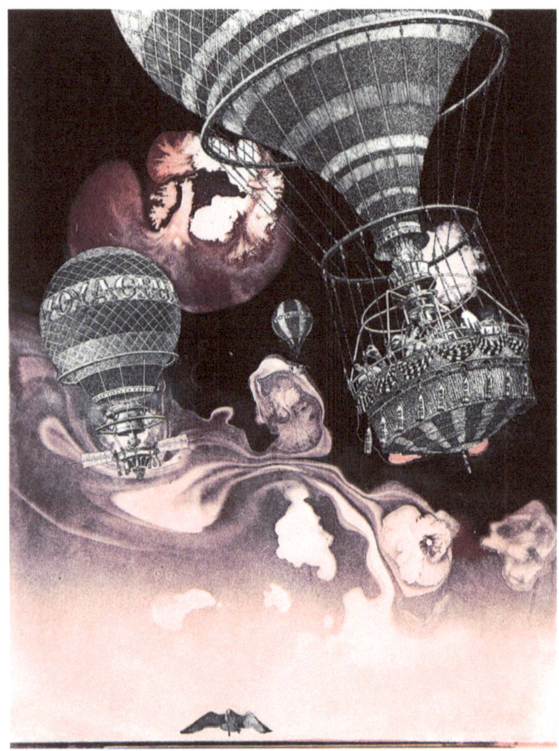

Ken Kerslake
"The Journals of Voyageur: Adrift Near the Source"
Photo Etching/ Aquatint 19 ½ x 15

Ken Kerslake was one of a handful of printmaker/educators responsible for the growth of printmaking in the southeast following World War II. Fresh out of college in 1958, Kerslake was hired by the University of Florida in Gainesville, to develop a printmaking program for its art department. Accomplishing that, he went on to have a thirty-eight year career at the University. He was active in national juried exhibitions during the Golden '70s. His prints at that time were some of the first to incorporate photo processing. These works were technical marvels and masterfully done. Kerslake continued his experimentation with digital printmaking techniques until his death in 2007. He has written this about his work, "figures searching for a connection, a sense of place, meaning and valid experience". Kerslake was Southern Graphics Council president from 1990-1992.

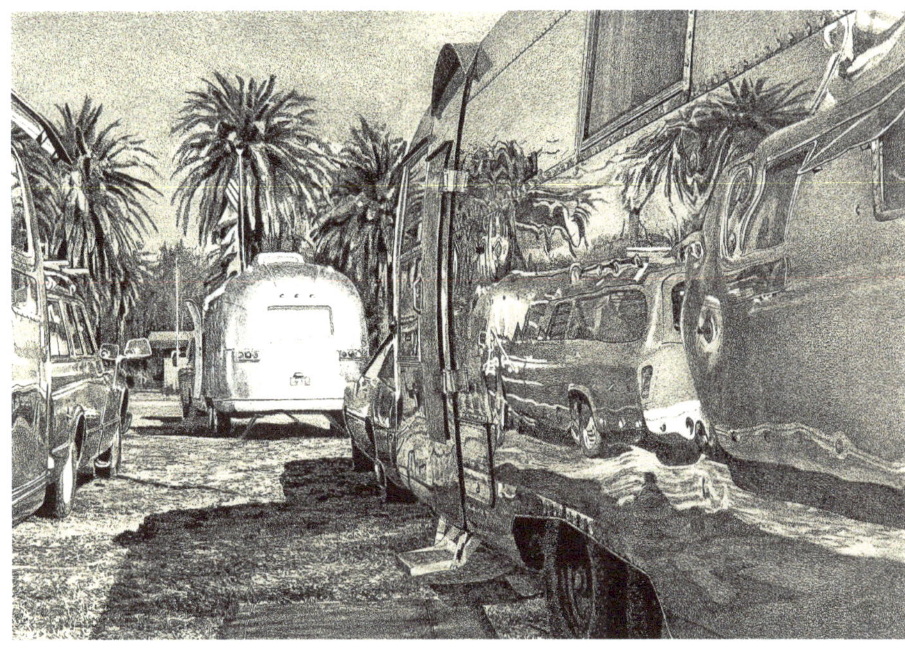

David Kessler
"Untitled (Trailer Park)"
Lithograph 13 x 19

David Kessler was born in Park Ridge, New Jersey, and presently lives and works in Arizona. He follows the Photo-Realist tradition, bridging the gap between what is real and what is illusion. His subject matter is waterscapes, as well as the Arizona desert landscape surrounding his home. "Untitled (Trailer Park)", pictured here, is an early lithograph that serves as a prelude to the refracted light of his present work which is done on aluminum sheets that enhance that light. He has stated; "As a painter, it is important for me to address the concerns of painting – what has been done – and what can I add to this".

Wayne Kimball
"Properly Mounted Texas Longhorn"
Lithograph 16 5/8 x 14 5/8

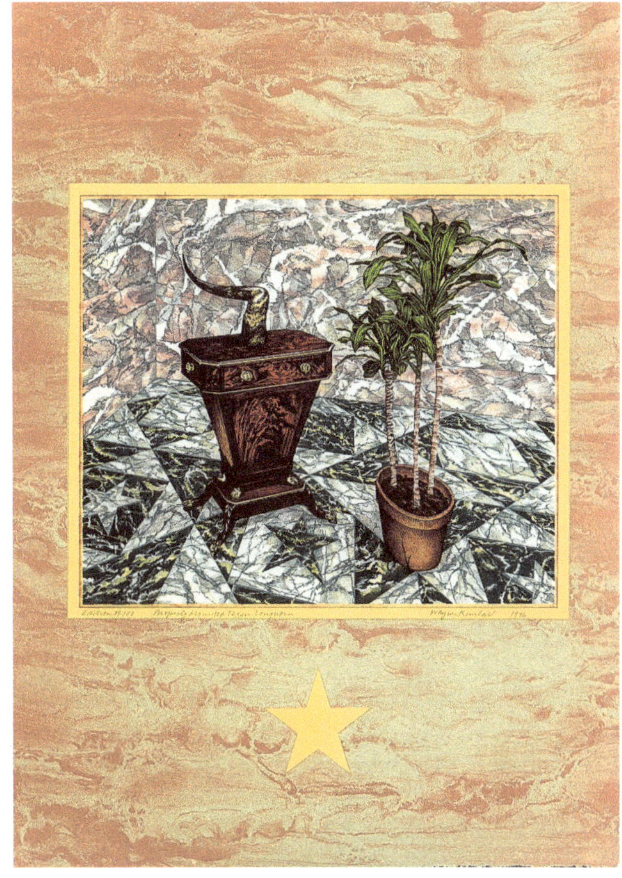

Wayne Kimble is a printmaker and a Tamarind Master Printer. His lithographs are small, meticulously drawn images, influenced by medieval icons. These images draw the viewer close, inviting one to enter the fantasy interiors that the artist has created. They are a visual delight, providing a romantic escape into an environment of enjoyable fantasy. There, they are left for the viewer to sort out in their own way. Kimball was an active participant in competitions during the Golden '70s and continues exhibiting today.

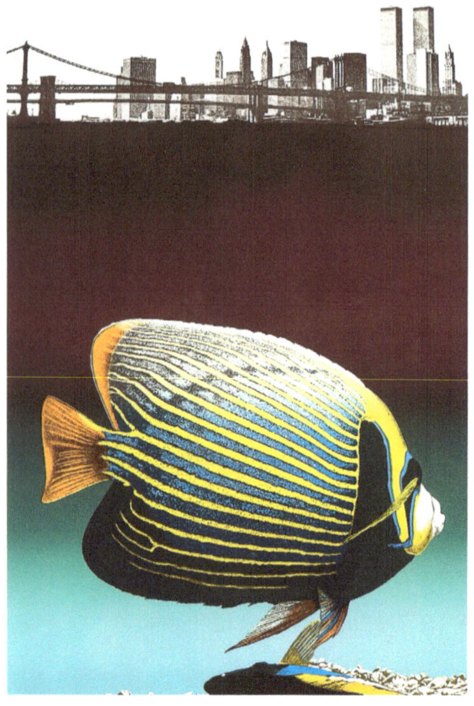

Michael Knigin

"Silent Witness" Lithograph 34 x 22

In 1968, Michael Knigin opened his own publishing company, Chiron Press. It was the first facility in the United States that combined lithography with silkscreen printing. He published prints for some of the major artists of the time; Andy Warhol, Roy Lichtenstein and Paul Jenkins. He was invited by the Israel Museum and the Jerusalem Foundation to establish the first professional lithography workshop in Israel, inviting and training artists from Israel, the United States and Europe. His contributions to Israel and America are well respected by artists, educators and collectors alike. His work is highly collected. Knigin passed away in 2011. He was a professor at Pratt Institute in New York City, and was married to the artist Joan Kraisky.

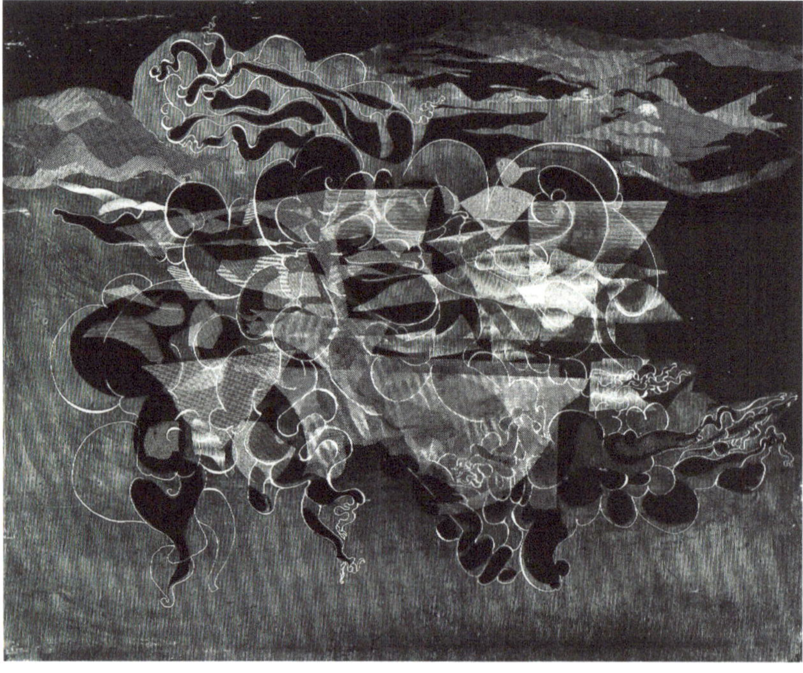

Misch Kohn

"Laocoon" Photo Etching 15 ¾ x 19 ½

Misch Kohn was a first generation pioneer in the Print Renaissance and a major figure in modern American art. He revolutionized printmaking and inspired generations of students and artists during a sixty year career. His constant experimentation with new techniques, along with the unprecedented scale of his prints, changed how printmaking was viewed. He thought that printmaking ought to be taken to a scale where it would rival painting. A true "basement printmaker", for many years his studio was his cellar, illuminated only by fluorescent lights. Kohn studied briefly with Hayter at Atelier 17 in Paris, and the two established a close friendship and spent much time together. In 1949 he began a twenty-two year career at the Institute of Design in Chicago, finally retiring from teaching at Cal State University – Hayward in1986. Despite his stature in the field, Kohn was a humble, soft spoken man and a patient teacher. He continued making prints until his death in 2003. His influence continues to be major.

Jacob Landau
"Crooked Sky" Wood Engraving 13 x 10 ½

Jacob Landau was best known for his evocative works on the human condition. Following World War II while in Paris, Landau met Leonard Baskin who taught him the medium of woodcuts. It would become his defining technique, and serve him well in his career as an illustrator and narrative artist. His work has been described as "unmistakably modern, and at the same time had its roots in the traditions of Goya and Blake". Landau taught at the Pratt Institute in New York City for more than twenty years, introducing many students to the art of printmaking, and the process of woodcut. Throughout his life, Landau's art increasingly addressed the self-inflicted turmoil of the Twentieth Century. Landau died in 2001.

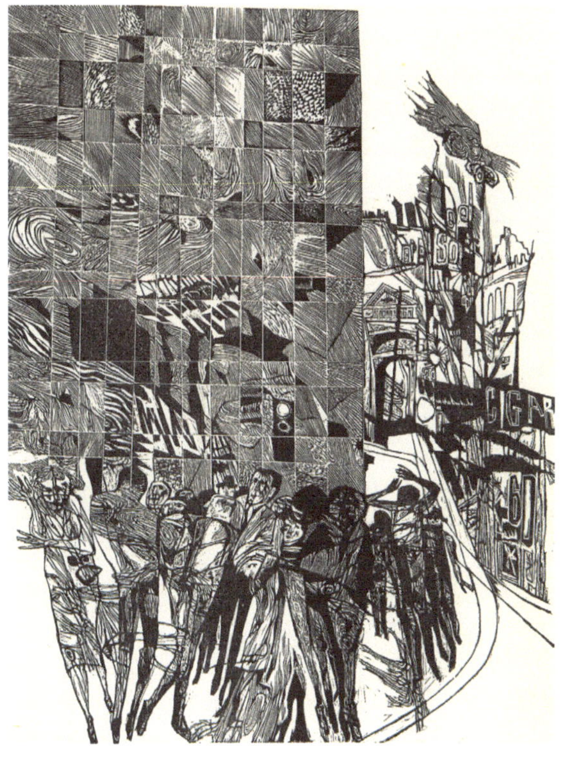

Mauricio Lasansky
"El Maestro" Intaglio Etching 15 x 14 ½

As a printmaker, Mauricio Lasansky was considered a "wizard" of printmaking technology, and has fittingly earned the title as one of the "fathers of twentieth century printmaking". Lasansky was a first generation forerunner in the evolution of the graphic arts in the US as a meaningful and critical art form. He was directly involved with Hayter and Atelier 17. As a printmaker, Lasansky was known for the grand scale of his images, and the vivid color and complex layering of multiple techniques in a single image. Some of his works involved 60 plates and measured 4 x 8 feet. He was instrumental in progressing the printmaking program at the University of Iowa, one of the country's finest. He was perhaps best known for his "Nazi Drawings" which examine the brutality of Nazi Germany. Lasansky passed away in 2012 at the age of 97.

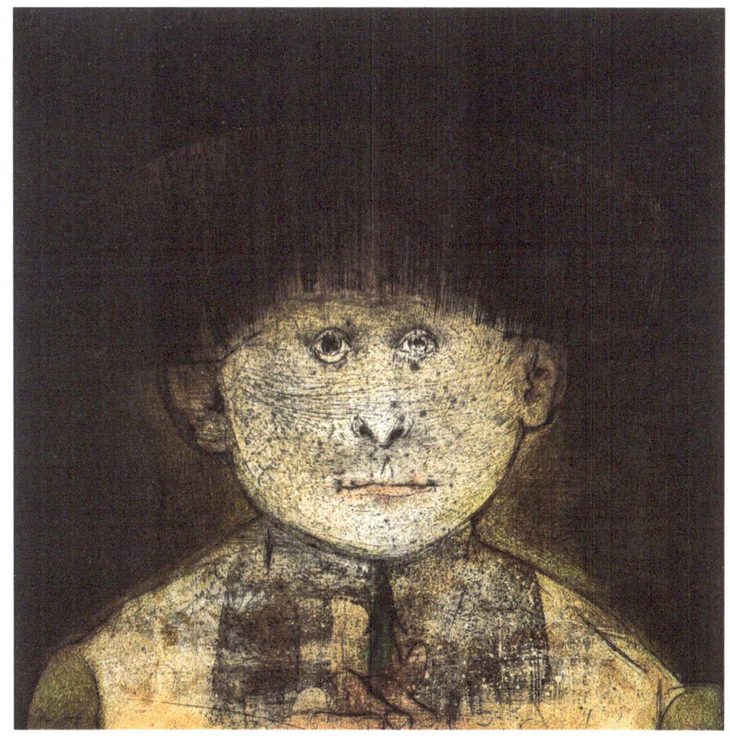

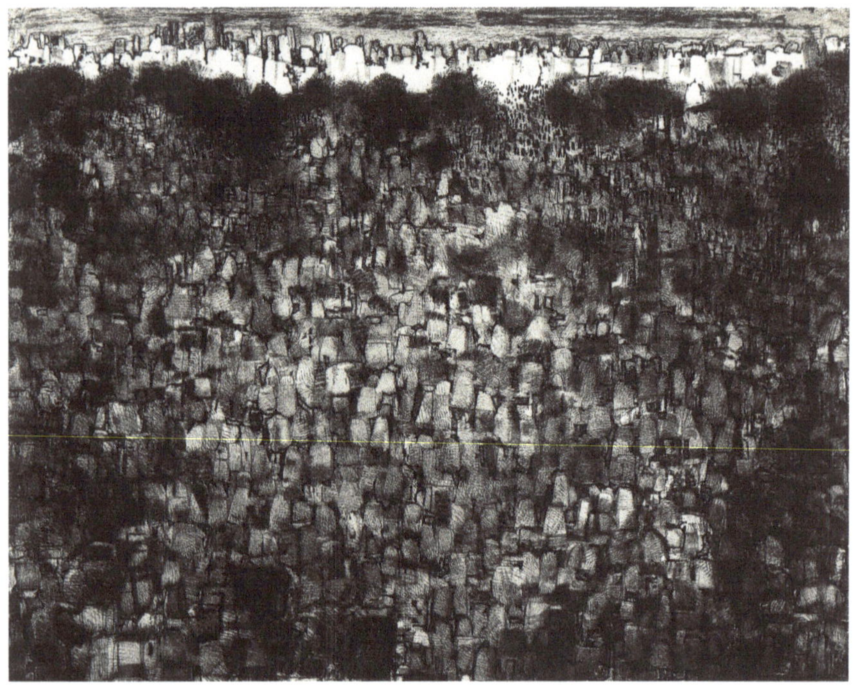

Gerson Leiber
"Along Ossuary Street, a Blind Man Taps His Cane"
Intaglio Etching 21 ½ x 28***

A painter and printmaker, Gerson Leiber studied with Gabor Peterdi at the Brooklyn Museum Art School, and with Will Barnet at the Art Students League of New York City. He later taught at the Printmaking Workshop established by Robert Blackburn. His emphasis turned to painting in the mid-fifties when he found inspiration in the gardens of a farm house property that he purchased with his wife Judith in East Hampton, Long Island. He designed and manipulated the natural shapes of the plantings to form a living, growing cubism, and these forms and colors became the focus of much of his art from that time on. He has stayed active and he continues to produce and exhibit his prints. Leiber was a past president of the prestigious Society of American Graphic Artists based in New York City.

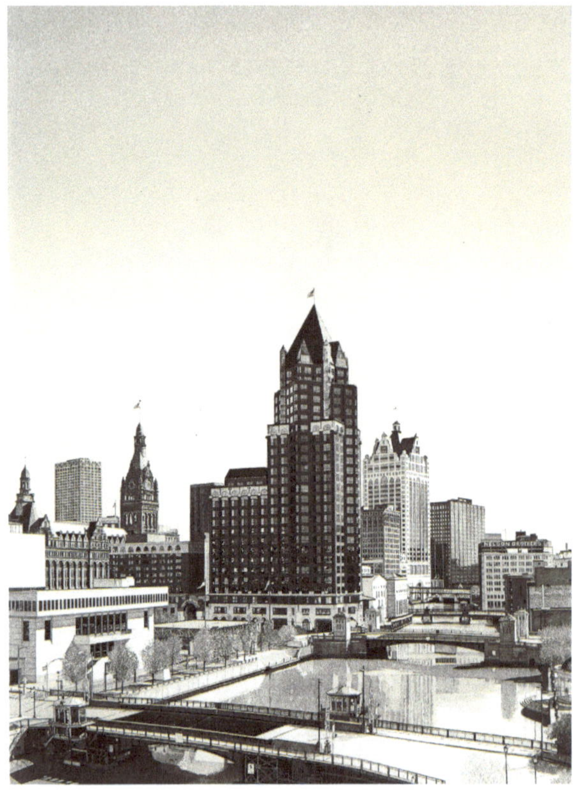

Martin Levine
"Milwaukee River" Etching 24 x 18

Artist, printmaker and educator, Martin Levine has been teaching at Suny Stoney Brook University since 1986. Levine was born in New York City and he presently lives on Long Island. Working mainly in etching and lithography, his subject matter consists of realistically rendered rural, and more recently urban landscapes, rendered in fantastic textural detail. Levine's masterful work gained national and international prominence in the Golden '70s, and it continues to amaze today. He is widely respected and his influence in printmaking has been substantial. He is a past president of the prestigious Society of American Graphic Artists based in New York City.

Evan Lindquist
"Thought" Engraving 12 x 11 ¾

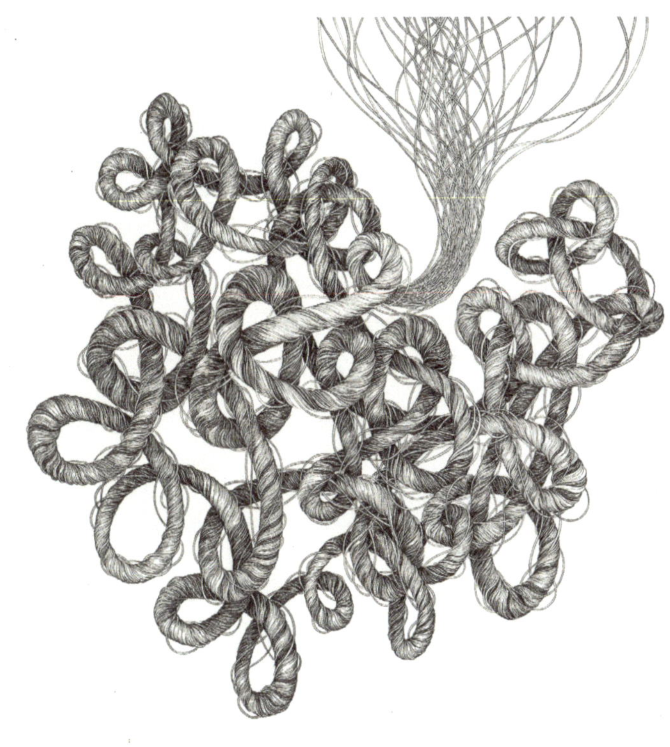

Born in 1936, Evan Lindquist had a distinguished forty year career teaching printmaking and drawing at Arkansas State University in Jonesboro, Arkansas. He retired in 2003 as Emeritus Professor of Art. Lindquist is a master of the traditional process of engraving using the burin. He works in series, researching his subject matter tirelessly. His image pictured here, "Thought", was based on a series depicting string. It is a superb example of his technical virtuosity. One reviewer described his work as "metaphors of the mind". Lindquist was a consistent exhibitor and prize winner in exhibitions in the Golden '70s. He has had a major influence on students and colleagues alike. One of many honors, he has been named as Arkansas' first Artist Laureate for the years 2013-2017. A tireless worker, Lindquist continues to be an inspiration to his past students and to his peers.

Nicola Lopez
"Iceberg City" Relief 10 x 11

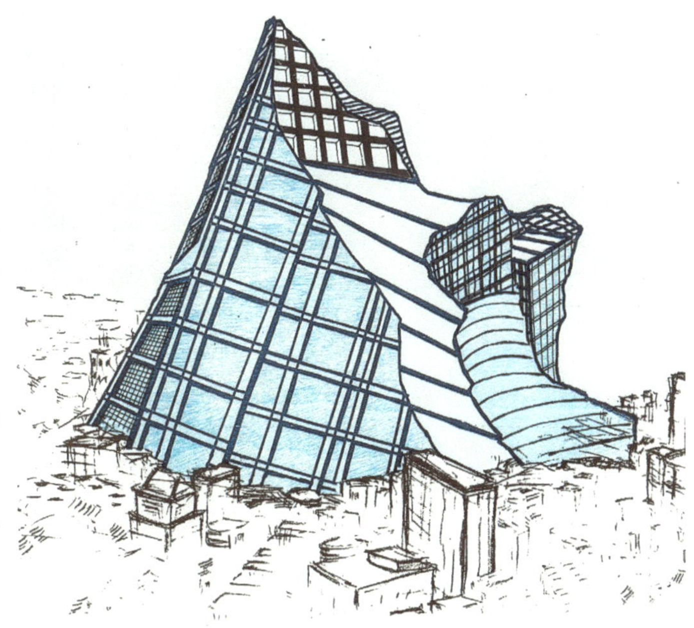

"Pay attention to what is out there and what is happening – in all of its strange, overwhelming, terrible and thrilling awesomeness". So stated Nicola Lopez, born in Santa Fe, New Mexico, and presently lives and works in Brooklyn, New York. She teaches at Columbia University in New York City. Her subject matter is primarily urban-landscape, stemming from an interest in urban planning, architecture and anthropology. While her work is strictly structured, and often suggest details of engineering plans, Lopez allows for a certain amount of process-based unpredictability in her work centering on a balance of order and disorder. She states; "The world reflected in my work is part here/now, part parallel reality and part near future". Hers are powerful and reflective images.

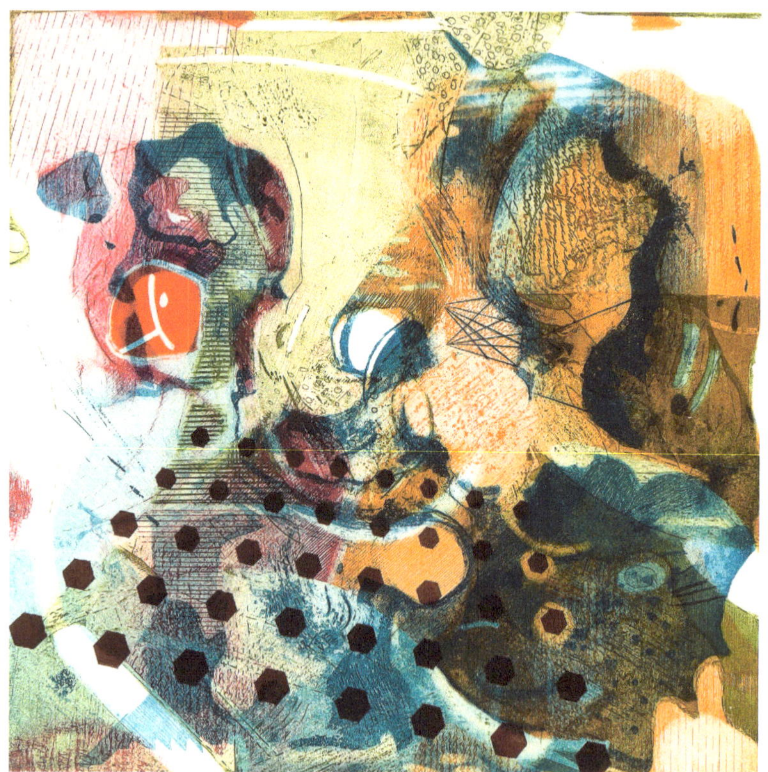

Marvin Lowe
"Andromeda" I
ntaglio Etching 23 ½ x 23 ½

Marvin Lowe studied with Mauricio Lasansky at the University of Iowa. In 1967, he and Rudy Pozzatti worked together building the University of Indiana Printmaking Workshop's outstanding reputation for teaching and research. Joined by Wendy Calman in 1976, they spent the next fifteen years building one of the most successful printmaking programs in the United States. His legacy to printmaking lives on through the many students whose lives he touched. His etchings are among the best examples in the medium. Powerful abstracted compositions of color and form, his images speak with an artistic message near shouting. They are exquisite visual statements of masterful eloquence. Marvin Lowe passed away in 2010.

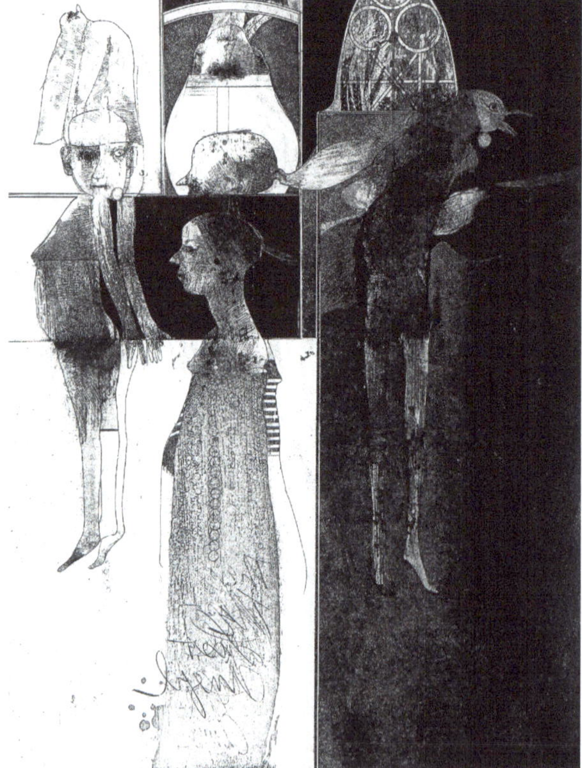

Robert Ernst Marx
"Church Window" Etching/Aquatint 18 x 14

Born in 1925, Robert Ernst Marx is an artist of great skills, and a master of the etching needle. He is part of a small group of important American figurative artists whose work addresses what it means to be human in an inhuman age. He says this about his work, "These people that I draw personify the human condition. They are people that are around us every day". His images are fascinating and haunting portraits of faces and figures, delivered through the use of his highly developed technical expertise of the etching medium. There is a beauty to his work that attracts the viewer, and also an ambiguity that invites interpretation and meditation. His influence has been major among students and peers alike.

Michael Mazur
"Confrontation" Etching 38 x 25

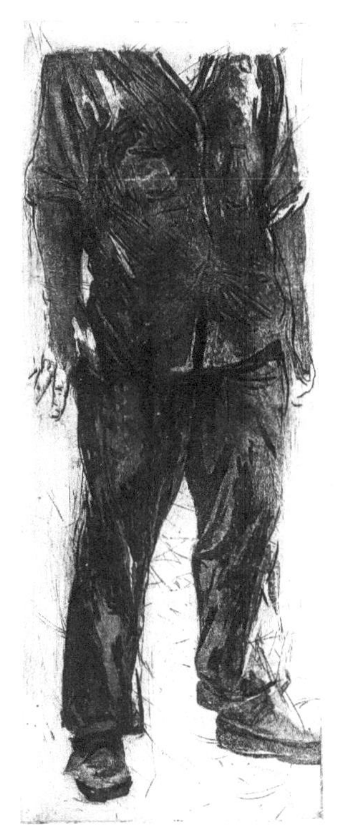
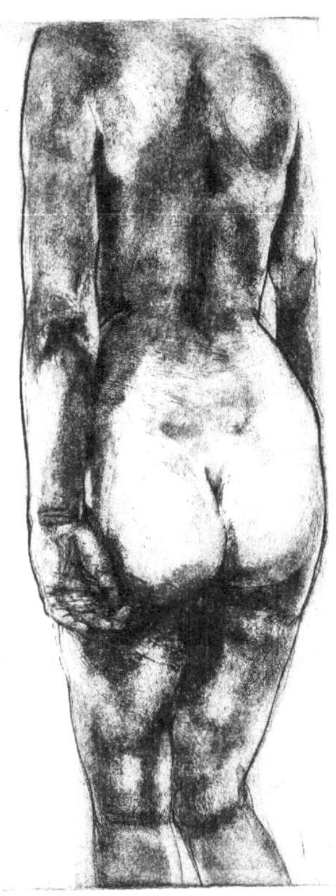

Michael Mazur first gained notice for his series of lithographs and etchings of inmates in a mental asylum, which resulted in two publications: "Closed Ward" and "Locked Ward". The artist has been described as a "restlessly inventive printmaker, painter and sculptor" whose work encompassed social documentation, narrative and landscape. Mazur is difficult to characterize as an artist because he was always trying new things. He continually reinvented himself over a fifty year period, never settling into a groove. Mazur taught at the Fine Arts Workshop in Provincetown, Massachusetts, and has been attributed with renewing the monotype process. His footprint on American printmaking is notable, and his influence far reaching. He passed away in 2009.

Bruce McCombs
"Gulliver's Lincoln"
Etching 22 x 27 ½

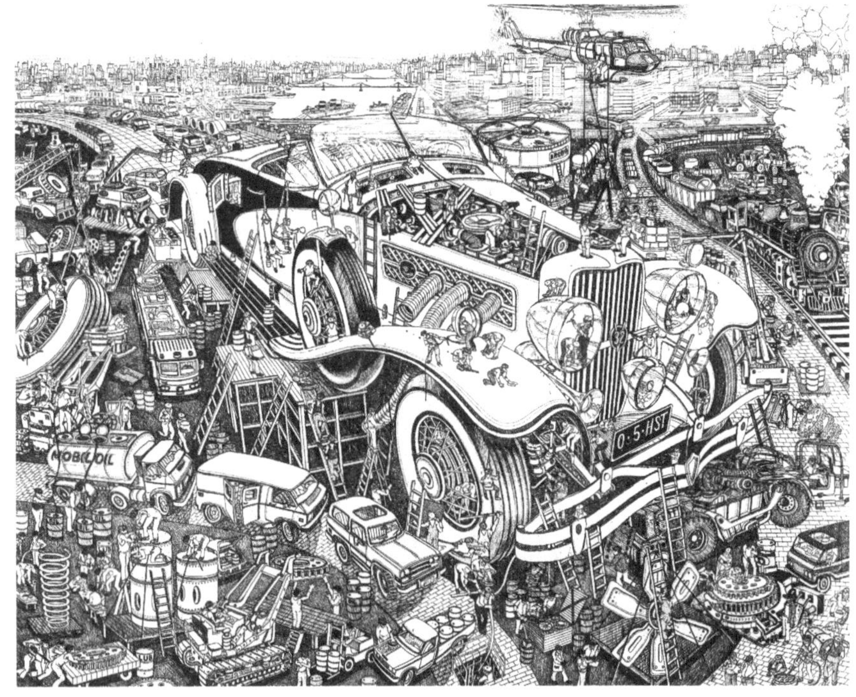

Bruce McCombs has been a professor at Hope College in Holland, Michigan since 1969, and is an acclaimed painter and printmaker. His etchings of masterfully handled urban perspective first gained notoriety in the Golden '70s, when he was a consistent prize winner in national juried competitions. He continues this same success today in the watercolor medium. McCombs is widely recognized for his super realistic imagery, rendering very detailed urban landscapes peopled by Lilliputian characters and vintage automobiles. His is a world of fantasy fully realized, and he is an artist and printmaker of great appeal and influence.

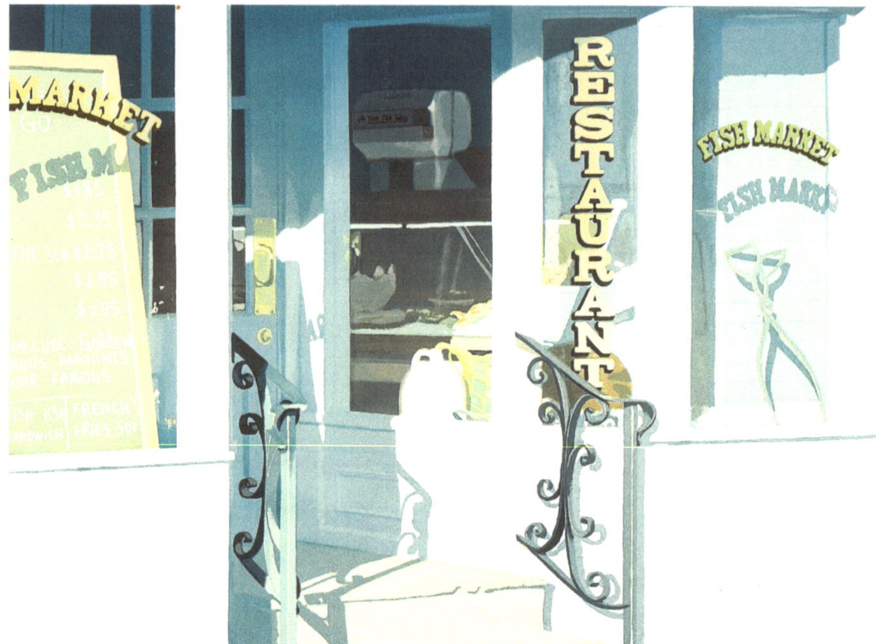

Nancy McIntyre
"Fish Market"
Silkscreen 19 x 29 ¼

Born in 1950 in Torrington, Connecticut, Nancy McIntyre attended the Rhode Island School of Design. Her near photo-realistic subject matter features store fronts, beach chairs and quaint beach houses. Her attention to detail is extraordinary. With "Fish Market", pictured here, McIntyre used 16 colors to create the final image. In some of her silkscreens she has used as many as 158 transparent layers of ink, creating subtle nuances of detail, with soft gradations of rich color. Together these layers form an exquisite interplay of light, shadow and a naturalness for the viewer, and create a sense of a particular moment captured in time. McIntyre shows a masters touch and understanding for the silkscreen medium, and it in turn answers to her bidding.

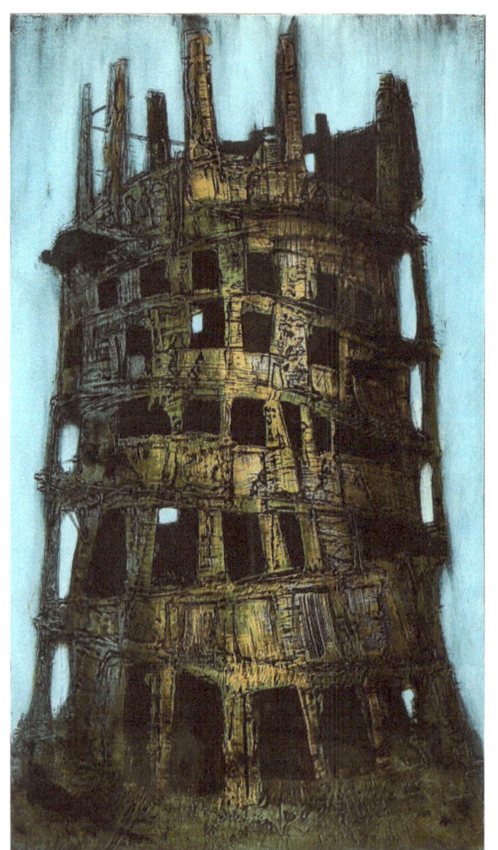

Dean Meeker
"Tower of Babel" Silkscreen/Intaglio/Collograph 34 x 19 ½

An internationally recognized printmaker, Dean Meeker was Professor Emeritus at the University of Wisconsin – Madison. A product of the GI Bill, he began his unprecedented forty-six year teaching career there in 1946. He spent time in Paris working at Atelier 17 with Hayter, and he established a close relationship with the India artist Kaiko Moti. He was a master of the silkscreen technique and transformed this once commercial process into a fine arts medium. He was a believer in exploration, never allowing known principles to limit his work. In 1950 he created the first ever university-affiliated course in serigraphy. He was to go on to be instrumental in accomplishing many firsts with the medium. In 1961 he began to apply a combination of silkscreen, collograph and intaglio to his own work, referring to them as polymer intaglios. During his tenure at the University of Wisconsin – Madison, the Department of Arts graphic program ranked as "world class" and "number one in the nation". His advice was focused, "Get up, go to work and keep your brushes clean". Meeker passed away in 2002.

Peter Milton
"First Gate"
Etching/Engraving *19 x 30*

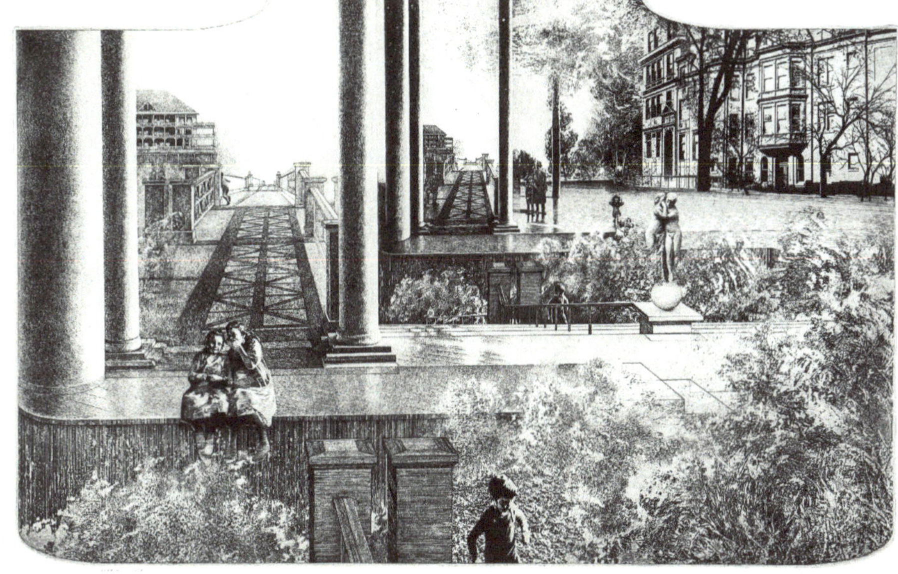

Born in 1930, Peter Milton is one of the most honored and respected printmakers of this era. He has been making prints for five decades, and has become the foremost living exponent of etching. His work stands in a league of its own. The rich black and white tonal scale of his prints are stunning and masterful. They capture the mood of mid-century cinema, and he has cited, among his major influences, film makers Ingmar Bergman and Fellini. His themes include architecture, history, myth and memory. Milton's prints display an extraordinary degree of photo-realistic detail, and his latest work has incorporated the new digital processes. His work is in every major museum collection here and abroad. Milton has been and continues to be a major dynamic force on an international scale in the printmaking world.

Lois Mogensen
"Three Chair Lineup"
Mezzotint 6 x 8

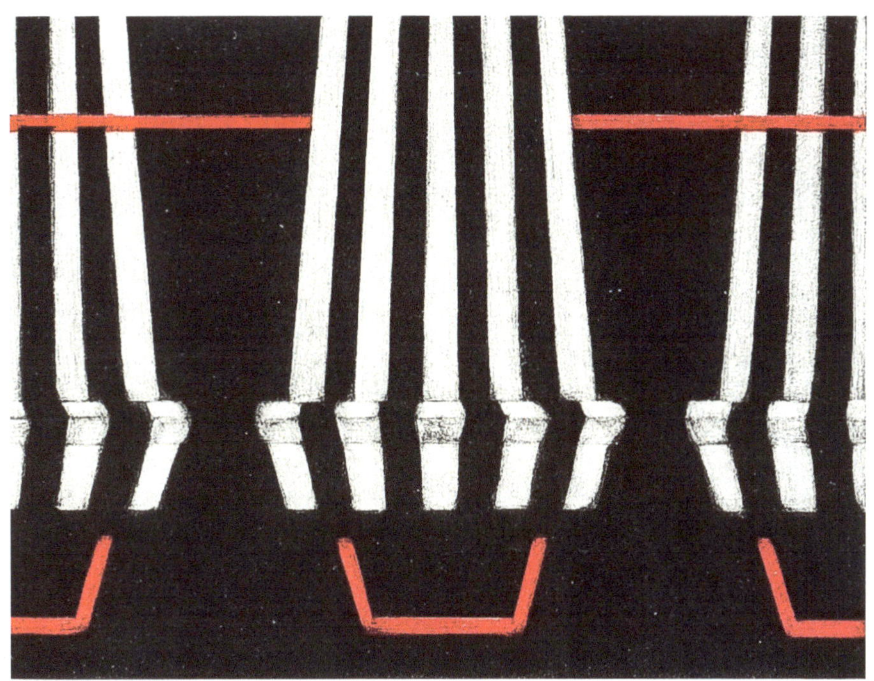

Lois Mogensen is a true "basement printmaker", producing mezzotint prints and drawings of exceptional quality and perception in her lower level studio. Mogensen has been making prints using a pair of deck chairs as her primary subject matter for the past twenty years. These are beautifully rendered compositions of red and black striations, evolved from recognizable shapes to pure hard edge abstraction. Her most recent prints are delicate studies rendered in a minimalist manner. This work has a strong linear graphic quality ideally suited for printmaking. She has stated, "I use the mezzotint process because I like the soft subtleties that can be achieved".

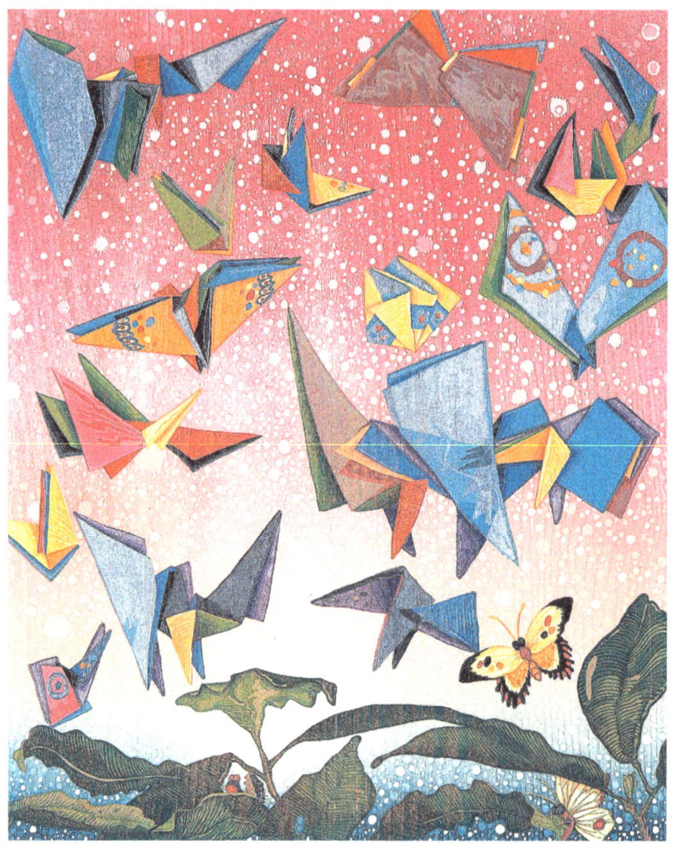

James P. Monson

"Origami Butterflies" Reduction Woodcut 21 x 17

In 1965, James P. Monson studied printmaking at the University of Iowa, under renowned printmaker Mauricio Lasansky. Upon graduation, he went to Paris to work with Hayter at Atelier 17, where he became Hayter's assistant and printer. Monson chose to focus on the woodcut medium, and used the reduction technique to create his prints. He lives and works in Southern France.

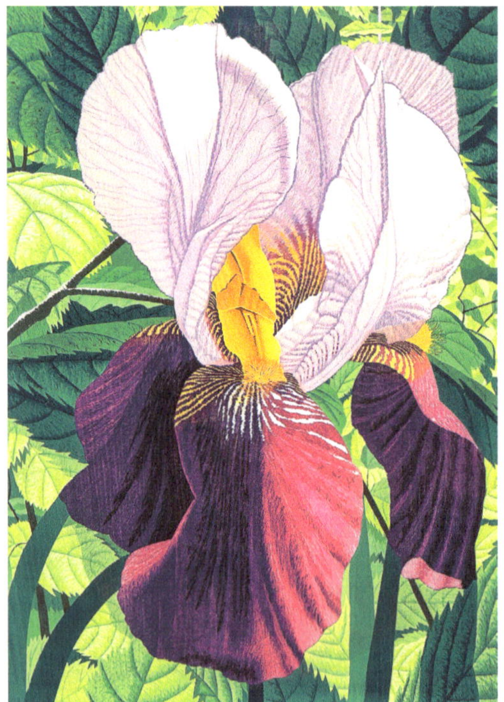

Gordon Mortensen

"Double Iris" Reduction Woodcut 26 x 19

Gordon Mortensen is a master of the reduction woodcut process, and is considered the premier artist of the medium in this era. He incorporates up to sixty-four colors and makes as many as forty-five press runs to complete a single print. Mortensen came to prominence in the Golden '70s, consistently winning awards in national juried exhibitions. His subject matter is the landscape; marshes, woodlands, canyons and prairies. His realistic interpretations have made his work highly collectable, and he has gained wide acceptance with museums, private collectors and the general public. He has stated, "My chief interests are color, shape and texture". This work is exceptional, and a tour de force of the medium.

Barry Moser
"Charles Dickens" Wood Engraving 6 x 4 ½

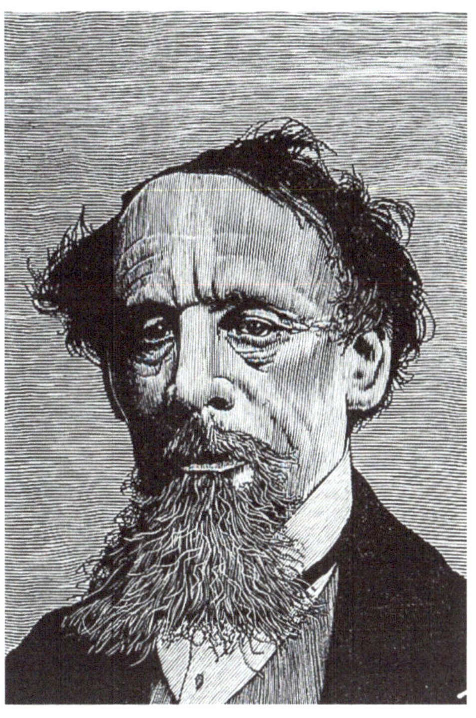

Barry Moser studied the craft of wood engraving under the tutelage of Leonard Baskin. A celebrated illustrator, Moser has more than 250 illustrated works to his credit including Lewis Carroll's Alice in Wonderland and Through the Looking Glass. He has also illustrated the Bible and Moby Dick. He is currently Professor in Residence and Printer to the college at Smith College, Northampton, Massachusetts. His works are masterful renderings of illustration seldom matched in their field.

Kaiko Moti
"Persian Cat" Aquatint 22 x 30

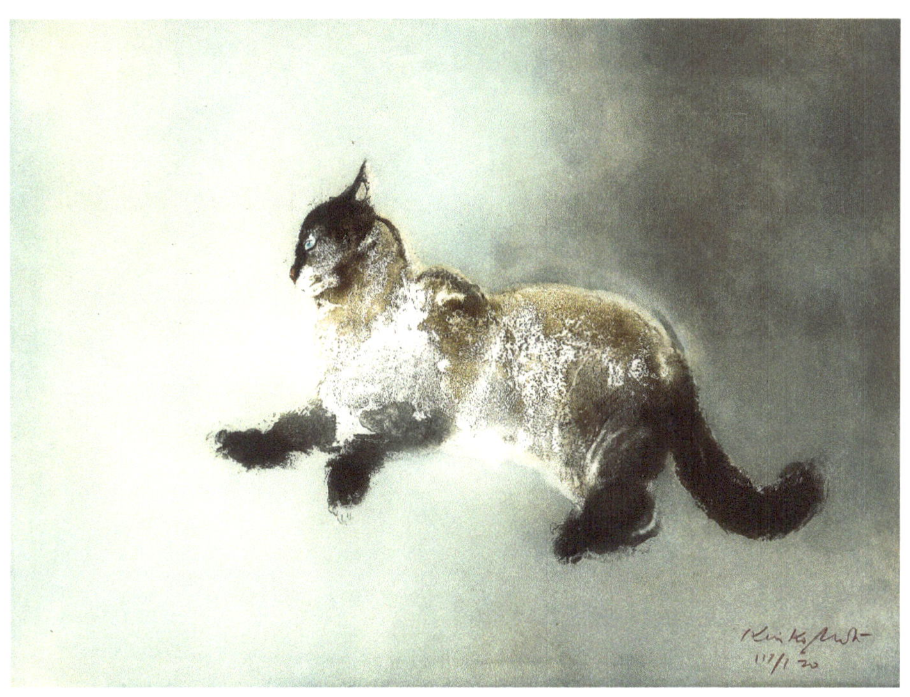

Kaiko Moti was born in Bombay, India. Moti began studying engraving with Stanley William Hayter at Atelier 17 in 1952, where he pioneered many techniques in the process of viscosity printing. He was a master of aquatint etchings, and is recognized today as having been one of the premier practitioners of that process in the world. He claimed to have no secret techniques, only to have refined the basic methods, learning from each of his created works. Moti's work has been highly collected by museums, private collectors and the general public. He died in Paris in 1989, but leaves a large legacy to the printmaking field.

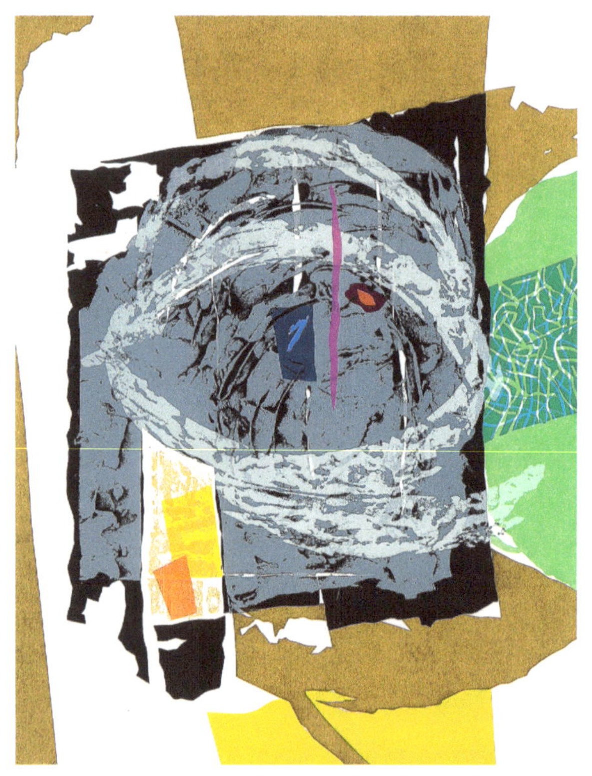

Seong Moy
"Eye of Vishnu" Lithograph 24 x 18

A Chinese born American printmaker, Seong Moy came to the United States in 1931 at the age of ten. Moy was primarily a painter until he received a fellowship to work at Hayter's Atelier 17. There he discovered the qualities of printmaking, and began making prints. His woodcuts from 1955 were notable for their incorporation of subject matter from Chinese classics. He combined this old world culture with the techniques of Abstract Expressionism. Bold in both color and form, his woodcuts are beautiful renditions that contain an Oriental flavor. They are classics in their own right.

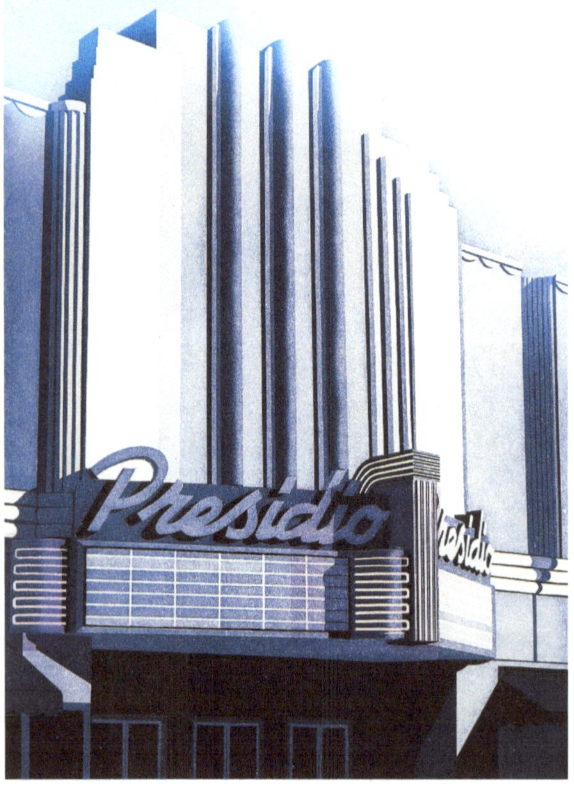

Frances Myers
"Presidio Palace" Aquatint 19 ¾ x 15

Frances Myers was an artist and printmaker of exceptional abilities. She built a reputation and solid following with her subtly toned aquatints. She usually worked in series, studying and developing her subject matter in depth. As an artist, Myers was hard to define as she did not limit herself to any style or technique. She was a master of several mediums and chose what best suited her subject and her thoughts for its final presentation. Myers had recently retired from the University of Wisconsin-Madison, and continued a busy schedule of national and international exhibitions. She was married to artist Warrington Colescott, and they shared a studio in Hollandale, Wisconsin. Myers passed away in 2014.

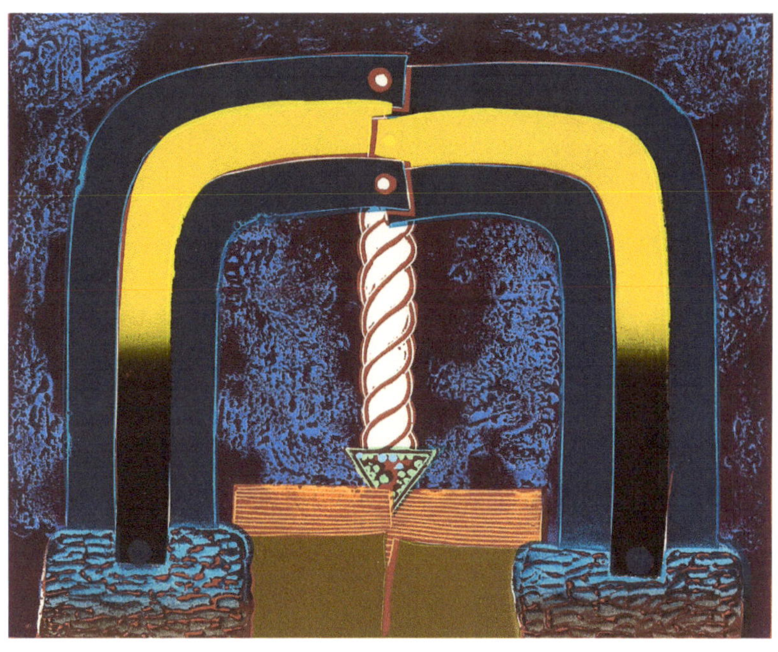

George Nama
"Monument for De Chirico"
Mixed Media 12 x 15

George Nama works in series, rendering bold and brilliantly colored, hard edged silkscreen abstractions. His imagery is that of the symbolist poet, thriving on combining works of ambiguity and clarity, to both reveal and withhold his intentions. He is obsessed with books, particularly old books. Nama collects them and then draws and paints on the pages. These works are an art of appropriation. He finds them, and then turns them into something new by adding his own personal imagery to the existing work. Nama has collected and made books all of his adult life beginning in Paris in 1966. He enjoys the intimacy of working with his hands on something that he can carry. He has a passion to collaborate with poets and writers, creating books that interpret their words with his works. He has taught at the National Academy in New York City.

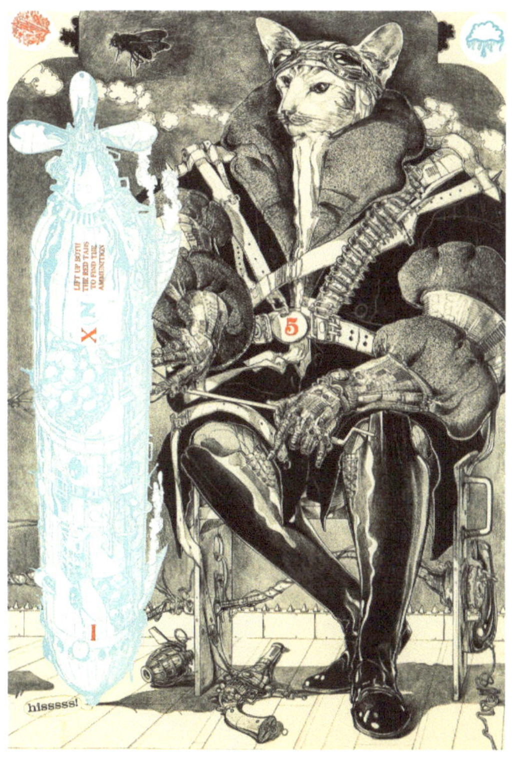

Robert A. Nelson
"Torpedo Tabby" Lithograph w/ collage elements 36 x 25 ½

Painter, sculptor, printmaker, collage artist and educator, Robert A. Nelson's art was described by one writer as "logic disarmed". Cats, birds, mice and other metamorphosed creatures are combined with mysterious patterns of notations and numerations. His surreal compositions dazzle the eye, constructed with a combination of masterful drawing and collage elements. His creatures find a place within these fantastic settings to tell their story. These are ambitious works of art, and they are a delight to the eye. In forty years of teaching, Nelson has influenced students and colleagues alike. He is revered in the printmaking field.

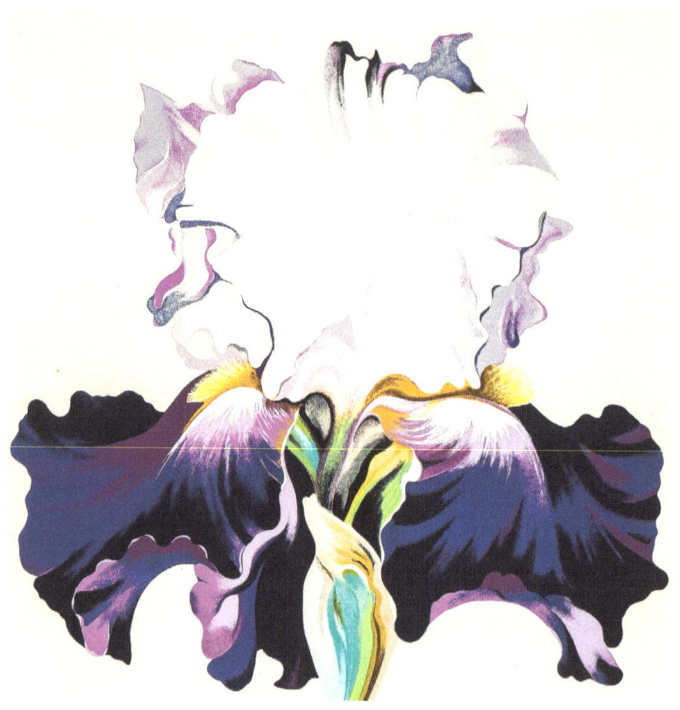

Lowell Nesbitt

"Blue Iris" Silkscreen *30 x 30*

Lowell Nesbitt was best known for his oversized floral works of art. They are his most beautiful and poetic images, and are readily known worldwide. Dramatic, implicitly sexual and a little ominous, they earned the artist a popularity with the general public that tended to overshadow his reputation within the art world. Nesbitt has been grouped with the Photo-realists, but his imagery is more interpretively distorted and somewhat more loosely rendered. His style and subject matter has influenced more than a few practicing artists, and his work continues to have many imitators. His giant colorful subjects were a perfect fit with his use of the silkscreen printing process.

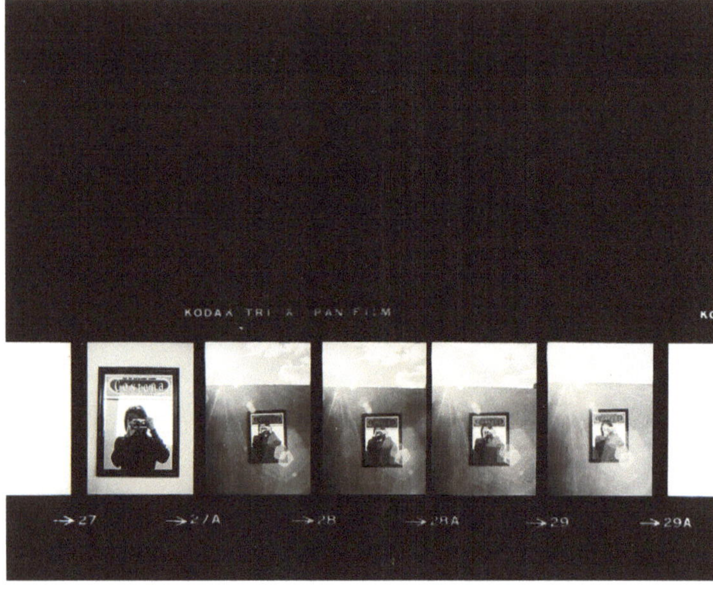

Tetsu Okuhara

"Costena" Photograph 8 x 10

Tetsu Okuhara is a Japanese American photographer born in Los Angeles, California and presently residing in New York City. He is noted for his large scale photo collage pieces that investigate the figure, seeking new ways to view, depict and experience it. Photo-collage is the medium Okuhara is most noted for, cutting and pasting individual segments together, and constructing them within a carefully composed grid. Some of these works are as large as 48 x 180 inches. His work has been described by critics as "interpretive", "intuitive", "whimsical" and "ironic". The artist has stated: "Art is a reflection of an internal reality and should engage and hopefully elevate the spirit, emotions and mind. It is manifested for me through the medium of photography". His influence has been far reaching in the medium and continues.

Katja Oxman
"Passage of Time II" Etching 30 ¾ x 23 ½

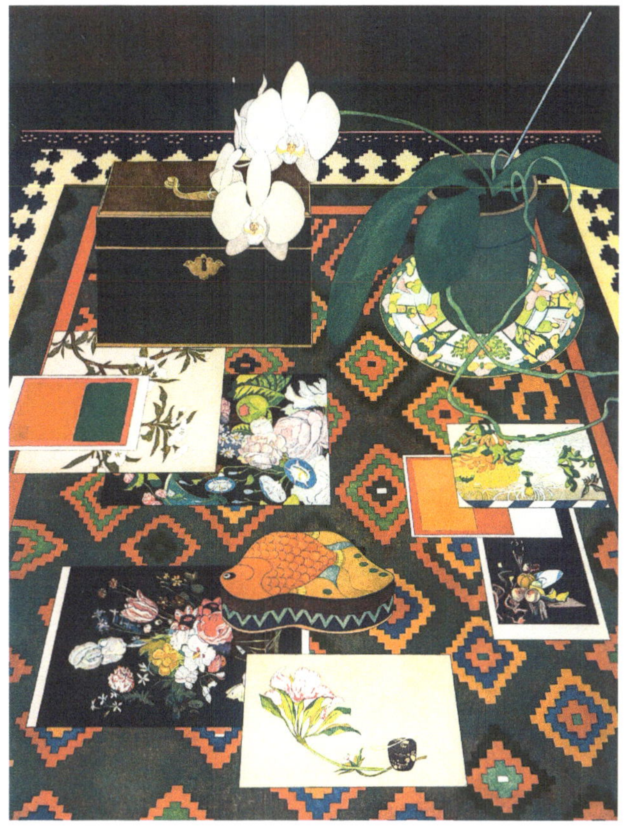

Katja Oxman was born in Munich, Germany and immigrated to the United States at the age of nine. Her multi-plate aquatint etchings present complex still lifes of richly patterned Oriental rugs populated by an overwhelming array of the artist's treasured objects. These are masterful works of minutely detailed surfaces that exude a warm, earthy range of tones. Her thought provoking titles are often quotations from Emily Dickinsen verse. Oxman's prints are awesome in their technical virtuosity. She is a master of the medium.

Eduardo Paolozzi
"Omoggio a Michaelangelo"
Etching 22 ¾ x 19 ¼

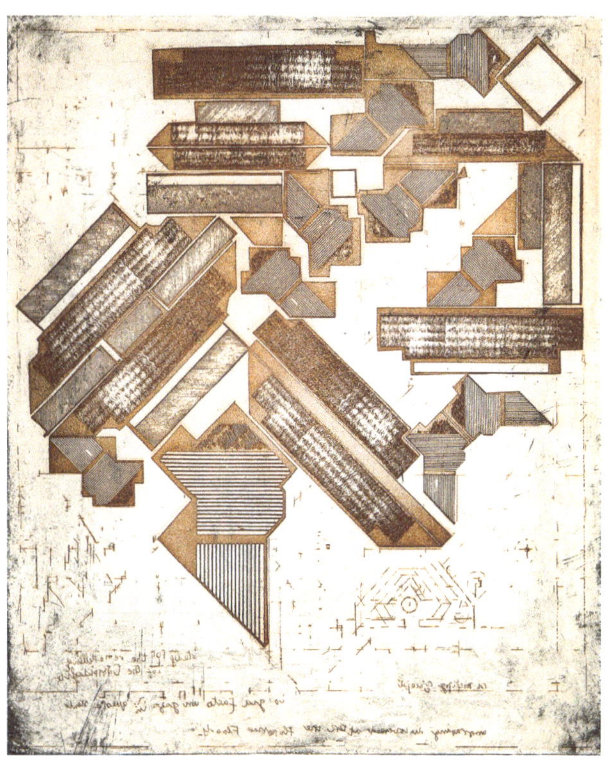

Eduardo Paolozzi was a major figure in the international art scene. A self-subscribed surrealist, he worked in a wide range of media throughout his career: sculpture, ceramic, film, printmaking, and writing. He was also an educator. His graphic work was highly innovative, exploring and extending the possibilities and limits of the silkscreen medium. His imagery combined collage elements of popular culture and contemporary machinery. Paolozzi is heralded as the founder of British Pop Art, and as such has had immeasurable influence among artists in the United Kingdom and also worldwide. Paolozzi died in 2005.

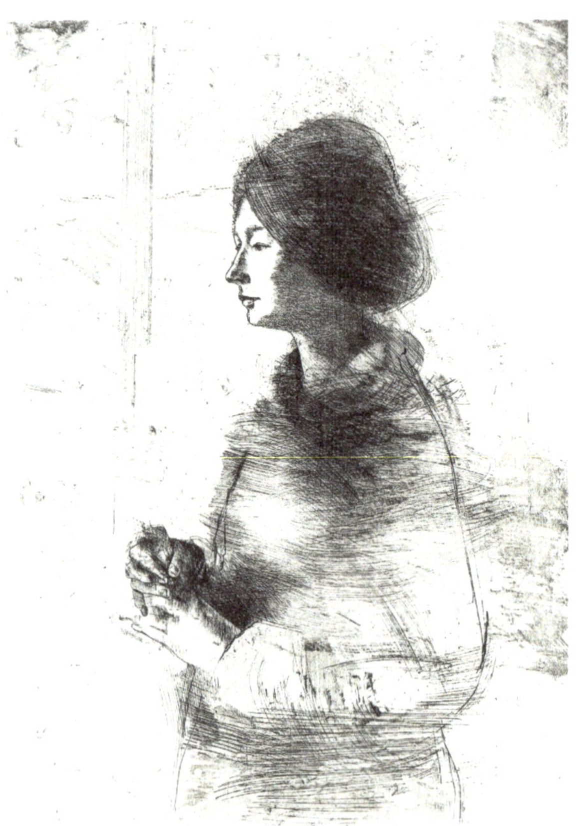

William Patterson
"Woman by a Window" Intaglio Etching 27 x 20

William Patterson is an American realist. His subject matter is personal and close to home, familiar renderings of the landscape and figures that surround him. "Woman by a Window", pictured here, is an excellent example of his figurative work that brought his prints to prominence in the Golden '70s. Pensive and beautifully drawn, this sensitive portrait is a masterful rendering of the intaglio medium. His recent work has centered on landscapes, painted in exquisite detail, and inspired by his trips to Italy and also the familiar places that surround his home in Deerfield, Massachusetts. Patterson states, "All my work emanates from day to day life experiences". His present landscape work is reminiscent of the masterful landscapes of George Inness.

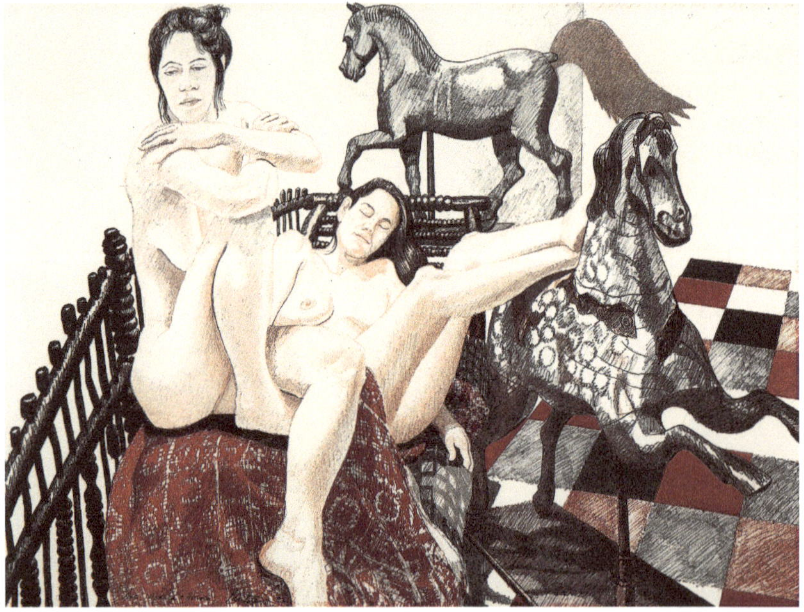

Philip Pearlstein
"Models and Horses"
Lithograph 20 ¾ x 28

Philip Pearlstein was born in Pittsburgh, Pennsylvania and presently resides in New York City. A painter and printmaker, Pearlstein is recognized by many as the pre-eminent figure painter of the 1960s to 2000s and was a key figure in the sharp-focus realist movement in America during that time. His subject matter is foremost the nude female figure. These figures are characterized by a non-traditional informality, unexpected postures and unusual perspectives, including the radical cropping of the figure within the picture plane. In many works he has introduced elaborate backdrops of richly patterned fabrics and decorative floor patterns. The artist has stated, "I am simply interested in the way ordinary people look". Pearlstein's works are beautiful renditions of the human body. His influence has been and continues to be substantial.

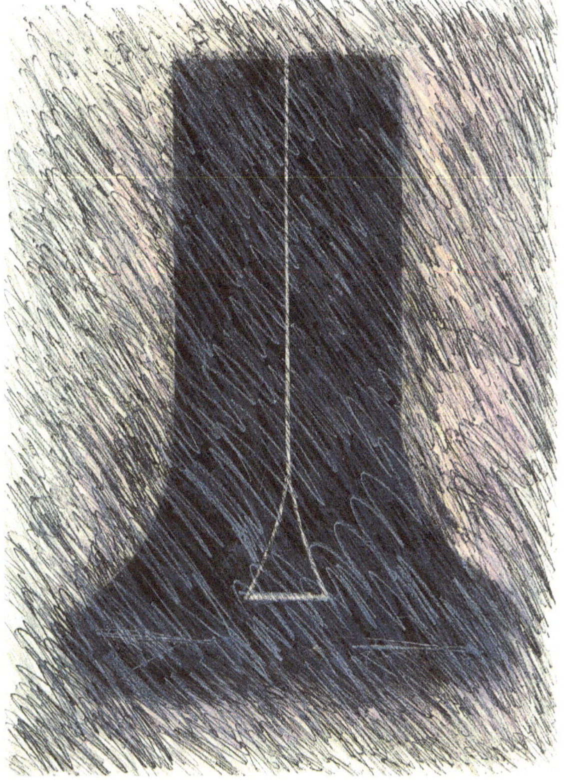

Beverly Pepper
"Sculptural Form" Lithograph 22 x 16 ¼

Beverly Pepper is best known for her sculptures, which are located and enjoyed throughout the world. She studied with the renowned artist Fernand Leger. The lithograph print shown here is a study for her monumental work in granite, located in Florence, Italy, titled "Borgia Altar", and completed in 1998. Besides her worldwide reputation as a sculptor, Pepper is also active as a printmaker of etchings and lithographs.

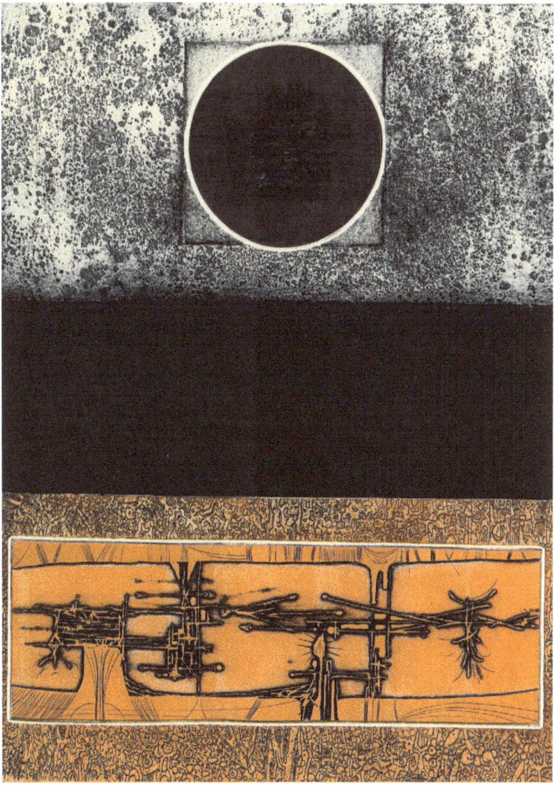

Gabor Peterdi
"Land, Sea, Moon" Intaglio Etching 23 ½ x 17 ½

Hungarian born, Gabor Peterdi was an American painter, printmaker, author and educator. He established and directed the Graphic Workshop at the Brooklyn Museum Art School. Peterdi was a first generation pioneer of the Print Renaissance and worked with Stanley William Hayter at Atelier 17 in Paris. A master of printmaking techniques, his subject matter was predominantly landscape, and became more abstract in nature over time. Peterdi's book, "Printmaking Methods Old and New", was published in 1959 and remains a standard technical reference for both printmaking students and professionals alike. His influence on printmaking is significant and its scope is worldwide. Peterdi died in 2001.

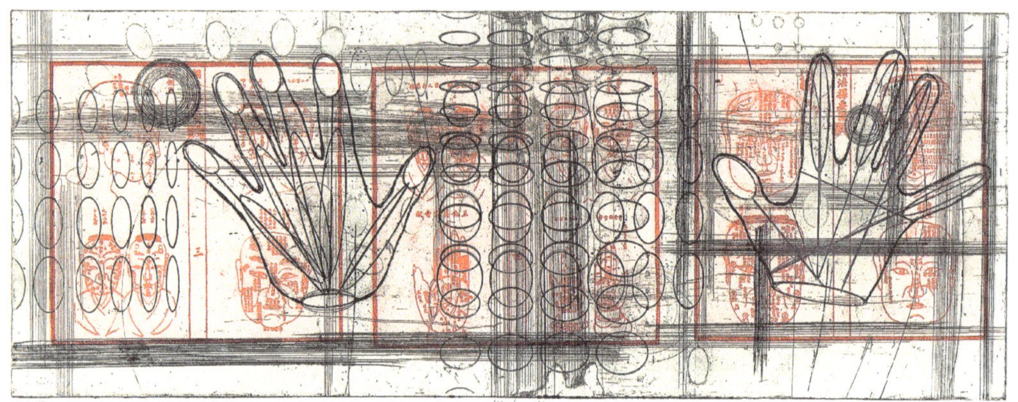

Judy Pfaff
"Wu Fu Wu"
Etching/Mixed media 10 x 28

Born in London, England, Judy Pfaff is an American artist known mainly for her Installation Art. Her works are dynamic, exuberant and large scale, incorporating many different media. Her pieces have been described as "collages in space". Pfaff's print work is contemporary and ambiguous, and technically masterful. About the commercial viability of her work, she has stated, "I've always done prints and drawings. No one buys those installations, so when you see things that are portable that I'm not physically attached to, they're probably two dimensional. If you get an installation of mine, you inherit (my assistant) Ryan, myself, a crew, the dog, the noise, the dirt. We wreck the house. So, if you don't want that, then you get prints and drawings". Pfaff is a force on an international level in the contemporary art scene.

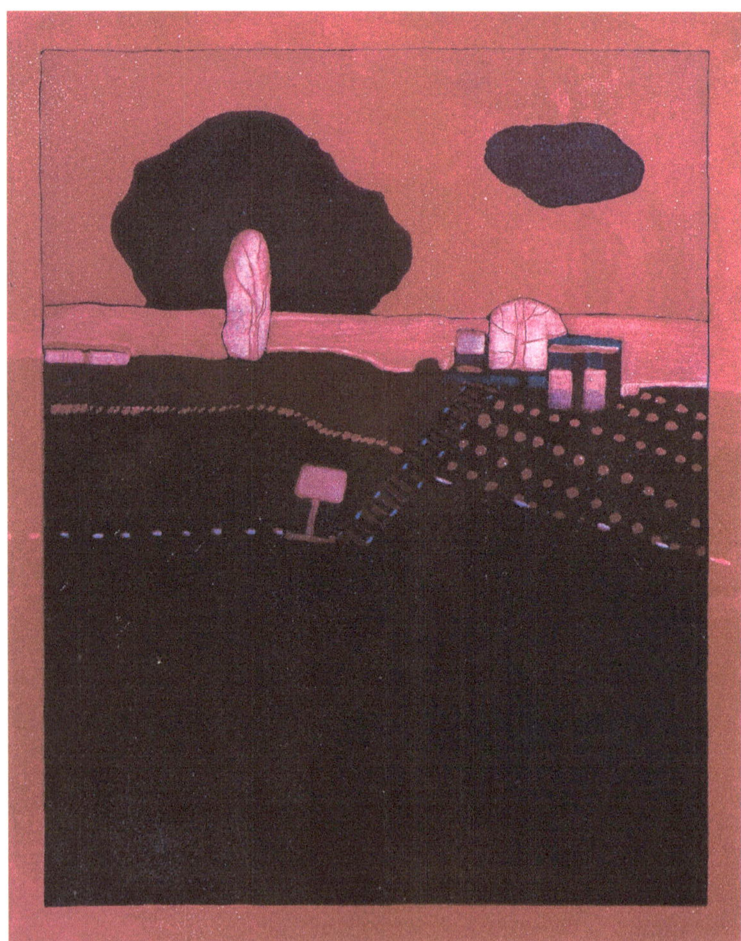

Linda Plotkin
"One Morning" Etching/Aquatint 24 x 19 ½

Born in 1938 in Milwaukee, Wisconsin, Linda Plotkin was well known for her still life subjects of recurring objects in breakfast table arrangements, and of magical landscapes of substance, both real and surreal. Plotkin describes her work as; "dreaming, a time when images, seemingly random, can be appealing, but more often sinister and disturbing, and combine in unexpected and mysterious ways. The true meaning is always just out of reach". Plotkin was a frequent exhibitor in the Golden '70s. Her work pictured here, "One Morning", is an excellent example of her surreal landscapes, and an exceptional print.

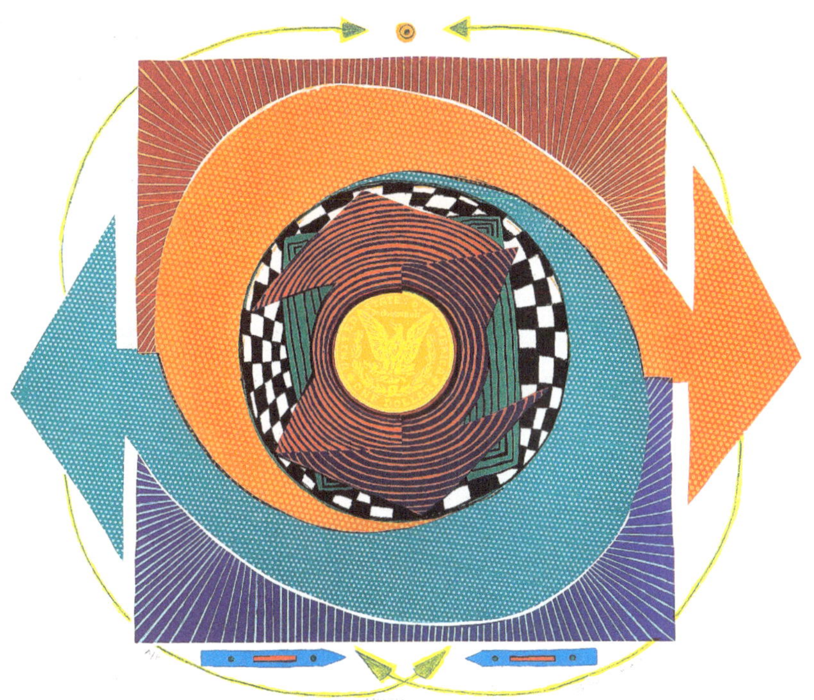

Michael Ponce de Leon
"Untitled"
Mixed Media Collage 22 x 25

Michael Ponce de Leon was born in Miami, Florida in 1922. A printmaking innovator, Ponce de Leon often made his own paper, and turned it into three dimensional prints imbedded with impressions of discarded material. Found objects were inked and printed and became an important part of his work. He combined etching with collage, made white on white prints and collaborated with other artists. His editions were often five prints or less. Ponce de Leon was an instructor at the Art Students League in New York, and his innovations in the printmaking process had a significant influence on both his students and peers.

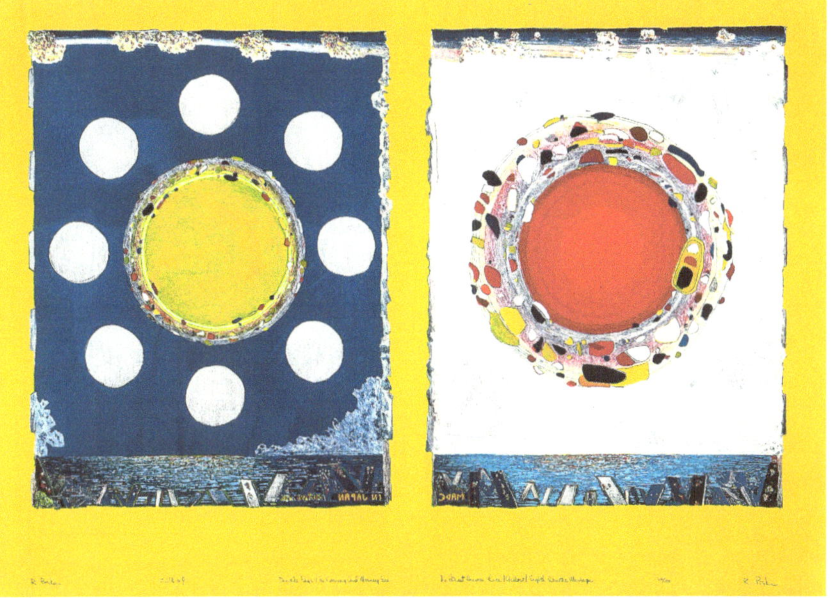

Roland Poska
"The Great Human Race Series - Yellow"
Lithograph 30 x 40

A painter, sculptor, papermaker, printmaker and publisher, Roland Poska has had a significant influence on the art community on a national level. Poska's pioneering work in the field of handmade papermaking established him as an important figure in America. For nearly five decades his work has explored themes of color, nature and egalitarianism on a monumental scale. Poska was a founder of the Milwaukee Institute of Art and Design. He also founded the Fishy Whale Press Workshop in Milwaukee in the 1960's, the first of its kind in Wisconsin. He immediately gained recognition for attracting leading printmaking artists from across the country. Poska's most ambitious publications are a series of suites based on the "Great Human Race" theme, which has become the workshop's defining topic. The suites address the cultural development of particular disciplines such as Medicine, Law, Architecture and Business. They pay tribute to the most profound physical and spiritual aspirations of humankind. It is a remarkable endeavor, and a theme of worldwide importance. Poska continues his work in his studio now located in Rockford, Illinois.

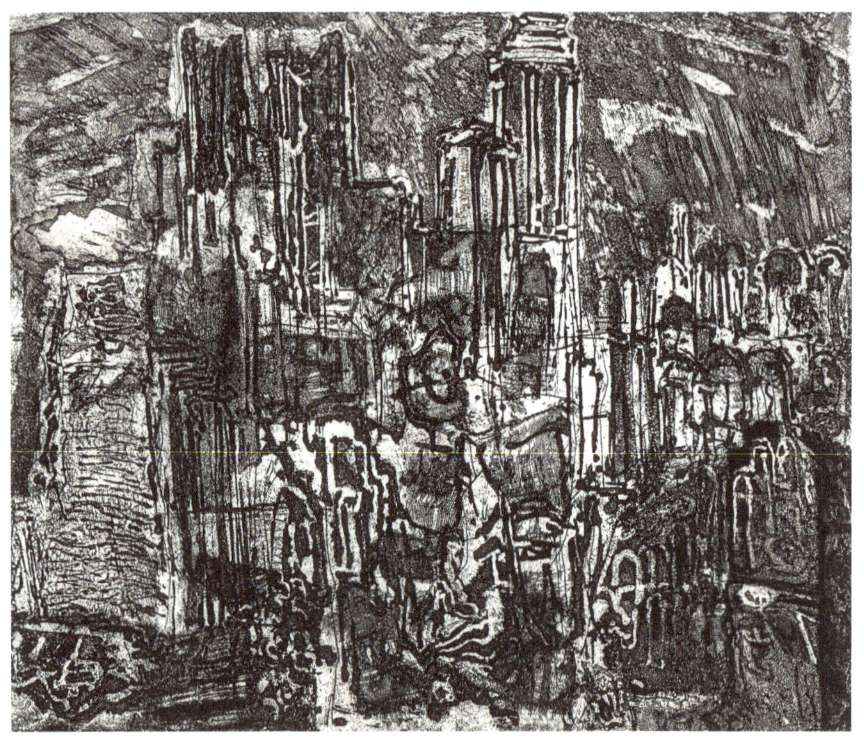

Rudy Pozzatti
"Night in Etruria" Etching
13 ¾ x 16 ½

A second generation pioneer in the Print Renaissance, Pozzatti has a defined place in American printmaking. A multi-media artist and educator, Pozzatti has a worldwide reputation as a printmaker. His subject matter is strongly influenced by Italy, and its centuries old art and architecture. He worked alongside Marvin Lowe and together they built the Indiana University Printmaking Department Workshop's outstanding reputation for teaching and research, one of the most successful printing programs in the United States. Pozzatti has been cited as one of Indiana's living legends, and his influence is immeasurable.

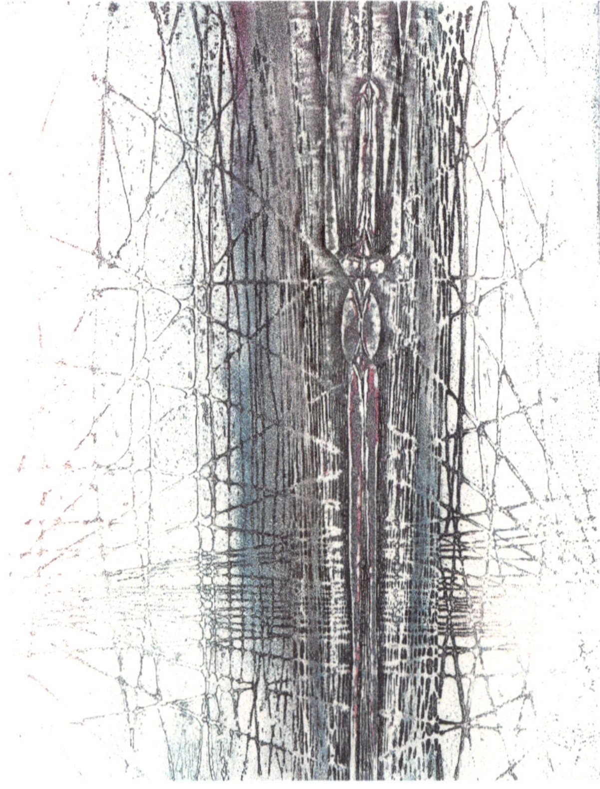

Krishna Reddy
"Praying Figure"
Viscosity Etching 17 ½ x 13 ½

Krishna Reddy is from India, and is considered a master in intaglio printmaking. His technique and style have distinguished him as one of the best printmakers in the world. Reddy rose to prominence in the 1950's, and has been Associate Director at Hayter's Atelier 17 in Paris since 1965. He pioneered and mastered the color viscosity etching process. Reddy lives and works in Paris, with frequent visits to the United States. He has been a force in the printmaking field, with an international presence.

Deborah Remington
"Davos" Lithograph 29 x 21

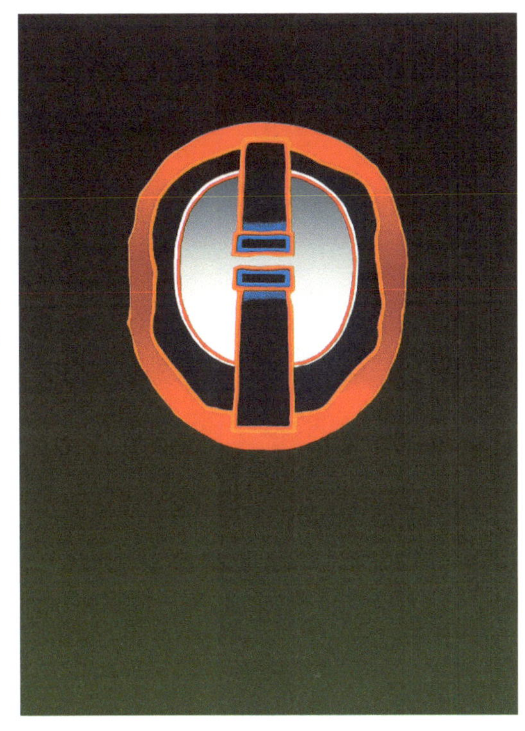

A Painter and printmaker, Deborah Remington studied painting with Clyfford Still. Part of the Bay Area Beat Scene, she rubbed shoulders with the likes of Allen Ginsberg. In 1965 Remington moved to New York, by which time she had gained renown for her imagery influenced by Abstract Expressionism. In 2001, Remington began producing the intense, emblematic and sensuous work by which she is best known. The work here, "Davos", is a fine example of this personal vision. She felt that the recent gender focus in the arts was detrimental as it has the effect of separating artists. The artist died in 2010.

Minna Resnick
"Solitary Figure, Seated" Lithograph 22 ½ x 15

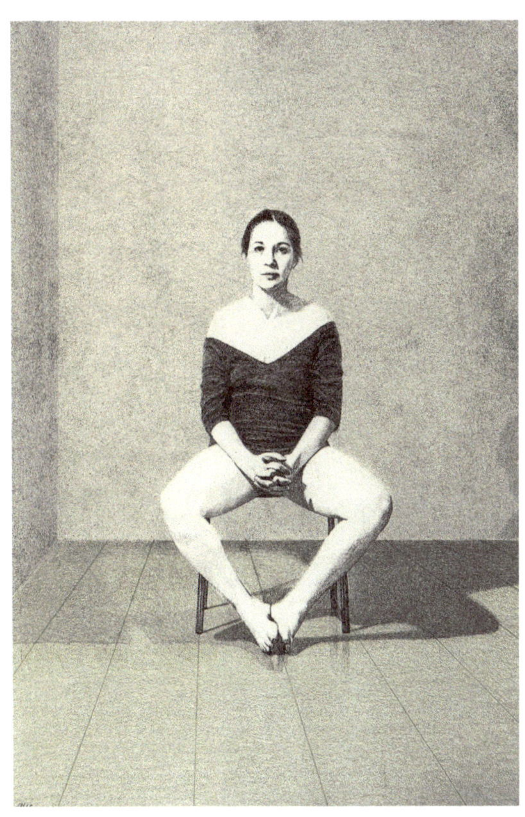

Minna Resnick has lived in Ithaca, New York since 1987, where she also maintains a studio. She works in primarily two mediums, lithography and drawing. Resnick was active and a frequent prize winner in National shows during the Golden '70s. Her work focuses on language; body language in her early work, and actual text to connect and give substance to the pictorial image in her current work. Another interesting twist in her current work is the use of lithography printing as a base image and then drawing directly on this base, combining the two mediums. Resnick states: "In 1993, I began combining lithographic and drawn images to create narrative sequences. This fused the repetitive statement inherent in printmaking with the ability of restatement through drawing, which changed context." Resnick's works have a mature sensibility that go beyond the surface qualities of the image. Resnick gives lectures and workshops in the United States, and also teaches on a part time basis.

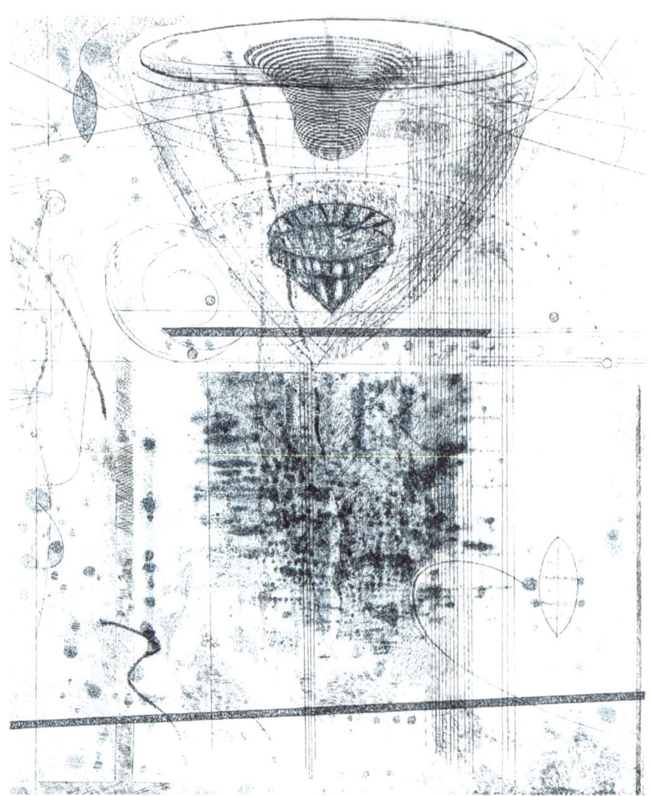

Roslyn Richards
"Descent" Etching 11 ¾ x 9 ¾

A painter, printmaker and educator, Roslyn Richards work explores the relationship between nature and technology. Abstract forms based on photographs and scientific diagrams are transformed into poetic, lyrical and expressive works of art. Her highly detailed prints are intimate statements with a profound message, and first came to prominence in the Golden '70s. They are gems of technical expertise. Since 1982, Richards has taught at Bucknell University in Lewisburg, Pennsylvania. One critic has noted, "Richards is an artist of experience and accomplishment".

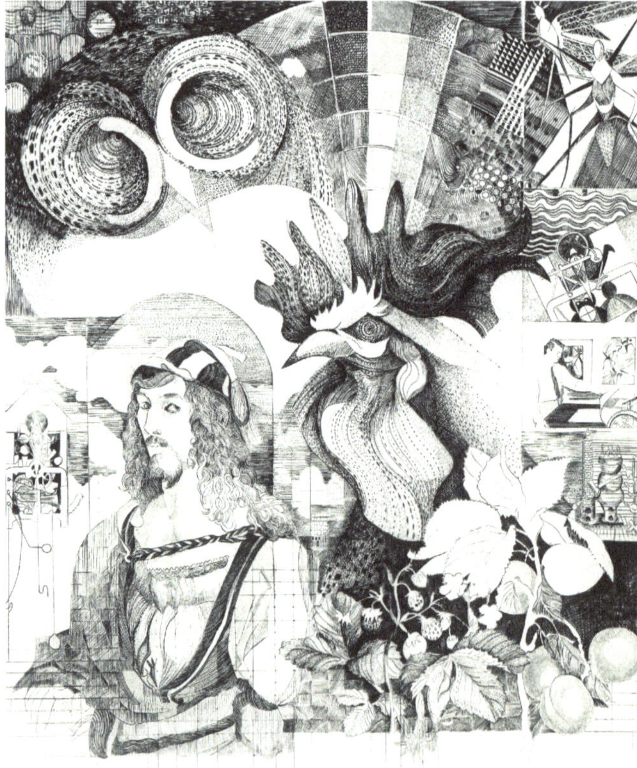

Walter Rogalski
"Homage to a Technique" Engraving 25 ½ x 21 ½

Born in 1925, Walter Rogalski was a printmaker and lecturer. He studied at the Brooklyn Museum School with Gabor Peterdi during the years 1947-1951. He was an Associate Professor at the Graduate School of Art and Design at the Pratt Institute. He authored the book, Prints and Drawings by Walter R. Rogalski. He was a master of the engraving burin. He passed away in 1996.

Frank Roth

"Four Green Shapes in Continuous Space" Silkscreen 17 ½ x 19

An American abstract artist, Frank Roth was born in Boston in 1936, and moved to New York City in 1954 where he studied with Hans Hoffmann. During the '60s and '70s, Roth began to use geometric compositions containing surreal forms and pure linear shapes on flat colored backgrounds as subject matter. Futuristic and appearing to be manufactured from dreams, his imagery places the viewer in a setting of what is going to be. His silkscreen work pictured here reminds me of the scene in the movie, "The Graduate", where the businessman offers advice to the young man for his future, "Plastics, my boy, plastics". Since 1963, Roth has taught at the School of Visual Arts in New York City.

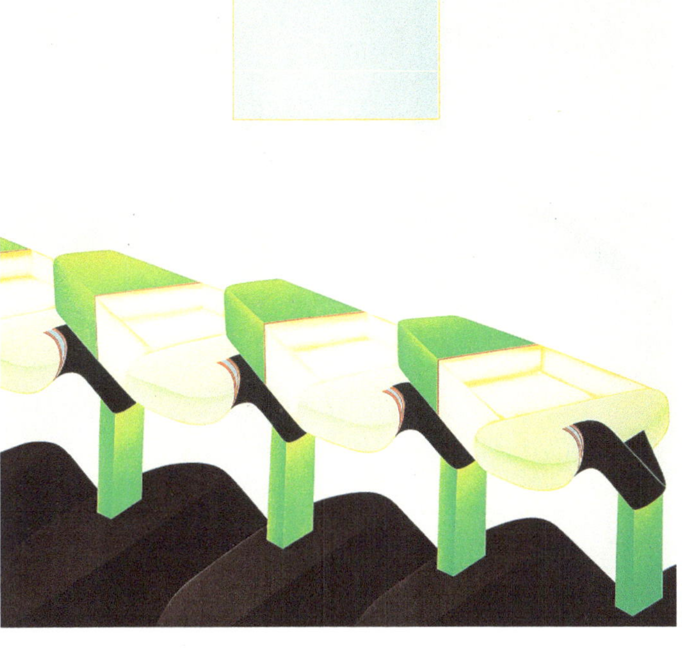

Harold Rotzoll

"Are Not Forgotten" Etching 22 x 16

A self-taught artist, Harold Rotzoll personifies the "basement printmaker". Working nights and weekends, after full work days, Rotzoll taught himself the technical aspects of the printmaking medium. Using patterns of dots, Rotzoll builds imagery that express his own personal experiences. His etching pictured here, "Not Forgotten" gives insight into his Viet Nam service with the Marine Corps and his lost comrades in arms. It is a strong visual statement that we are asked to share, and along with him, to not forget. It is an exceptional print, conveying a strong message.

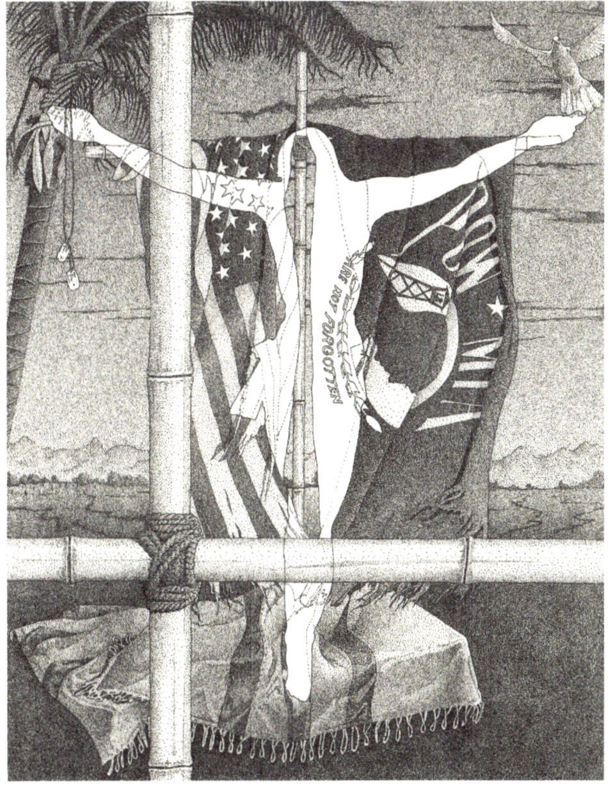

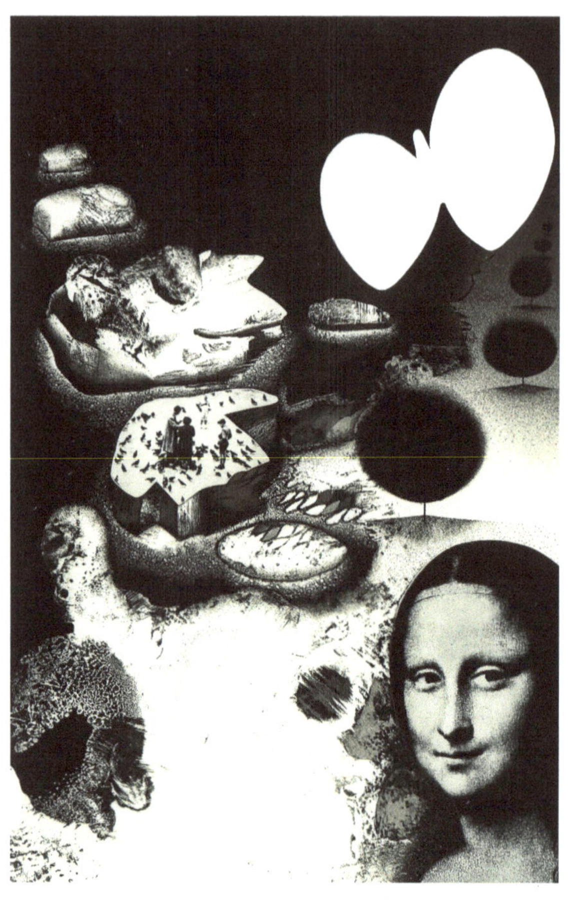

Dennis Rowan
"Big Sur-Real" Intaglio Etching 35 ½ x 23 ½

Dennis Rowan retired from the University of Illinois at Urbana Champaign as Professor Emeritus, after forty-two years of teaching. Rowan's print, *"Big Sur-Real"* pictured here, is a masterful demonstration of the intaglio process. Elements of straight line etching, aquatint, asphaltum work, embossment and photo transfer are noted. At least four plates were combined to complete the artist's statement. The technical aspects of the rendering is extraordinary, and a masterful rendition of combined processes.

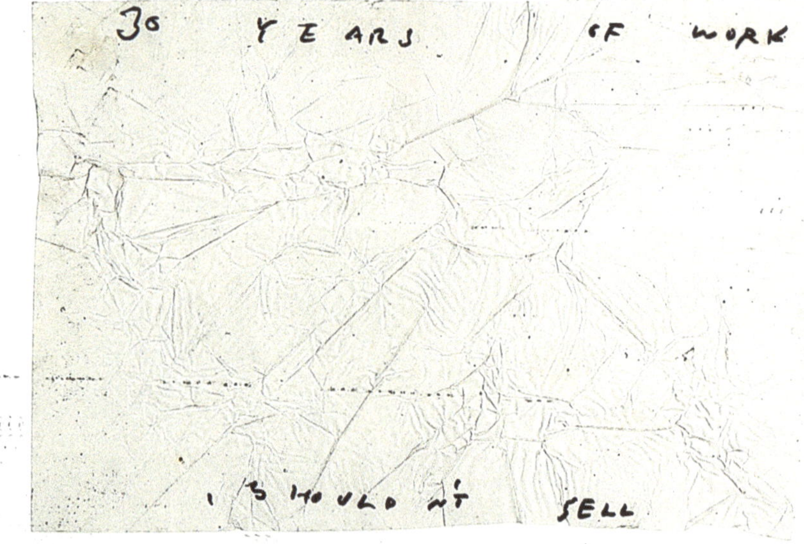

Ed Ruscha
(Attributed to) "I Shouldn't Sell"
Offset Lithograph on
Crumpled Paper 6 x 9

Ed Ruscha is an American artist associated with the Pop Art Movement. His work is all about text and image. Single or small groups of words overprinted on common imagery tell his story in a simple but profound way. The text in the image pictured here, "I shouldn't sell", followed by what appears to be a change of mind, the crumpled paper, has much to say. Ruscha is indisputably one of the most iconic American Artists of the 20th Century. He is a master printmaker, and has played a major part in the renaissance of printmaking. His influence is worldwide and he has had a profound influence on art history. His work can be found in every major museum in the world. He lives and works in Culver City, California.

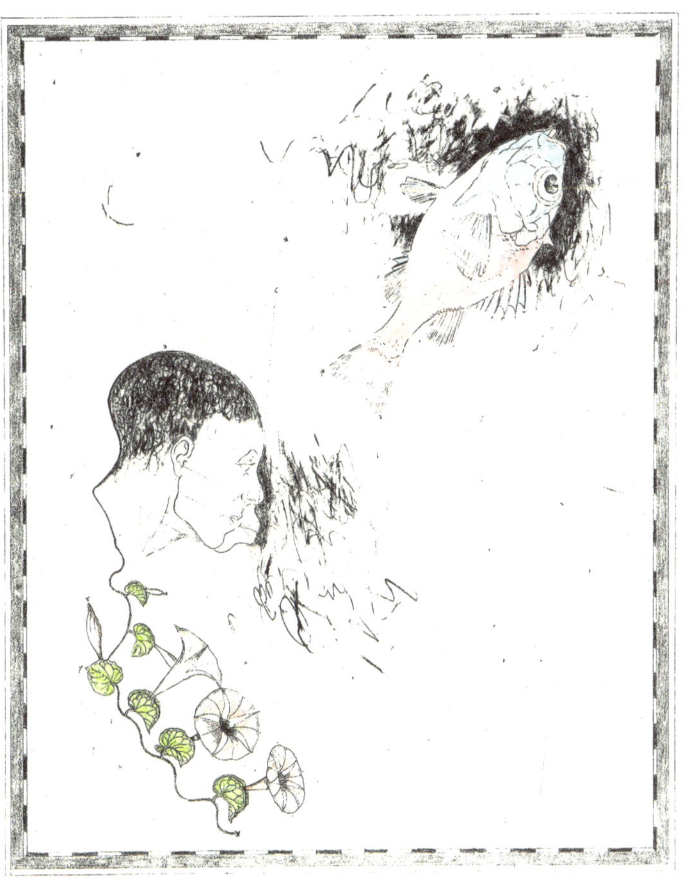

Donald Saff

"Fish" Etching *23 ½ x 18 ¾*

Donald Saff has been a major force in American printmaking since the 1960's with both his own prints and as an entrepreneur. In 1968, as professor and chairman of the University of South Florida Art Department, Saff founded Graphics Studio/The Institute for Research in Art on the campus of the university in Tampa. He built Graphics Studio into one of the most important printmaking ateliers in the country that is widely recognized for its innovative prints. Saff believes in collaboration and aggregate thinking. "You can do things that you would never do if left to your own devices", he has said. His own work centers on single realistically drawn objects such as, chairs, flowers, animals and figures that float in mostly open spaces. They are isolated, but seem to search for a connection with one another. They are mysteries that appear simple to understand, but in fact are complex pieces.

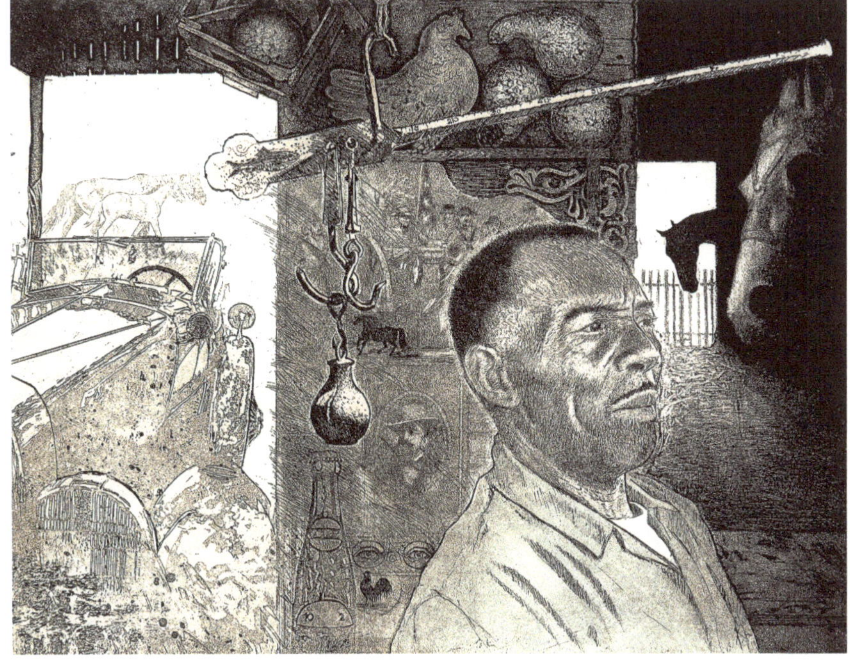

Boyd Saunders

"Guardian" Etching 15 ½ x 19 ½

Boyd Saunders had a 30 year career at the University of South Carolina. A Southern Regionalist, Saunders captures familiar southern images and everyday events. The result is powerful, yet intimate imagery, and gives the viewer a glimpse into the southern sense of place and identity. In 1972 Saunders organized the Southeastern Graphics Council, and served as its first President. Since that time, the organization has become international in scope and in 2010 became known as SGC International. SGC International is the largest print organization in North America and their annual conference is the most attended annual gathering focused on the field of printmaking.

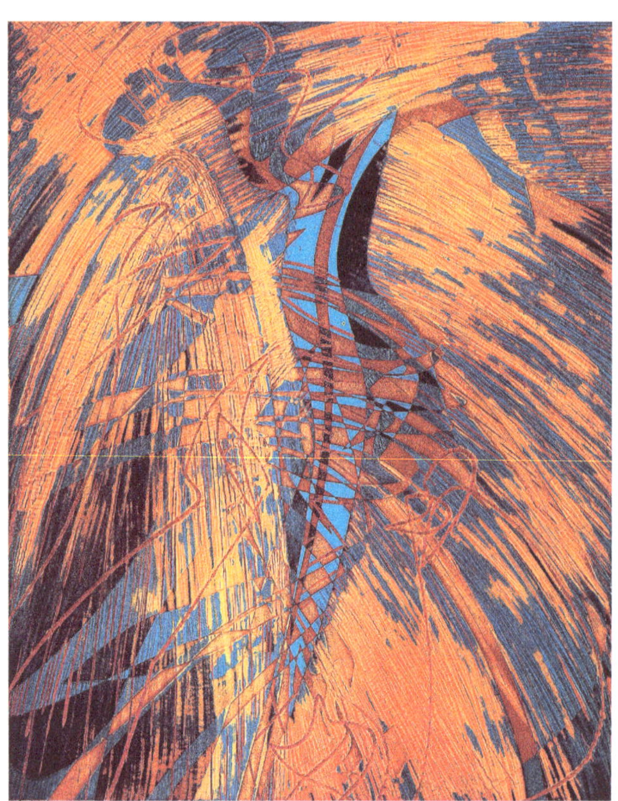

Hector Saunier
"Eruption" Viscosity Etching

Born in Buenos Aires, Hector Saunier moved to Paris and began studying printmaking with Hayter at Atelier 17 in 1966. During Hayter's absence, he would become Associate Director. Following Hayter's death in 1988, Saunier joined forces with Juan Valladaries to serve as co-directors of the atelier that they renamed Atelier Coutrepoint. His viscosity etchings are a celebration of the expressive power of line, texture, and space. His color sensibility is unrivaled. He continues to ceaselessly experiment with the simultaneous polychrome technique and has made new discoveries hitherto undreamt of in sophistication and subtlety. Saunier is unique among printmakers and his influence is immeasurable.

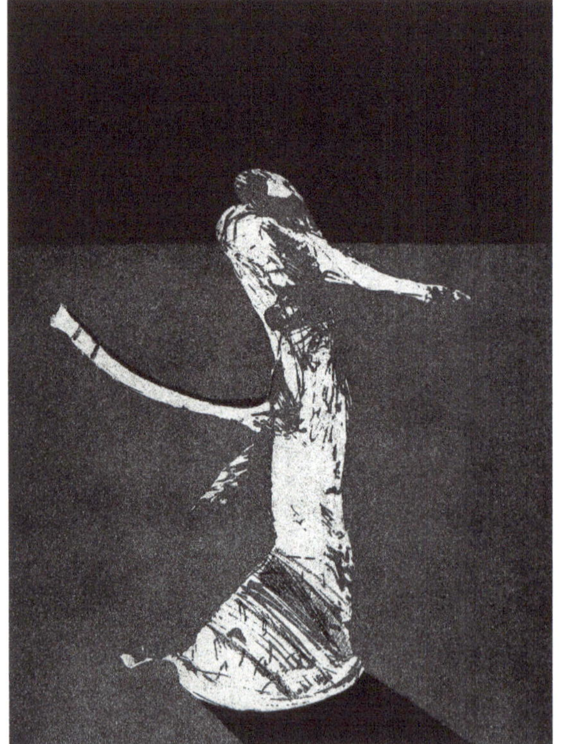

Fritz Scholder
"Mystery Portrait in Barcelona #1"
Etching/Aquatint *21 ½ x 16*

Fritz Scholder has been a major influence for a generation of Native American artists. His revolutionary work broke away from stereotypical roles and forever changed the concept of "Indian Art". His style is well known for its distortions, explosive brushwork and vivid colors. Though primarily a painter, Scholder was equally adept in the printmaking medium. His etchings and lithographs are held in high esteem. Scholder worked in series, exploring themes. His "Mystery Portrait in Barcelona #1", shown here, is a prime example of his mastery of the printmaking medium. Scholder was one of the most renowned and influential Native American artists of the 20th century. He died in 2005.

Karl Shrag
"Dark Trees at Noon" Etching/Aquatint 24 ¾ x 18 ¾

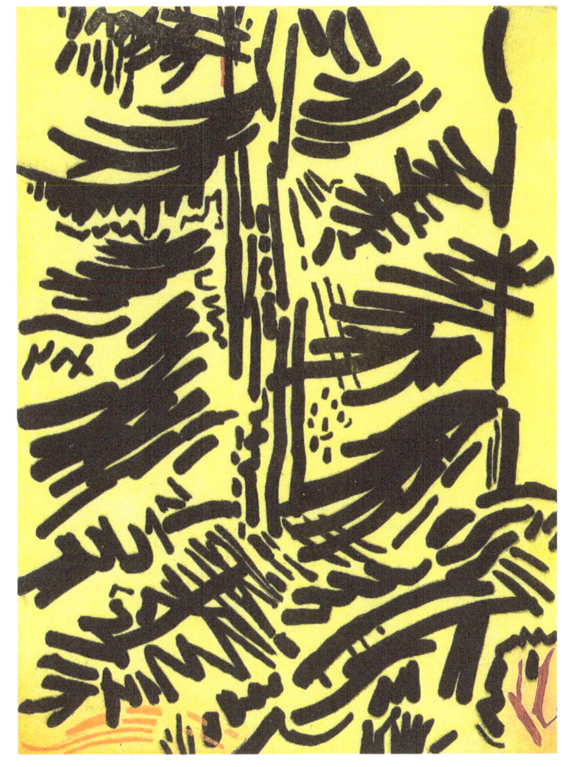

Karl Shrag was a first generation pioneer of the Print Renaissance, and had a major influence on the print resurgence in America. Shrag taught at Cooper Union in New York for many years, and was closely associated with Hayter and Atelier 17, working alongside artists Miro and Jackson Pollack. When Hayter left to return to Paris in 1950, Shrag was made Director of the atelier in New York. Nature was his subject, and night scenes fascinated him. Bold strokes were his detail, and trees came to life with a few drawn lines. Strong in structure and minimal in execution, he was able to deftly meld realism with abstraction. Shrag died in 1991, but left an indelible mark on the printmaking field.

Thomas Robert Seawell
"Michigan"
Collograph/Etching/Aquatint 17 ¼ x 17 ½

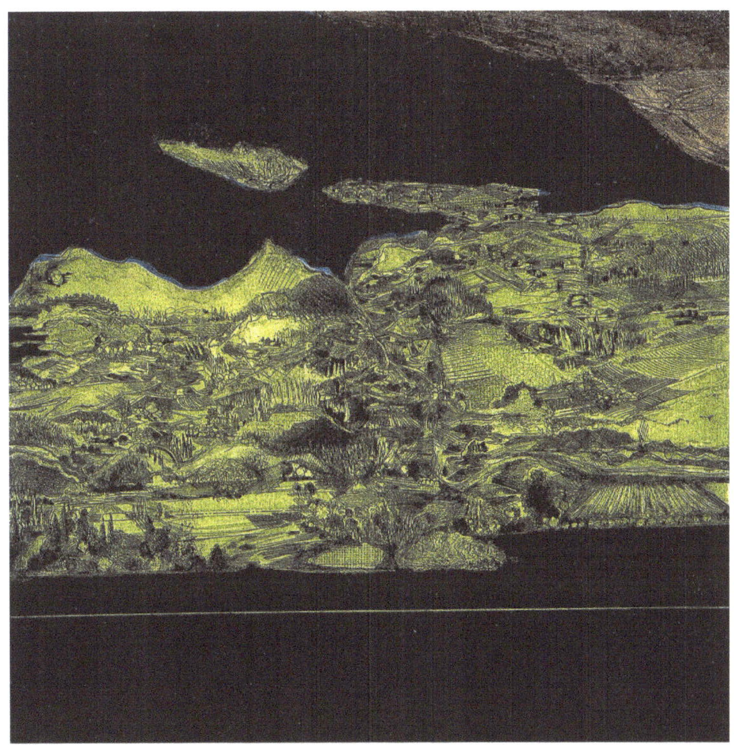

Thomas Seawell's silkscreen prints are complex overlays of printmaking techniques, colors and glazes. Technically innovative, Seawell was instrumental in the development of the collograph, but later concentrated on multi-color serigraphs of urban Pop culture. He was active and a frequent exhibitor during the Golden '70s. Seawell taught printmaking and drawing at the State University of New York (SUNY) at Oswego for thirty years before retiring in 1991. He has had significant influence in the printmaking field.

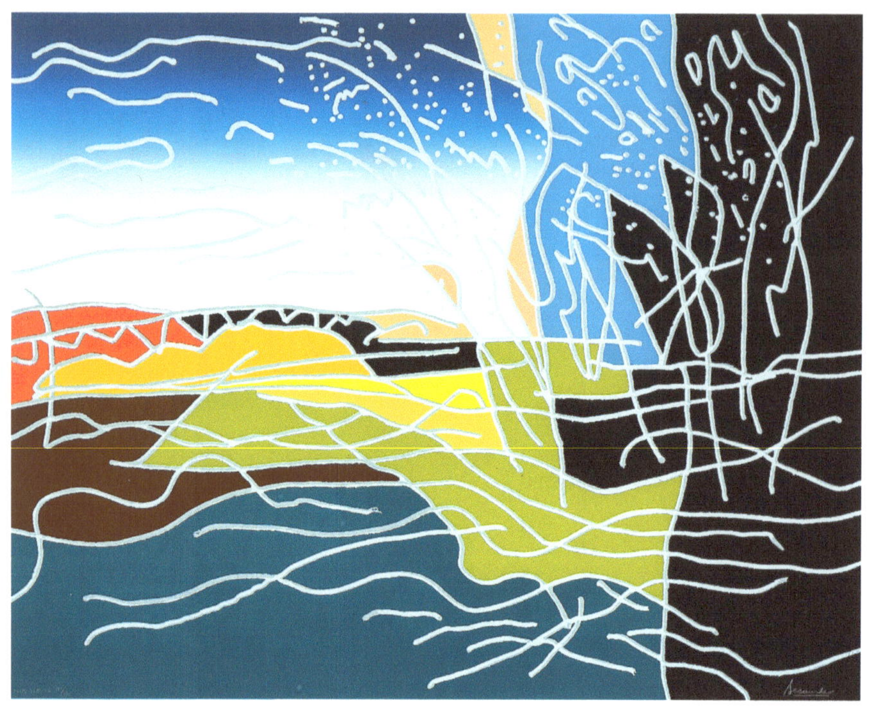

Arthur Secunda
"Four Seasons" Silkscreen 31 x 39

Arthur Secunda is an internationally renowned artist whose career has spanned five decades. His graphics have been acclaimed for their lush color and the artists own technical inventiveness. He considers himself a landscape artist and has a highly developed recognizable style in representing nature, the land and its forms. Secunda has a large following and enjoys wide commercial success and influence. After years of living in Paris, Secunda maintains a studio in Scottsdale, Arizona.

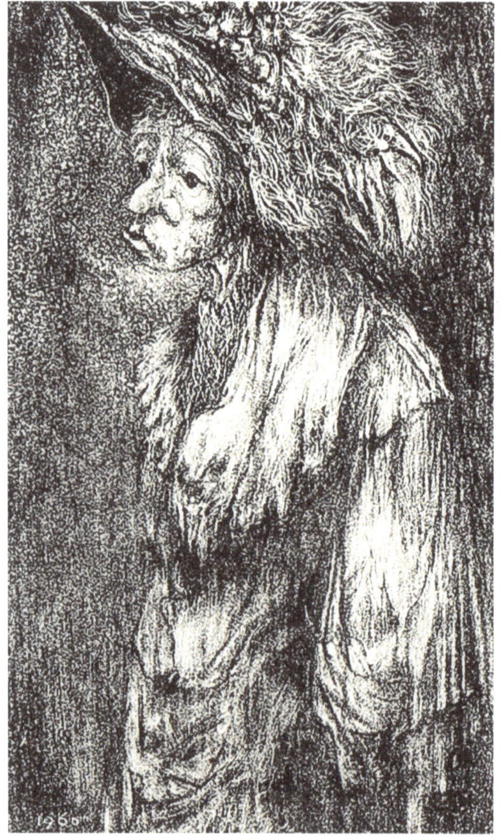

Alfred Sessler
"Sarah" Lithograph 7 x 4 ½

Drawing cartoons during the 1920's sparked Alfred Sessler's interest in art. He was the consummate printmaker, ultimately becoming best known for his lithographs, etchings and woodcuts. His imagery was often caricatures of faces and figures, and fantastic representations of trees and natural growth. Sessler was inspired by nature and everyday people. He stated, "My main interest is in commentary concerning the human life around me". He is credited with the invention of the color reduction process for creating woodcuts using a single wooden surface. In the mid-forties, at the same time that Mauricio Lasansky was carrying the gospel of intaglio printing to the University of Iowa, young Alfred Sessler was bringing etching and lithography to the University of Wisconsin – Madison. There he set a tone of tolerance, humanism and liberality and established a ground breaking graphics program. This program provided the University with a position of leadership in the field of printmaking, and made it the largest and most progressive in the country. The period confronted massive challenges in the printmaking field, and Sessler was said to be "a man of consistency in a time of change". His influence and contribution is notable and far reaching. He was a dedicated and caring teacher and inspired these same traits in those around him. Sessler passed away in1963.

Lynn Shaler
"Duality" Etching/
Aquatint 5 ¼ x 6 ¾

Lynn Shaler is known for her intricate color aquatint etchings. Prominent throughout her work is a vivid combination of pattern, texture and contrast. Shaler was a frequent exhibitor and award winner in national shows during the Golden '70s. She currently lives in Paris.

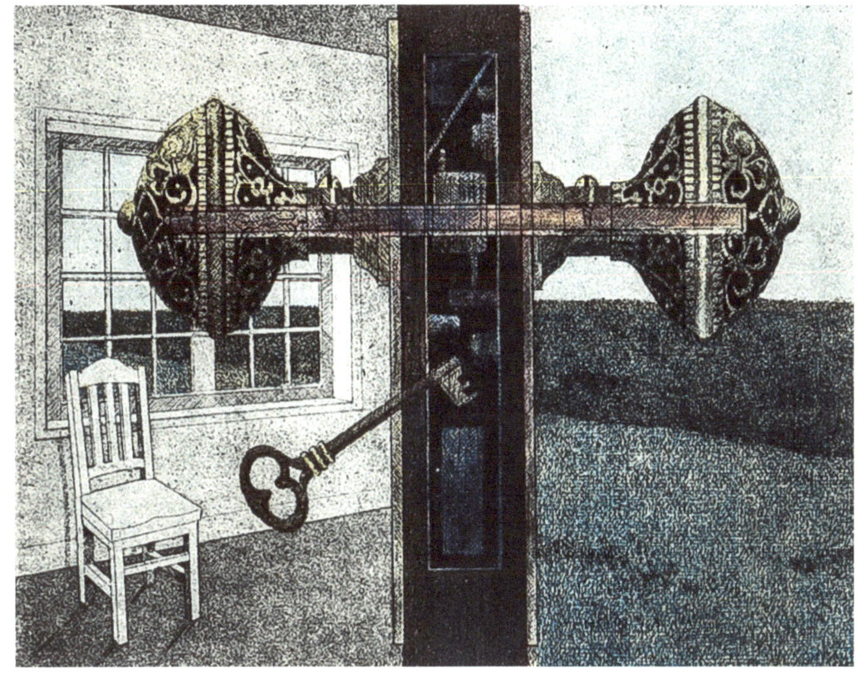

Jeanette Pasin Sloan
"La Terrazzo" Lithograph 20 x 15 ½

Jeanette Pasin Sloan is an American painter and printmaker born in Chicago, Illinois. Sloan is known for her still life compositions that border on Op art, and display a masterful technical virtuosity. The artist uses a photo – realistic style to depict reflective objects set against patterned backgrounds. Hers are striking works that at first puzzle and then please the eye. Sloan has stated, "I've always thought that my best work was right on the edge of disorder. I think that it is as much about disorder as it is about harmony and balance." These are works of an artist who has complete command of her vision. Sloan's imagery and delivery are exceptional.

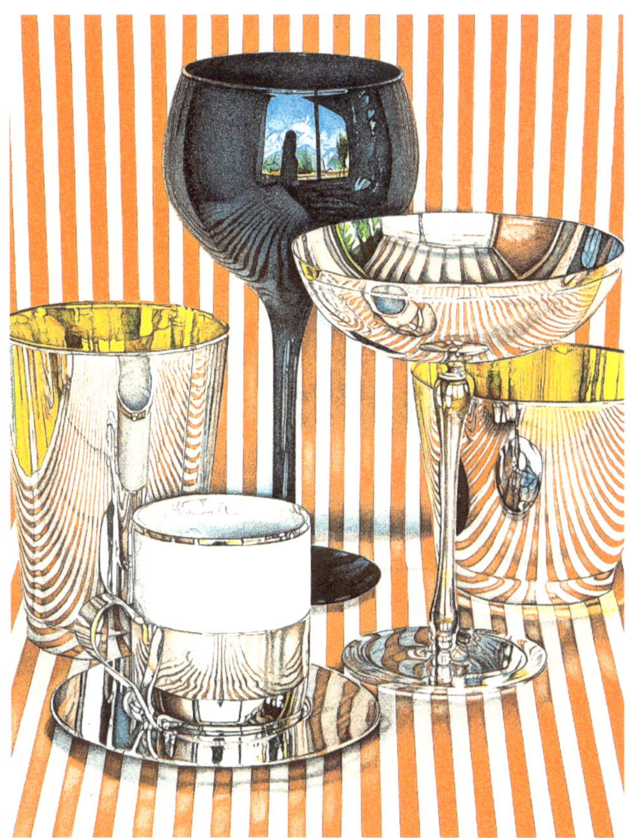

Jean Solombre
"Early Morning" Aquatint 15 ¾ x 12 ½

French painter, illustrator, poet and printmaker, Jean Solombre is a master of the aquatint medium, and he is known worldwide for his romantic and mysterious landscape imagery. A Surrealist, his prints evoke dream states, giving comfort, and it has been said that "you can hear, as well as feel, their resonance of silence". His work has been described as magical and mystical.

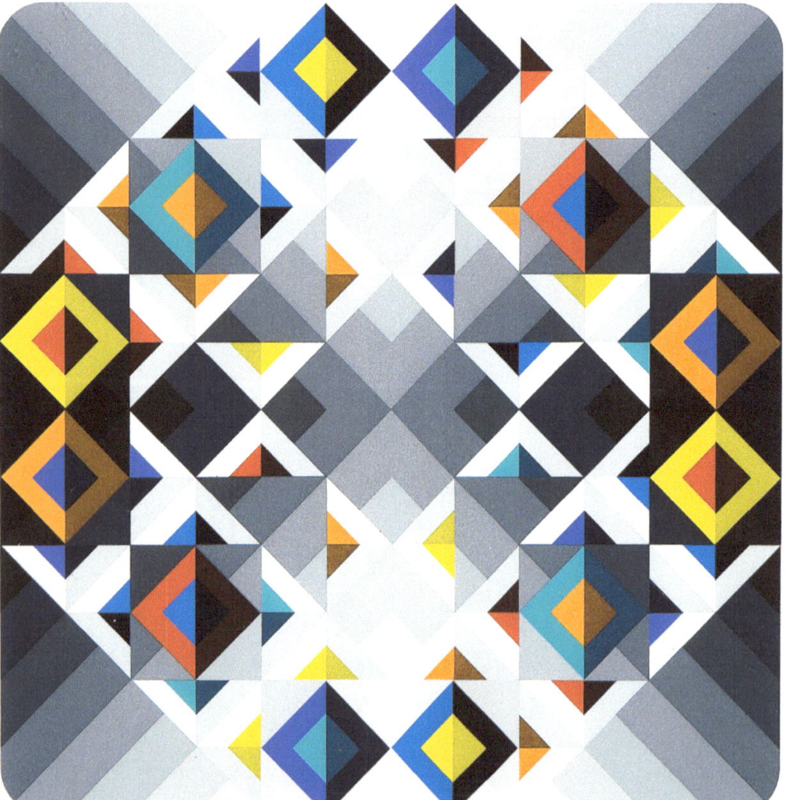

Marko Spalatin
Silkscreen "Pulsar VI" 20 ½ x 20 ½

Marko Spalatin was born in Zagreb, Croatia and immigrated to the United States in his late teens. His work is often associated with Optical Art. Working with geometric forms, Spalatin develops variegated color surfaces that capture light, creating the illusion of volume and space. The artist draws sensations, mysteries on the edge of chaos, but one of controlled chaos. Spalatin's work is always about light, and this light makes his work imposing. He has stated, "I like to create a sense of something beyond the ordinary. I want to provoke the viewer to question, what is it that I'm looking at?" Spalatin's work has universal appeal, and has been highly sought after by museums and collectors worldwide. His work is imaginative, and his color and form choices are dramatic.

Robert Stackhouse
"Working Sketches"
Lithograph 21 x 30

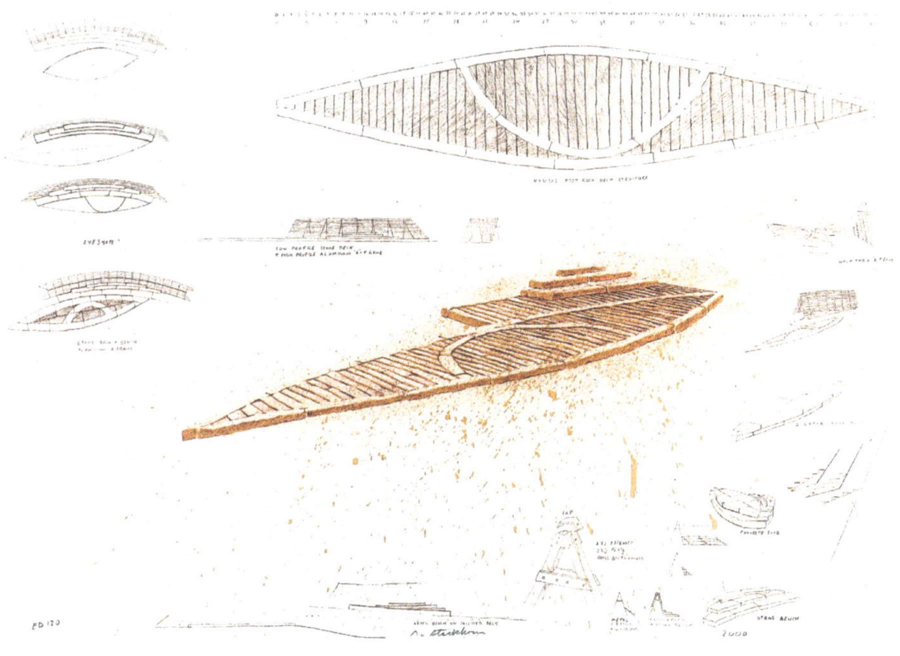

Although best known for his sculpture, Robert Stackhouse is also a prolific painter and printmaker. Skeletons of ships or boats, house like structures and snakes dominate his subject matter. His images and structures frequently have a transcendental quality of things long dead rising to a new and higher form. There is a rebirth, the building of the new from the old. "Working Sketches", pictured here, is a prime example of his work. Stackhouse has stated, "Drawing is an integral part of my work". And he is a master of the medium. His are impressive works, and his influence is far reaching.

Donald Sultan
"Lips" Etching 3 x 4 ¼

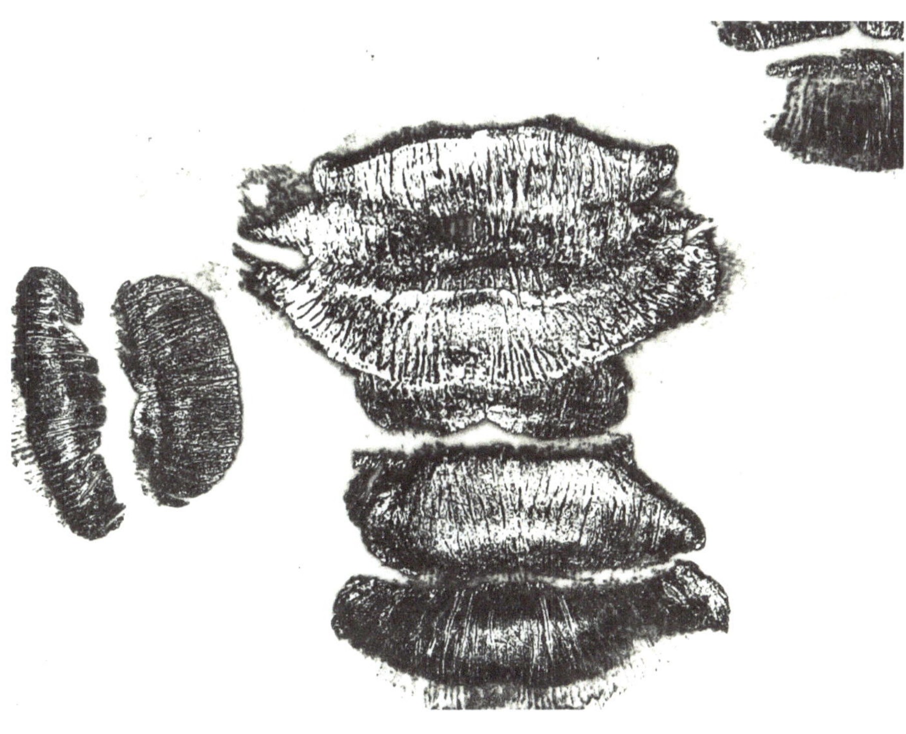

Donald Sultan was born in 1951 in Asheville, North Carolina, and presently lives and works in New York City. He is considered one of the leading contemporary still life artists in America. Despite the representational objects in his imagery, Sultan proclaims that his works are first and foremost abstract. With his unique artistic methods, and his innovative approach to traditional subject matter, Sultan is considered to be at the forefront of contemporary art. He is internationally acclaimed and his work is collected by museums and private collectors throughout the world. Sultan has said of his work, "It turns you off and turns you on at the same time".

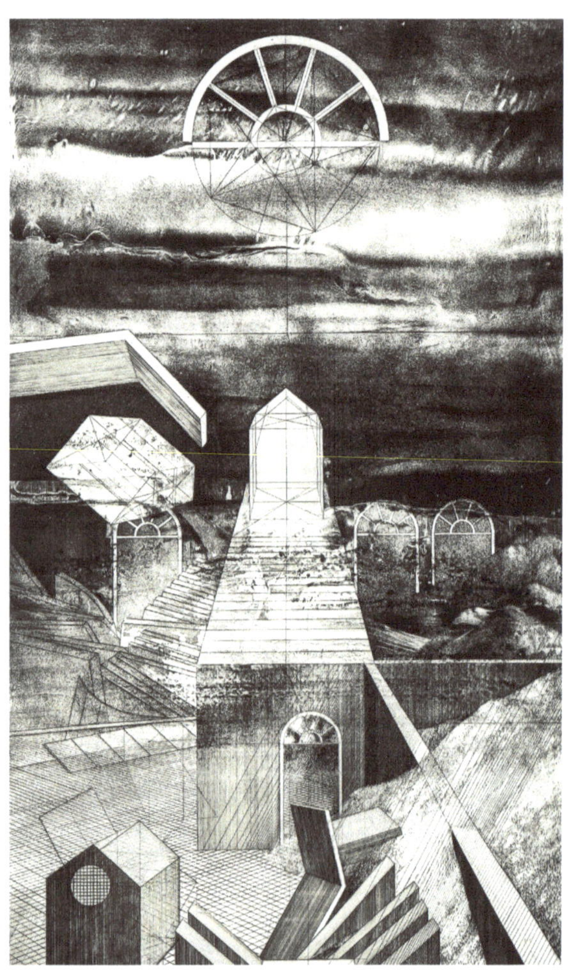

Evan Summer
"Landscape L" Etching/Drypoint 35 ½ x 21 ½

A master printmaker, Evan Summer has been making prints, exhibiting in national and international shows and winning awards for over four decades. He continues to do so. The combination of drawing and the technical challenges of printmaking were ideally suited to his abilities, and early on in his career, became his main interest as an artist. Nature, science and architecture are his subject matter and that has not changed over the years. His initial prints in the Golden '70s were collographs, which at the time was a relatively new medium. These prints were large interior scenes of decaying rooms, reminiscent of past memories and also reminders of our own mortality. He has since moved on to exterior landscapes with outlined forms that remind one of buildings and base structures still in progress. They are dreamlike surreal settings, and they are now drawn on copper plates with etching, drypoint engraving and aquatint as his medium. These are awesome works of art, rendered with masterful technical virtuosity, and they are a delight to view. Summer is currently teaching at Kutztown University in Pennsylvania. His influence is significant with his many students after forty years of teaching, and he has earned the respect of his peers.

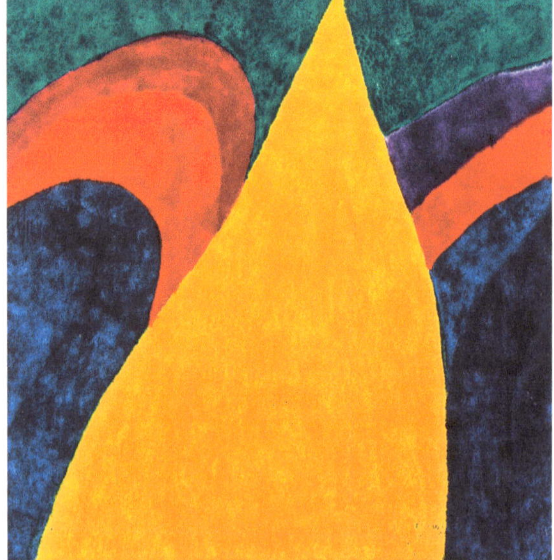

Carol Summers
"Swedegon" Woodcut 12 ¼ x 12

Carol Summers is renowned for his vivid colors and the revolutionary woodblock techniques that he introduced in the 1960's. Woodcuts became his specialty around 1950. His subject matter is predominately landscapes anchored by broad, abstract shapes with saturated fields of bold color. Summers is a master of the woodblock technique, developing an innovative and recognizable personal way of printing to convey the unique luminescent glow that is a hallmark of his work. He has stated, "The notion that there is a right way to make a print strikes me as exactly backwards, since any method tends to dictate a specific result". Summers work has been widely collected for decades.

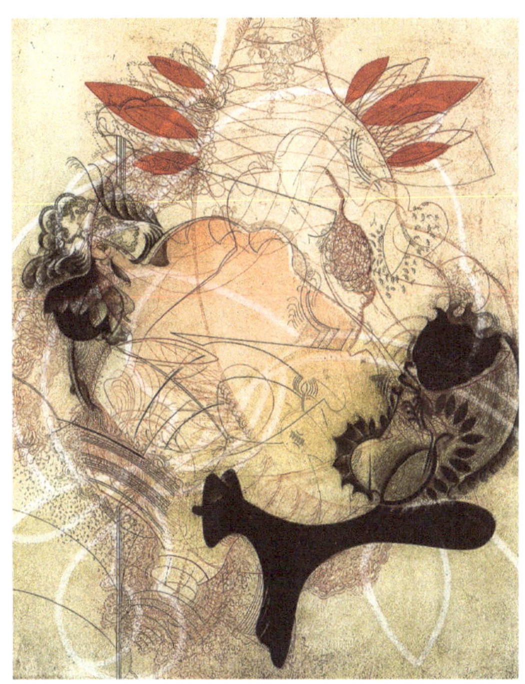

Shelley Thorstensen

"Je ne sais quoi"
Etching/Relief 15 x 11 ¾

A printmaker and educator, Shelley Thorstensen presently teaches drawing and printmaking at the Tyler School of Art. A master of the processes of printmaking, Thorstensen's multi-media work is presented with a technical virtuosity that is impressive. Her ornamental based imagery is pleasing to the eye, combining powerful forms in elegant settings. They are concentrations of layered variations of color, using lush blacks in fields of elegant pinks and soft greys. The results are deceptive; delightfully presented, but with an edge. She is a past President Elect of the prestigious Society of American Graphic Artists based in New York City. With both her students and peers, Thorstensen's influence is significant.

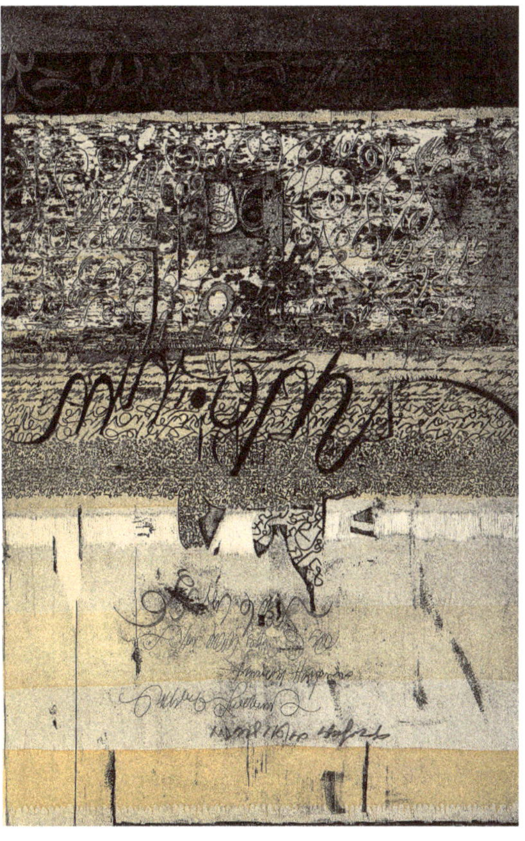

Arthur Thrall

"Ceremonial Document" Intaglio 29 ½ x 22

Arthur Thrall is a painter, printmaker and educator, with an international reputation. His masterfully rendered images are inspired by music, the art of calligraphy, manuscripts and other graphic sources. Thrall transforms sensuous lines into graceful compositions of elegant curves and flowing shapes. A second generation pioneer of the Print Renaissance, Thrall achieved substantial recognition during the 1960's on the printmaking scene in national and international juried shows. He taught at Lawrence University in Appleton, Wisconsin for twenty-six years before retiring in 1990. He remained active until his untimely death in 2015, working in his studio in Milwaukee, a remodeled factory building which was formerly a nut packaging facility, and which he fondly referred to as "the nut factory". His influence has been substantial for students and peers alike. He has taken the art of printmaking to a higher level. His print, "Oval 10", graces the cover of this publication.

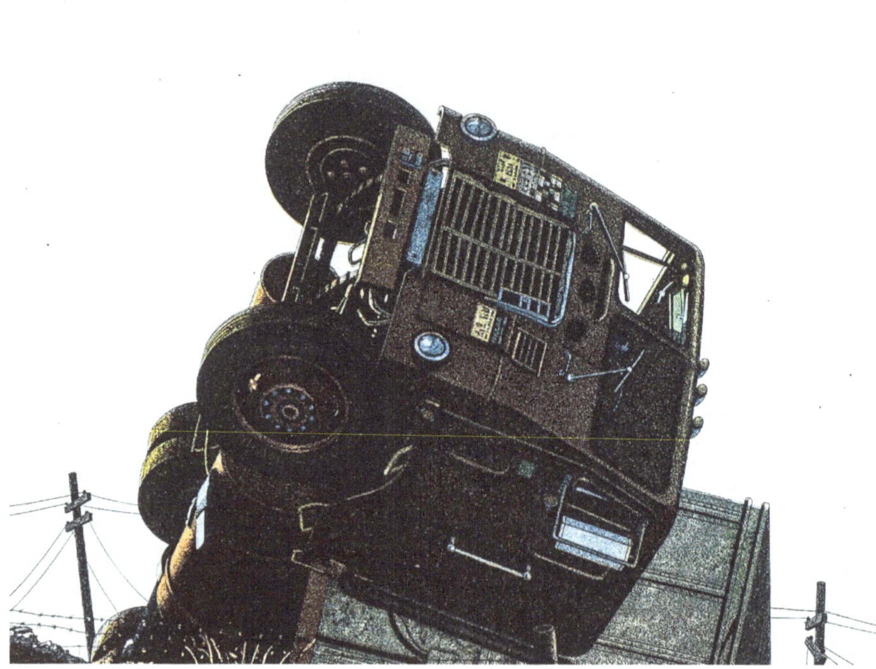

James Torlakson
"Asleep at the Wheel"
Aquatint 12 x 12

James Torlakson is best known for his photo-based realism. His imagery is centered on everyday America using various objects such as trucks, railroad cars, drive-ins, and images related to a repeated motif of architecture. A product of the Golden '70s national juried shows, Tolakson's new interests are video production, computer generated imagery and experiments with a more graphic surrealist style. He states, "Given a personal and honest perspective, most anything is worth consideration". His work continues to impress.

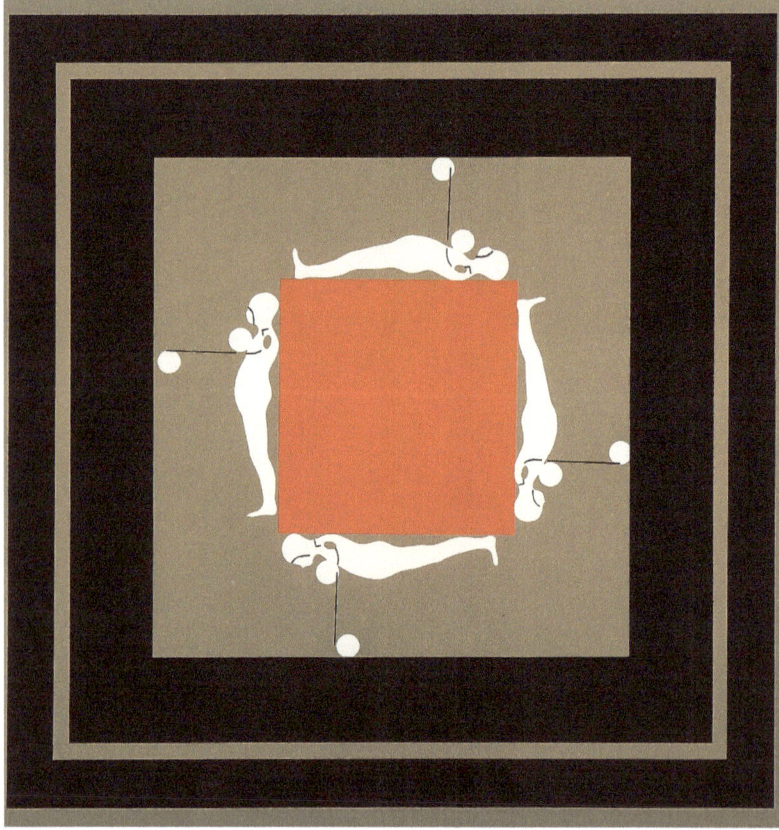

Ernest Trova
"Untitled (Falling Man)"
Silkscreen 25 x 25

Ernest Trova was a self-taught American surrealist, Pop painter and sculptor. He was best known for his signature image and figure series, "The Falling Man", created in 1964. He viewed this symbol as personifying human fallibility. Serialization was essential to his work, and Trova considered his entire life's output a single "work in progress". He stated, "All of it, all the sculptures, paintings and prints, are one work". The commercial success of the imagery led to charges by critics of commercialism and that his work was period kitsch. Though misunderstood by a few, Trova gained international renown as an artist, and lived his entire life in his hometown of St. Louis, Missouri. He passed away in 2009.

Don La Viere Turner
"Puppet and the Puppet Dragon" Woodcut 21 x 32 ¼

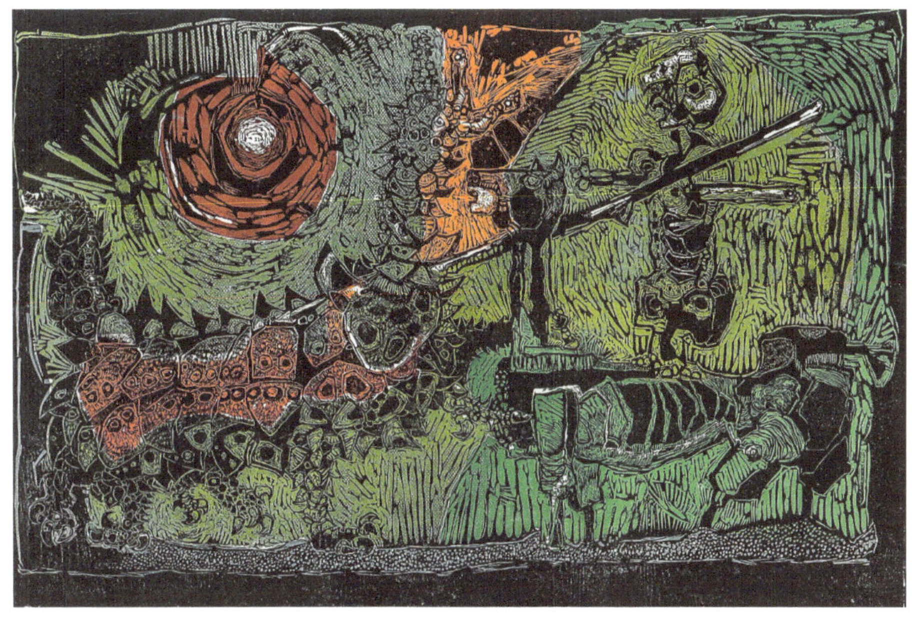

Born in Milwaukee, Wisconsin in 1929, Don La Viere Turner was a painter, sculptor, printmaker and educator. He attended the University of Wisconsin-Madison and studied under the late John Wilde. In 1971 he began teaching there. Fine draftsmanship is the essential element in all of Turner's work. His use of line covers the fine delicacy of silverpoint, which he is credited with redefining, to the bold blacks of the woodcut. His subject matter reveal profound concern for the human condition. His work shows a strong German Expressionist influence. Turner passed away in 1997.

Carol Wax
"Lepidoptiks" Mezzotint 9 ½ x 6

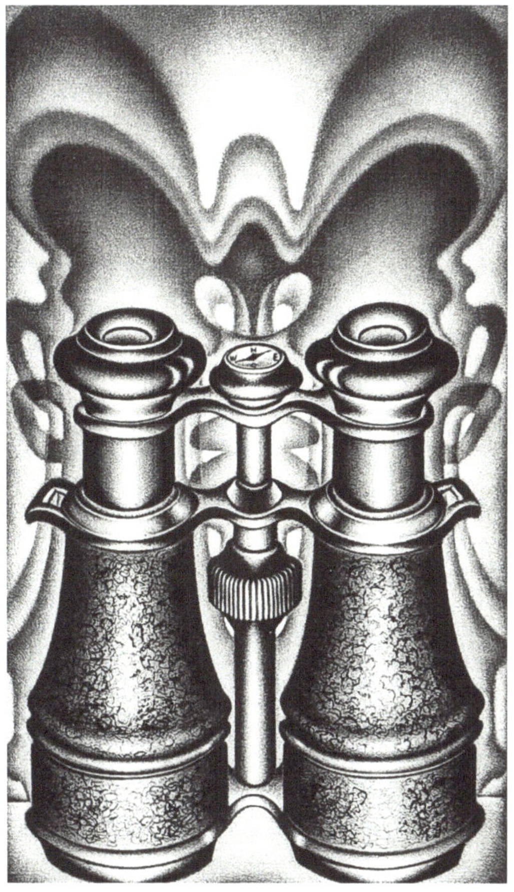

Carol Wax is an American artist and author. The New York Times has called her, "a virtuoso printmaker and art historian" for her works in mezzotint and her writings on the history and techniques of the medium. She has been a major force in the process, influencing innumerable artists with her defining publication, "The Mezzotint: History and Technique", published by Abrams 1990-96. It has become the standard reference work for mezzotint practitioners. Wax was born in New York City in 1953 and has never strayed far from there. She was an active participant in national juried shows in the Golden '70s, and continues to widely exhibit her work. Mezzotints by Wax are highly collected by museums, private collectors and the general public. Her works are true masterpieces of the medium.

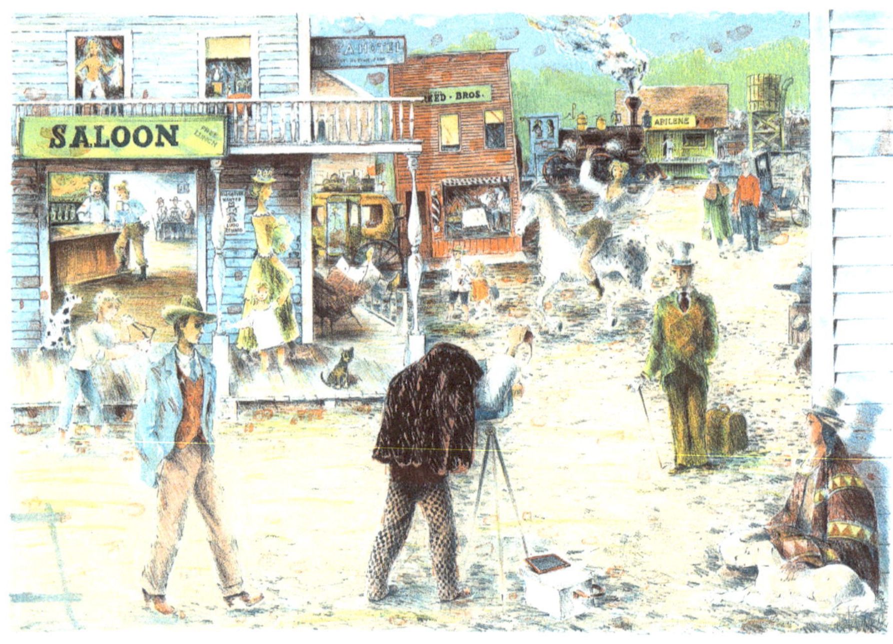

Emil Weddige
"Meeting Place"
Lithograph 18 x 27

Emil Weddige completed his education at the University of Michigan in 1937, and spent the next 38 years as a working professor there, influencing close to four decades of students and peers alike. During this time he built a reputation as a master of both color and the media of lithography. Weddige's subjects have a regional air, as they are classic Americana. His images remind one of the playfulness reminiscent in the works of Chagall. Weddige was born in 1907 and passed in 2001.

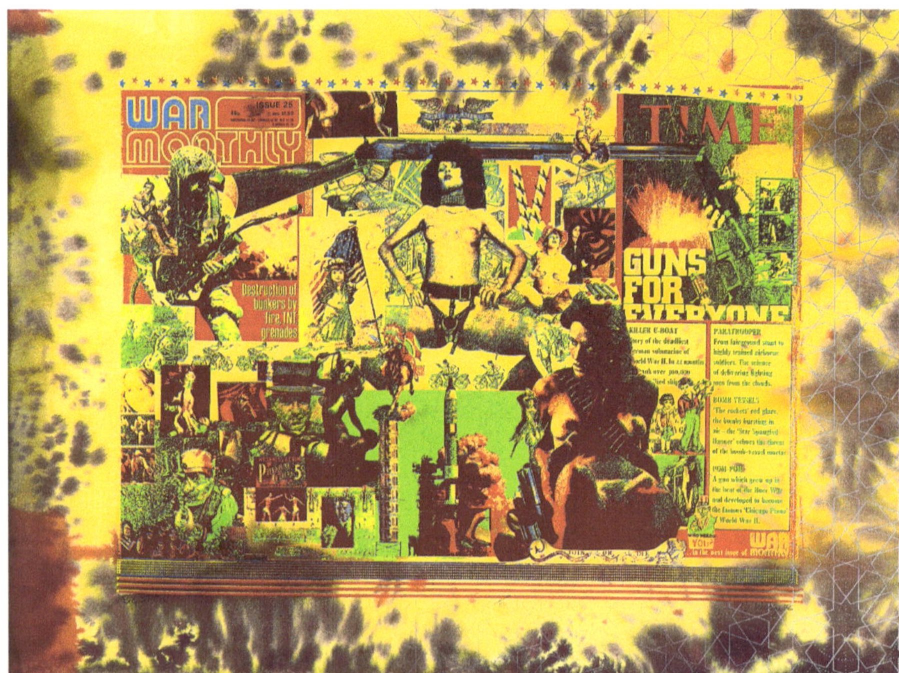

William Weege
"Big Stick"
Lithograph 21 ½ x 29 ½

William Weege is Professor Emeritus at the University of Wisconsin-Madison Art Department and founder and artistic director of Tandem Press, which was set up in 1987 and termed an "artistic laboratory". Tandem Press is one of only three workshops in the United States affiliated with a University. Weege is best known for his large abstract paper prints, and is one of the early practitioners in the revival of making handmade paper, which started in the 1960's. He is highly regarded in the printmaking field on an international level. Weege continues to teach at the University of Wisconsin-Madison and is still creating and developing innovative processes for making art. His stated philosophy of art is simple and direct: "Do it".

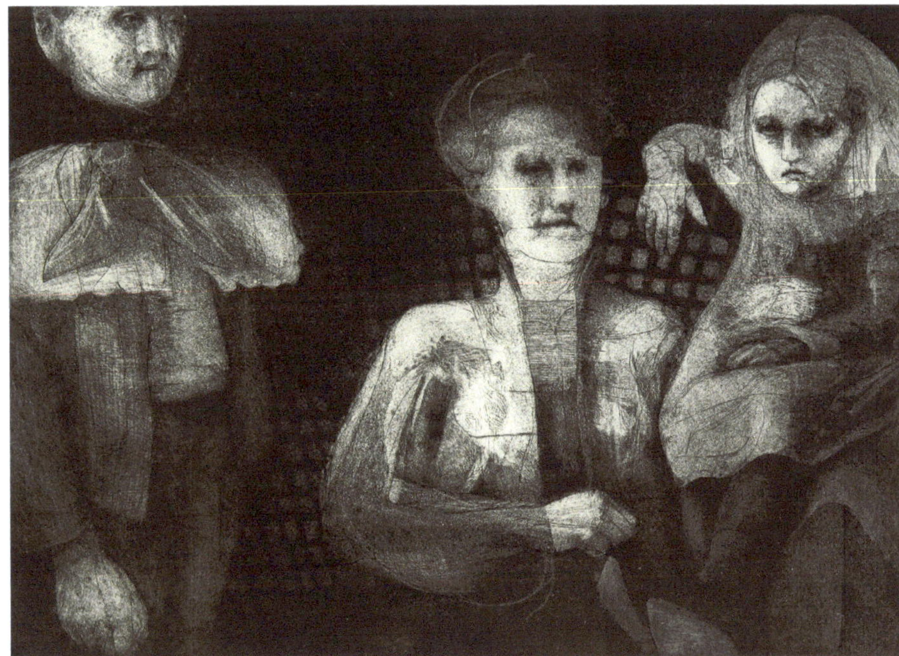

Charles Wells
"Family Group"
Etching/Aquatint 18 ½ x 26

New York based Charles Wells is for the most part self-taught, and is mainly known for his sculpture. However, his print images match and in ways surpass the power and strength of his sculptural work. His subject matter is predominately drawn portraits of famous artists of the past. Line dominates his printed imagery and his portraits literally jump off the paper. They are powerful renditions of their subject, going well below the surface of the skin. Wells is a master of line, and also of the etching medium. Once viewed, his images are not soon forgotten.

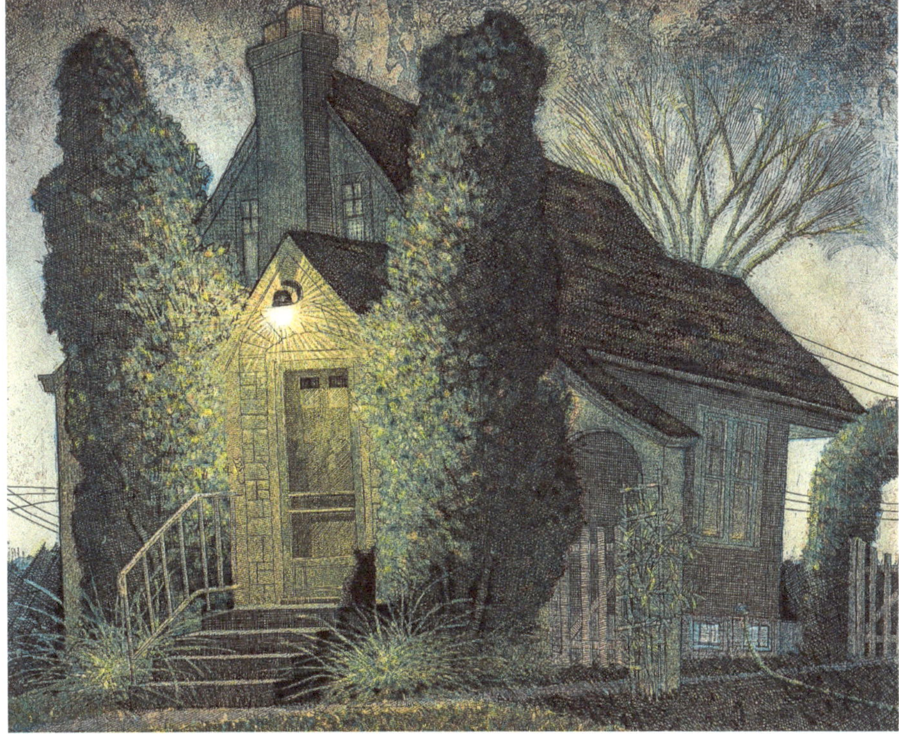

Larry Welo
"Dream House"
Etching 16 x 20

Larry Welo has been a full time artist since 1974. He makes his art in a converted opera house on the Main Street in Blue Mounds, Wisconsin. He is the consummate "basement printmaker". His first studio was a rundown storefront with no running water or heat. Carrying buckets of water from the adjoining neighbors and breaking formed ice on frigid mornings became a natural daily routine. Welo produces detailed and intricate realistic etchings inspired by various aspects of his life's surroundings; landscapes, urban areas and especially trees. His studies of nature are separated from others of that genre by the simple word, "truth". He states, "All of my imagery is rooted in the real world. My etchings are not intended to be duplications of what I physically see, but instead, interpretations of it". Welo is a seasoned and ambitious printmaker, and one who has dedicated his life to that pursuit.

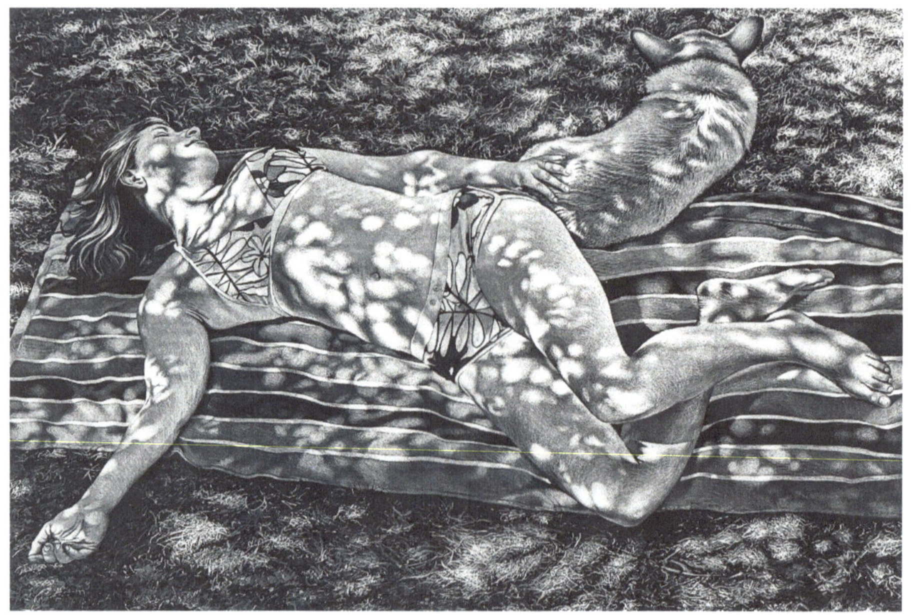

Art Werger
"Karla" Aquatint 23 ½ x 35 ½

Art Werger is a contemporary printmaker of exceptional abilities, who thrives in the technical complexities of the print media. He is active and has gained wide success in national and international exhibitions. Werger's prints show a keen observation of quiet and normally unnoticed moments. It has been said of his work that "he creates a dreamlike detachment from the events taking place". His subjects are urban mysteries, often narratives suggesting a story, left for the viewer to complete. Werger is presently Professor of Printmaking at Ohio University in Athens, Ohio. He is a frequent lecturer and guest teacher for workshops, and is highly regarded for his technical expertise in the mezzotint and aquatint mediums.

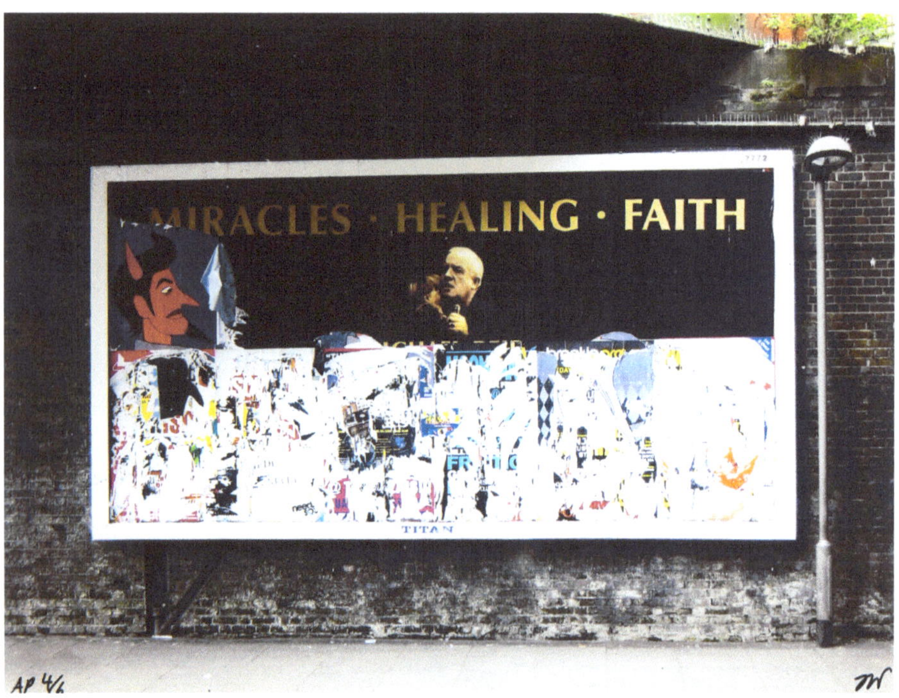

Tom Wilmott
"Sorry, can you say that again? I couldn't hear you coz' of the universal church of god damn fraud shouting shit all over." Photograph 5 x 7

Born in London, England, Tom Wilmott is a contemporary painter, photographer and writer. In this image he has combined the two mediums of photography and writing, for a very interesting tongue in cheek collaborative statement. The photo depicts a poster, advocating the services of faith healer Michael Reid. The left side of the poster has been torn away to reveal, purely by chance, a cartoon image of the devil from a previous flyer beneath. The title came from an overheard phone conversation of a girl having difficulty hearing, as a nearby church was using a van with a loudspeaker to make their announcements to the surrounding neighborhood. The artist states; "The phrase stayed with me and seemed to describe perfectly the billboard image I encountered years later." Wilmott seeks satisfaction from the pure act of making art itself, enjoying the physical and mental process. Everything is fair game. His are clever and thought provoking works.

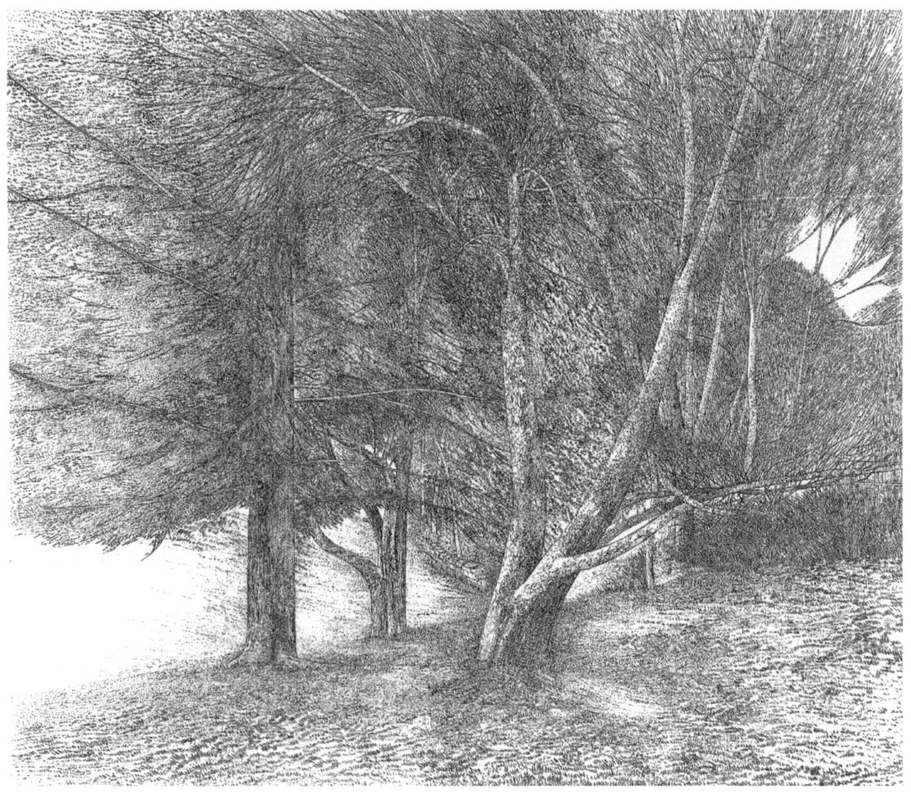

Richard Claude Ziemann
"Edge of the Clearing"
Etching/Engraving 20 x 23

Richard Claude Ziemann is a printmaker and educator. Nature and the landscape are his playgrounds, exploring in his work the play of light and the changes of form and textural variety of the seasons. The forest floor, fields of grass, flowers and foliage, and especially the trees have been interpreted with his etching needle. Ziemann has been called "the foremost etcher/engraver of landscapes in America", and has also been referred to as "the poet of landscape etching". He is Professor Emeritus at the City University of New York, CUNY, and has had great influence on students and contemporaries alike. Ziemann is a master of the etching medium.

*** Art work courtesy of the Kenosha (Wi) Public Museum. Gift of Ronald L. and Mary K. Ruble

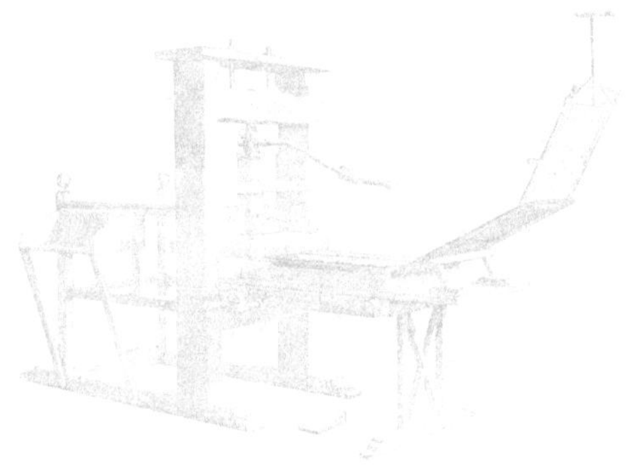

"I cannot imagine any living artist passing through this exhibition and remaining unaffected by it."

Hayter and Studio 17

"an event of consequence"

HAYTER AND STUDIO 17

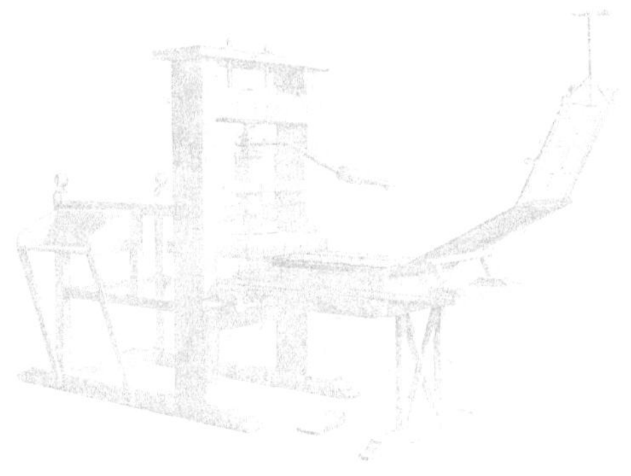

"a stunning presentation"

Hayter and Studio 17

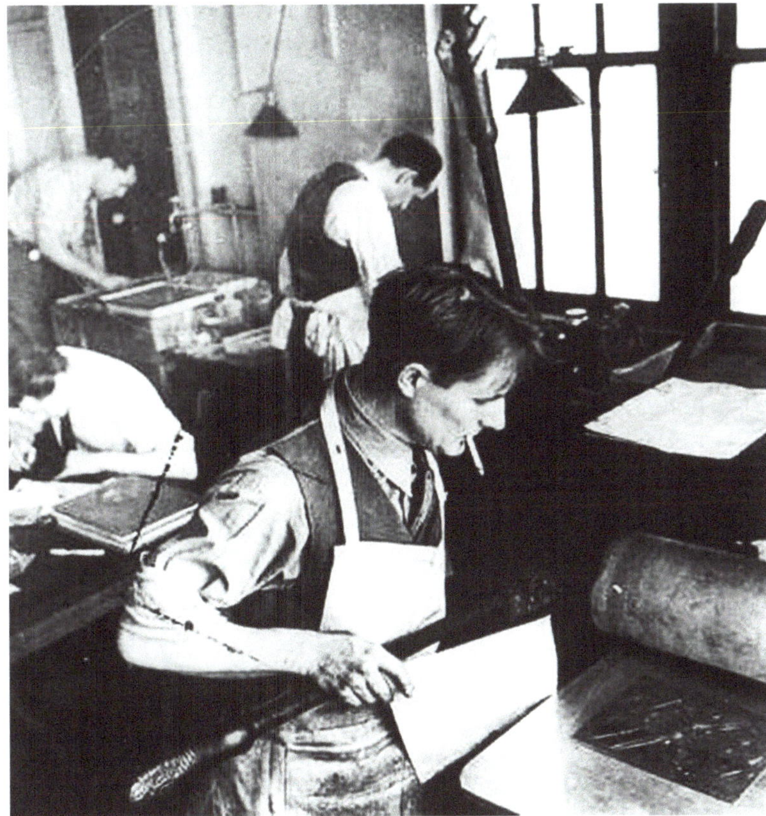

Stanley William Hayter at Atelier 17

As mentioned in other sections of this essay, the exhibit at the Museum of Modern Art in 1944 involving Stanley William Hayter and his followers from Atelier 17, was the catalyst that changed the fine art of printmaking forever. To capture the moment, I have listed excerpts on the following pages from the original catalogue of that historic event. I have included a reproduction of the cover, followed by pages from the catalogue listing the artists who were involved, and their exhibited works.

The show itself was titled "Hayter and Studio 17", and was a part of the "Art in Progress" exhibition to celebrate the fifteenth anniversary of the Museum of Modern Art in New York City. The exhibit was what we would term a "Blockbuster" today. There were several different sections to the anniversary exhibit, with printmaking being one of them. The others were painting and sculpture, industrial design, photography, film, dance and theatre, and architecture. It was a comprehensive survey of the contemporary art scene at the time. I can only conclude that the printmaking exhibit not only held its own with the other exhibits, but most certainly stood out, as it launched what was to be called the Print Renaissance in America, which is the basis for this book. The "Hayter and Studio 17" exhibit has been described as being "an explosion of sorts" for its immediate impact on the art world.

What I found most interesting and exciting were the press comments from the brochure. Emily Genauer summed it up rather emphatically in The New York World Telegram:

> "...the most beautiful display in the museum's history...a stunning presentation."

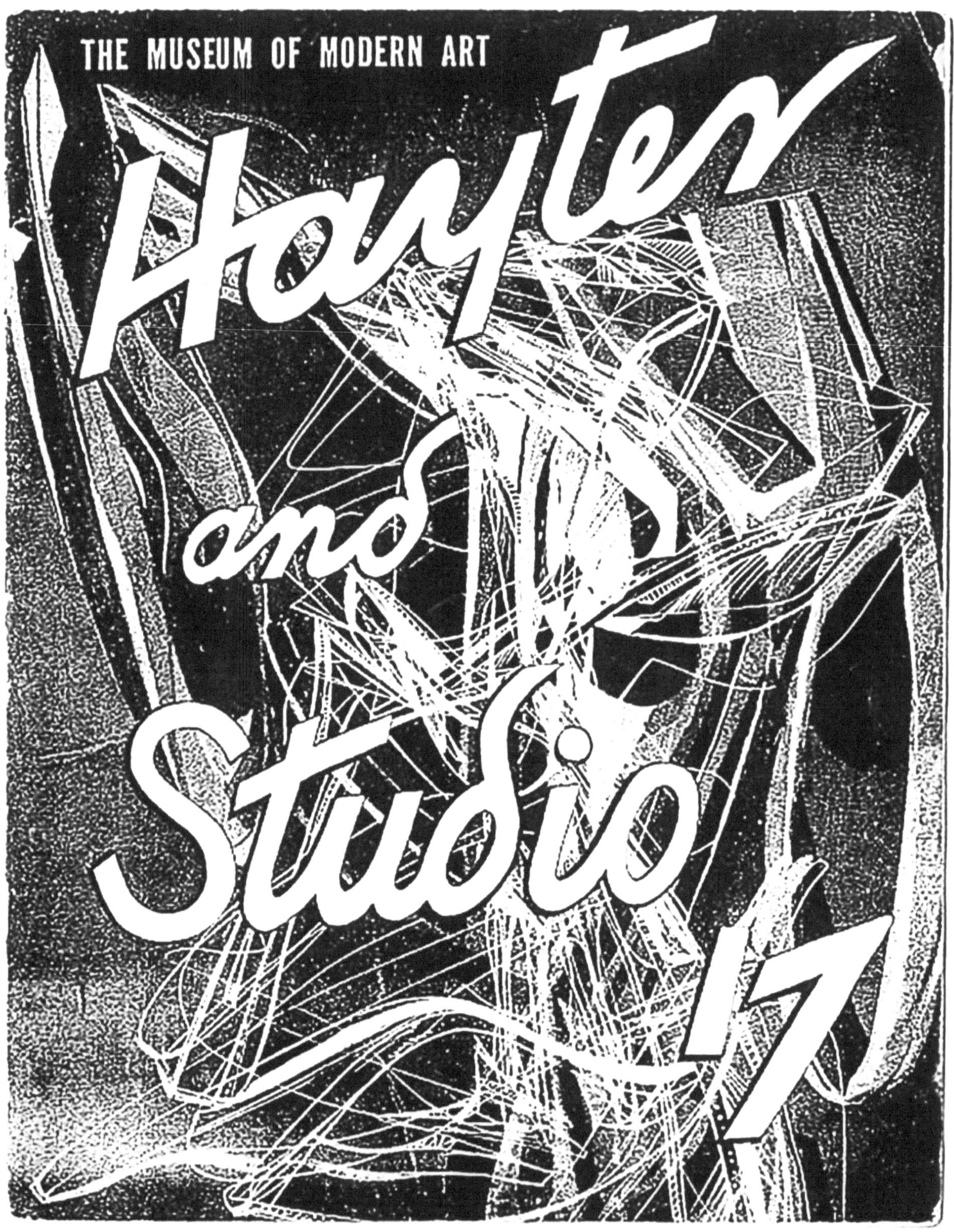
THE MUSEUM OF MODERN ART
Hayter
and
Studio 17

CHECK LIST

All works are lent by the artists unless otherwise credited. Names in parentheses are those of individuals and galleries through whose courtesy the prints have been assembled. In dimensions height precedes width.

The following abbreviations have been used:

drypt.	drypoint
engr.	engraving
etch.	etching
s.g.e.	soft ground etching

ADLER, Jankel

1. Interior. 1938, engr., 7⅞ x 9⅞". (Hayter)

BECKER, Fred

2. Dancer, 1942, etch., 7¼ x 5".

BUCKLAND-WRIGHT, John

3. Combat. 1937, engr., 6⅛ x 7¾". (Hayter)

CALDER, Alexander

4. The Big "I." 1944, s.g.e., 6⅞ x 8¾". (Wittenborn & Co.)

CHAGALL, Marc

5. Chevalière. 1944, s.g.e., 9 x 6".
6. Femme Violincelle. 1944, s.g.e., 8⅞ x 6⅞".

DREWES, Werner

7. On Different Planes. 1944, engr., 11¾ x 6". (Wittenborn & Co.)

FINE, Perle

8. Weathervane. 1944, engr., 4⅜ x 5".
9. Calm after Storm. 1944, etch., 7⅞ x 5⅞". (Wittenborn & Co.)

FULLER, Sue

10. The Sailor's Dream. 1944, relief etch., 9 x 6".
11. Cock. 1944, color engr., 8 x 5⅞". (Wittenborn & Co.)
12. Mosaic. 1944, s.g.e., 9⅞ x 7¾".
13. The Emperor's Jewels. 1944, s.g.e., relief print on plaster, carved, 8 x 6".
14. The Connoisseur. 1944, s.g.e. in color on plaster, carved, 11 x 8¾".

HAYTER, S. W.

15. Flight. 1944, engr., s.g.e., 15 x 9¾". (Wittenborn & Co.)
16. Laocoön. 1943, engr. on plaster, carved, colored, 23½ x 14".
17. Prestige of the Insect. 1942, engr. on plaster, carved, colored, 13 x 12⅝".
18. Tarantelle. 1943, engr., s.g.e., 21¾ x 13". (Buchholz Gallery)
19. Laocoön. 1943, engr., s.g.e., 12½ x 21⅞". (Willard Gallery)
20. Le Viol de Lucrèce. 1934, engr., s.g.e., 11½ x 14".
21. Masques. 1937, engr., s.g.e., 4⅛ x 7¾".
22. Mirror. 1942, engr., s.g.e., 7½ x 4¾".
23. Centauresse. 1944, color engr., 6 x 4". (Buchholz Gallery)
24. Myth of Creation. 1941, engr. and s.g.e. on plaster, carved, 10 x 8".

HUGO, Ian

25. Jackal of the Moon. 1943, engr., 6⅛ x 14⅞".
26. Night Gods. 1943, engr., 9 x 6".
27. Rage of the Prophet. 1944, engr. relief print on plaster, carved, 15 x 10".

KOLOS-VARI, Maximilian

28. Bull. 1939, engr., 7 x 9¼". (Hayter)

LASANSKY, Mauricio

29. Horse. 1944, engr., 13⅝ x 5½". (Wittenborn & Co.)
30. La Lagrima. 1944, color etch., 9 x 11¾".
31. Doma. 1944, engr., 19⅞ x 13⅞".

LIPCHITZ, Jacques

32. Theseus. 1943, etch., engr., aquatint, 13¾ x 11⅜". (Buchholz Gallery)
33. Le Chemin de l'Exil. 1944, engr. and aquatint, 13⅞ x 9⅞".

MASSON, André

34. Petit Génie du Blé. 1942, s.g.e., 13⅞ x 10". (Buchholz Gallery)
35. Le Génie de l'Espèce. 1942, drypt. ,and engr., 14½ x 10¾". (Buchholz Gallery)

MAYO

36. Petite Composition. 1936, etch. and engr., 7½ x 5⅝". (Hayter)

MEAD, Roderick

37. River. 1940, engr., 7¾ x 7¾".

MIRO, Joan

38. Print. c.1938, drypt., engr., 10½ x 9⅜". (Buchholz Gallery)
39. Print. 1938, drypt., 9 x 11½". (Buchholz Gallery)
40. Plate from Fraternité series. 1938, etch., 5⅞ x 3⅝". (Hayter)
41. Plate from Solidarité series. 1937, engr., s.g.e., 4 x 3⅛". (Hayter)

NEGRI, Nina

42. La Fougère. 1937, relief engr., 4¼ x 7¾". (Hayter)

NORTON, Hubert

43. Civil Disobedience. 1942, engr., s.g.e., 3⅞ x 5⅜".

OLMSTED, Barbara

44. Le Negre et les Arbres. 1937, engr., s.g.e., 9⅞ x 7¼". (Hayter)

PETERDI, Gabor

45. Desespoir. 1942, etch., s.g.e., 10½ x 7¾".

PHILLIPS, Helen

46. Figure in Space. 1943, engr., 6⅞ x 5⅛". (Hayter)

PLATT, D. P.

47. Composition. 1943, engr., etch., 7⅝ x 9⅝".

48. Sea Bird. 1944, engr., s.g.e., 11⅞ x 8⅞".

RACZ, André

49. Mother and Child. 1944, color engr., 11¾ x 17¾".

50. Dejanira and Nessus. 1944, engr., etch. on plaster, carved, 10½ x 14¼".

RATTNER, Abraham

51. "Among those who stood . . ." 1944, color etch., 6⅞ x 9⅞". (Paul Rosenberg)

ROESCH, Kurt

52. Salome. 1944, etch., 17¾ x 11¾". (Buchholz)

RYAN, Anne

53. Centaur. 1943, engr., 7½" diameter (circle).

SZENES, Arpad

54. Le Carrousel. 1932, etch., 5⅞ x 7¾". (Hayter)

TREVELYAN, Julian

55. "Man is perhaps . . . " 1932, s.g.e., 7 x 9⅛". (Hayter)

56. Metropolis. 1937, etch., gouache, 7⅞ x 14". (Willard Gallery)

UBAC, Raoul

57. Le Drame Nocturne. 1938, engr., 9⅞ x 7¼". (Hayter)

VIEILLARD, Roger

58. Le Temple de la Liberté. 1937, engr., 9¼ x 7". (Hayter)

59. Phaeton II. 1938, engr., 7¾ x 6¼". (Hayter)

YARROW, Catherine

60. Head. 1936, etch., aquatint, 10¼ x 8".

NOTE: In addition to the prints above, the Museum Exhibition includes a number of the original copper plates, an uninked plaster cast from Hayter's plate *Runner*, and two books with covers and illustrations printed from original plates by Hugo.

PRESS COMMENT ON **ART IN PROGRESS** EXHIBITION

New York World Telegram, Emily Genauer—" . . . the most thrillingly beautiful display in the museum's history . . . a stunning presentation such as no other institution in the country could or would have assembled."

The Sun, New York, Henry McBride—" . . . the Museum of Modern Art . . . celebrates its fifteenth birthday with unusual splendor. . . . It sounds the modern note triumphantly and proves that the best men of today have caught the tempo of the times we live in just as brilliantly as the ancients did theirs. . . .

The special merit of the Modern Museum's show is that it connects its exhibits with present living conditions. This obviously, is the chief business of any modern museum, and it is heartening to find it so easily accomplished as it now is on 53rd street. . . .

I cannot imagine any living artist passing through this exhibition and remaining unaffected by it. For that reason the event takes on extreme importance . . . apparently New Yorkers have an all-summer job on their hands in getting reacquainted with their museum. . . ."

New York Herald Tribune, Carlyle Burrows—"Any of five or six sections of 'Art in Progress,' at the Museum of Modern Art, could be isolated and by itself be considered an event of consequence."

New York Times, Edward Alden Jewell—"The Museum of Modern Art has spent its first fifteen years, upon the whole, most profitably. It has had its vicissitudes. It has made its mistakes. It has been severely—sometimes, I think, unjustly—criticised. . . .

Taking an unbiased view of accomplishment to date, and recognizing what the museum stands for as a rounded, progressive cultural force in the community, I should think the town would be, on this occasion, inclined to stand up and cheer."

The Art Digest, Maude Riley—" . . . somehow, subtly, within the full-house exposition of art and its collaterals, the Modern seems to have recaptured the spirit of the original idea upon which it was founded. There is dignity and rightness in the quiet arrangements that progress easily from room to room and from floor to floor of this Anniversary Show."

New York Times, Editorial, May 24, 1944—" . . . a genuine source of public enjoyment and profit. Expansion of the museum's program has been phenomenal. . . . The Museum of Modern Art has won the confidence of the community, as expressed in a degree of public interest that increases day by day."

ON COLLECTING

"The Art of the Deal"

O
N

C
O
L
L
E
C
T
I
N
G

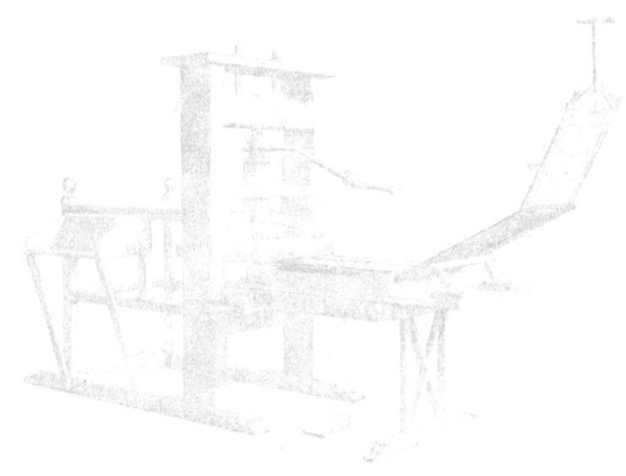

"Each piece has its own story as to how it landed on my doorstep; also, ways to acquire your own fine arts print collection with modest means."

On Collecting

Collecting is an art in itself, and one that gives great pleasure. People have been collecting objects since the beginning of time. Perhaps it has to do with our basic need to be hunter gatherers, I don't really know. We accumulate many things: match book covers, bottle caps, and ships in a bottle; rocks, sea shells, and fossils, but the payback is the enjoyment that one can only find in the possession of whatever it is that we deem special.

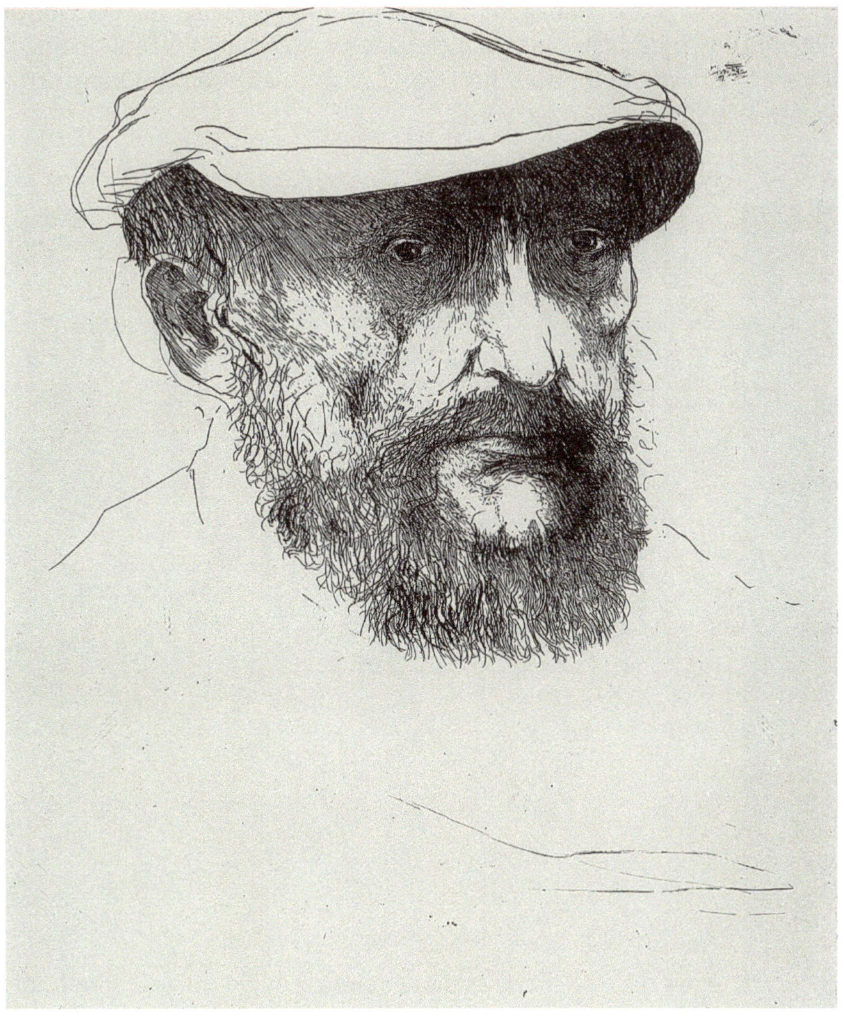

Leonard Baskin "Barlach" Etching 17 ¾ x 14 ½

I personally enjoy art, and specifically fine art prints. For me, collecting these prints has become a pleasurable habit, growing as the years pass. I enjoy the journey of the hunt, searching for that special print by that special artist, and I celebrate each successful outcome. Every fine art piece that I have acquired has its own story as to how it finally arrived on my doorstep. These stories are personal, and add special meaning for the objects collected. My need to be the temporary caretaker of something fine and unique has become something close to an obsession.

Building a substantial collection of art work was not my initial intent fifty years ago. My habit started innocently enough, when I did a favor for a friend who owned a frame shop in Kenosha, Wisconsin. Imagine my excitement when he gave me a Leonard Baskin etching, titled "Barlach", as a thank you gift. At the time I had no knowledge of the artist or the medium, but it was an elegant and stunning image, and I was impressed that it was hand signed by the artist.

Several years later my personal focus as an artist shifted from painting to printmaking. I became a "basement printmaker", and my art centered on various printmaking media. In the 70's, I began to enter national and international juried shows and was encouraged not only by my work being selected for exhibition, but also by winning major awards. I also became more knowledgeable regarding the work being done by my peers, and the many mediums they used to produce fine works of art. I enjoyed watching certain artists develop over the years, and it inspired me in my own work.

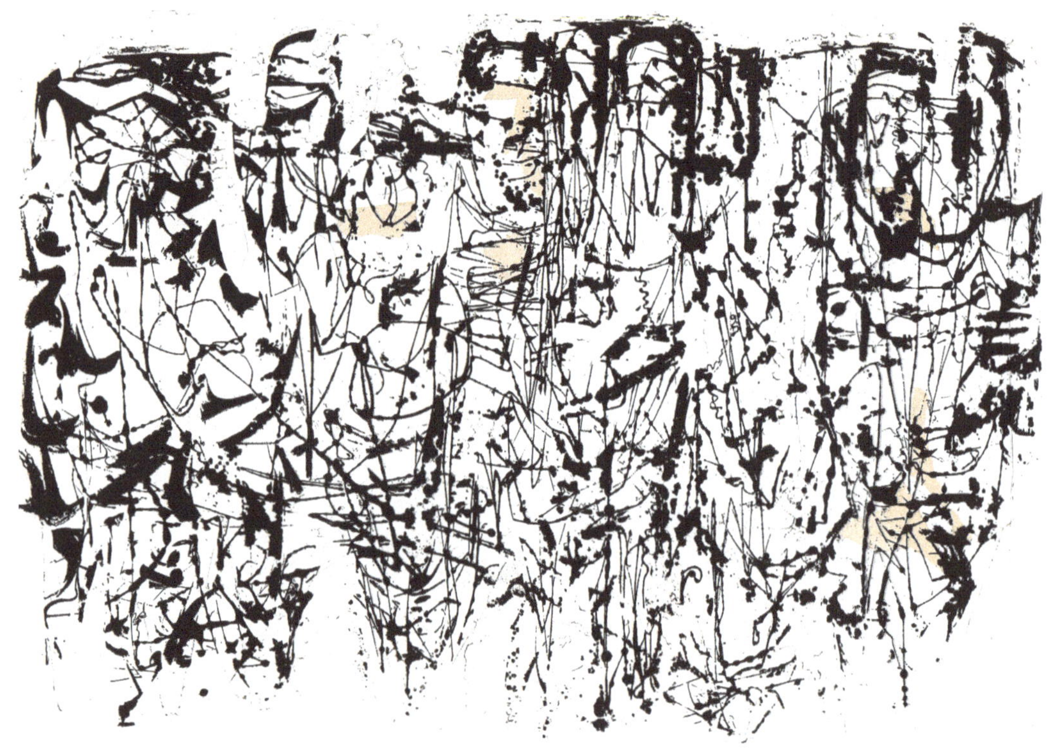

Misch Kohn "A Convocation of Strangers" Chine Colle 14 ¼ x 19 ¾

At some point, it occurred to me that other artists that I admired might be willing to trade works of art with me. I started by writing letters to a few select printmakers, and was heartened by the response. I found that, for the most part, artists are very generous people and were receptive to the idea of trades with their peers. One trade led to another, and soon a collection of sorts was born.

I was encouraged by these successful trades, and what started out as a casual interest evolved into a passion. I expanded my reach by negotiating with dealers who carried my work, trading my prints for pieces by other artists that they handled. For more commercially successful artists, I would sometimes add cash to the transaction. I also hunted through local thrift and second hand stores, and antique shops. I then discovered EBay, which is a treasure trove of prints. I scoured them all, perpetually searching for the jewels, and I was fortunate to find my share. I purchased and resold anything that I perceived as having value, using any profits for seed money to buy prints on my wish list. Meanwhile, the collection grew, and so did my enthusiasm.

Over time, I realized the immensity of the printmaking world, and the impossibility of having it all. My collection was also varied in its content, having works by Piranesi and Pierre Bonnard, as well as many modern foreign printmakers. I had a collection of prints, but there was no direction. As I reflected on the many pieces that I had accumulated, I realized that for the collection to make any sense, I would have to develop a theme, and a more centered approach. It finally dawned on me that I was living in the midst of a period of time that was actually unique in art history, the revival of printmaking. It was the *Print Renaissance*, and it was in full play all around me, involving a growing number of American printmakers. I was also directly involved in it. What could be more appropriate?

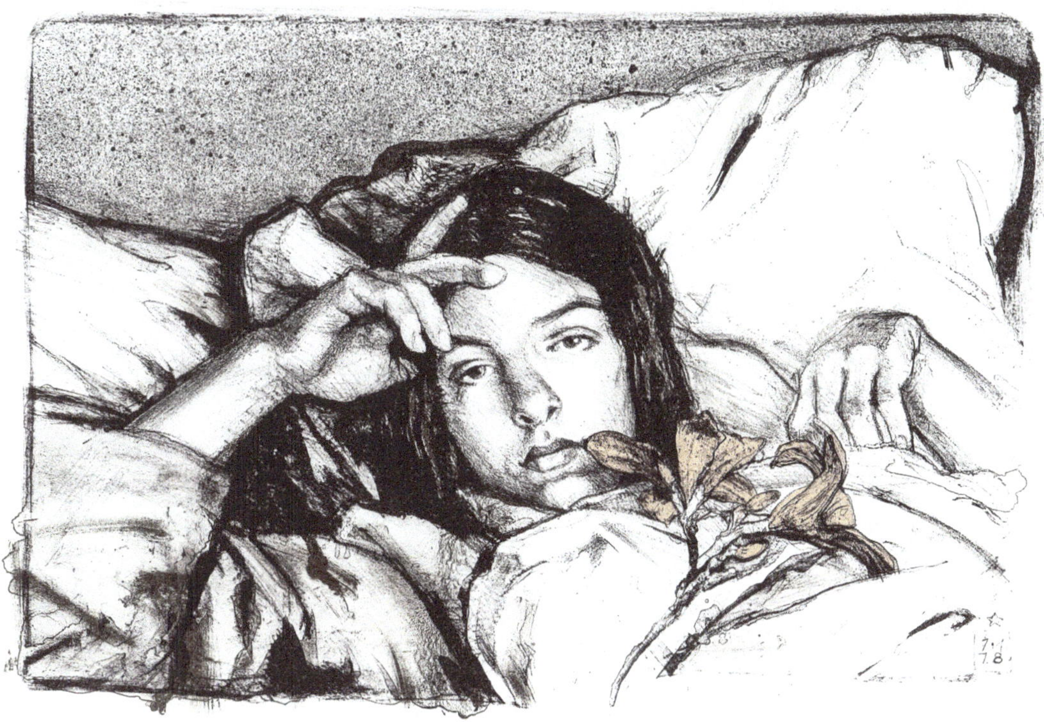

Sigmund Abeles "Tiger Lily" Lithograph 15 x 22

So, the *Print Renaissance* became my theme, encompassing the time period from Stanley William Hayter's Atelier 17 blockbuster exhibit in 1944 at the Museum of Modern Art, to the present. It was and continues to be a defining period of time in the history of art, ultimately leading to the resurgence and acceptance of printmaking as a fine arts medium. I now had my theme and a slice of time. The parameters were set. My collection was focused and centered, with a sense of purpose.

I continue to collect, and it has become more of a passion than ever. Collecting has given me great pleasure, and has fueled my desire to learn more, acquire more, and also to share more. Some of the results of my addiction are on display in this book. For me worth is not always measured in dollar value, and this collection is proof of what can be achieved at a modest price.

My hope is that you gain some knowledge of this slice of art history, and in so doing, discover the world of printmakers, as they are our very own "National Treasures".

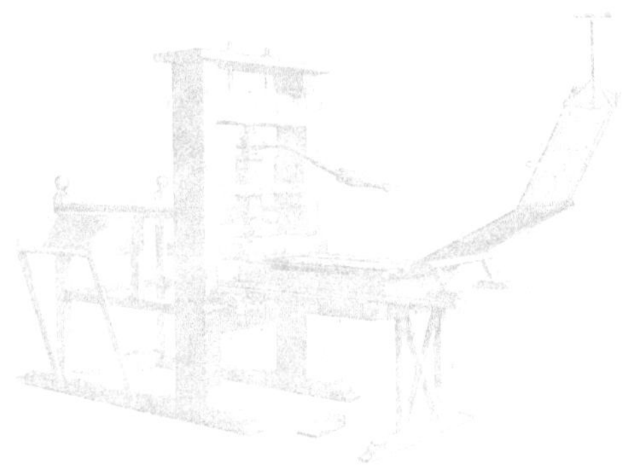

"No one owns the concept of art, or artistic processes. Take what you want, and build on it."

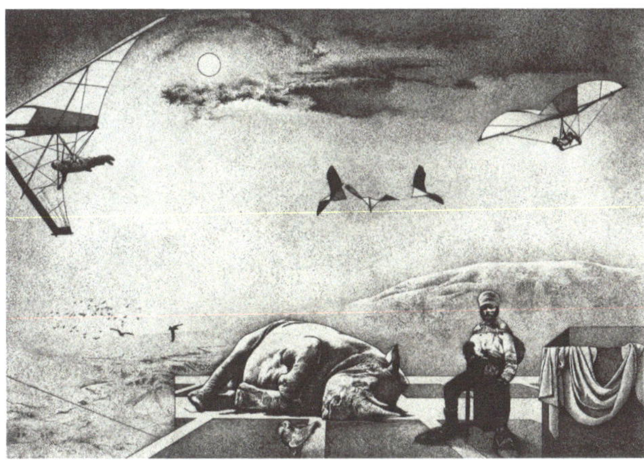

Ron Ruble "Dying Rhino" Etching 17 ½ x 25

"My art is narrative, combining realistic imagery of a symbolist nature with a touch of the surreal. My drawings are developed for the most part from photographs cultivated from family albums, news media, the internet, or wherever I can find them. Any image that grabs my attention is adapted for my work. I don't quite understand why one image will reach out to me and another doesn't. I seem to be drawn to images of a classical nature, putting them together somewhat like a collage, in settings that are ambiguous, even to me. I really don't seek to understand their meanings, but arrange them in compositions that just seem to fit.

Recently I have been experimenting with mixed media works, combining drawings, photos, manipulated computer images and also adding some collage elements. I do not burden myself with limits or rules. My goal is to get to the heart of my thought, to the final image, using any method or process that is available to me.

My only advice to other artists would be: don't hesitate to use whatever means are available to you to fulfill your vision. No one owns the concept of art, or artistic processes. Take what you want, from wherever you find it, and build on it.

I hope, that in the end, I have done good work."

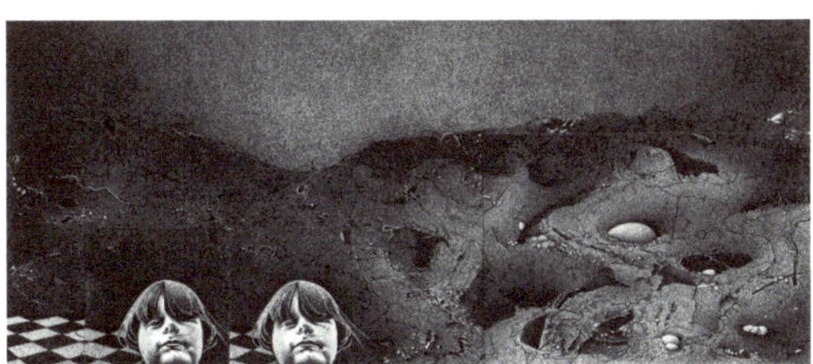

Ron Ruble "Two: 2" Hand Colored Lithograph/Collage 6 x 14

About the Author

Ron Ruble has been a successful business executive, fine arts painter, potter and a writer. Born in St. Louis, Missouri, he moved to Kenosha, Wisconsin at an early age, and spent his formative years there. He presently divides his time between Brooklyn, Wisconsin, and Punta Gorda, Florida with studios in both locations.

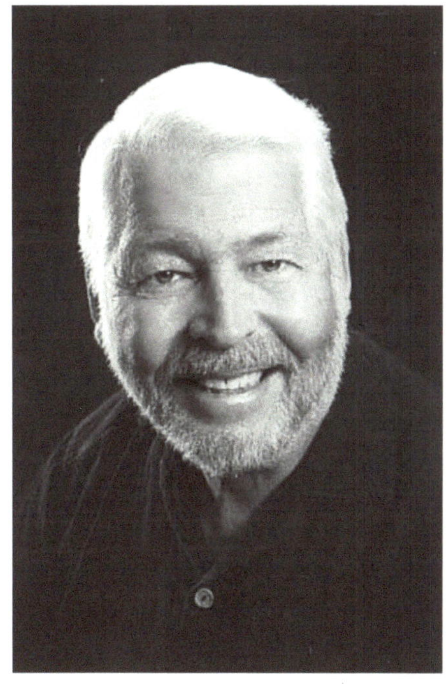

His work has been included in over 90 national and international juried art exhibitions and has been the recipient of 42 major awards. Ruble's work is included in more than 60 Museum and University art collections.

He is an elected member of the Los Angeles Printmaking Society, as well as the prestigious Society of American Graphic Artists.

Ron would love to hear from you.

CONTACT:

www.printrevolutioninamerica.com

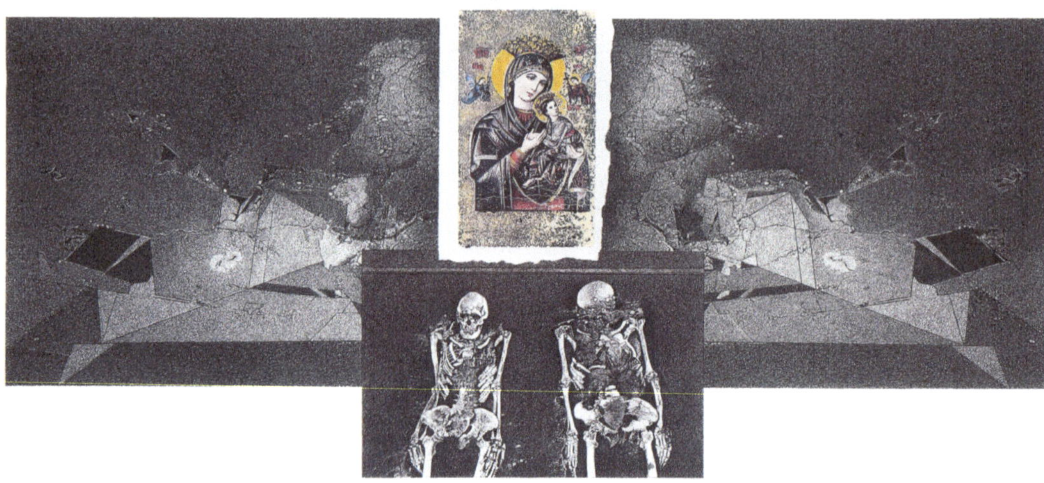

Ron Ruble "Day of the Dead" Mixed Media 14 x 29

Printmaking Quotes:
Collected from the Mid-America Print Council List

"The invention of the printing press was one of the most important events in human history."
Anonymous

"The act of printing has always seemed to me a miracle, just such a miracle as the growing of a tiny seed of grain to an ear – an everyday miracle, even the greater because it happens every day. One drawing is sown on the stone or the etching plate, and a harvest is reaped from it."
From Van Gogh's letters.

"For me there is no drawing surface like the Bavarian Limestone.....after graining and being the first human being to set my eyes on this layer of nature and drawing on its surface..... the experience becomes a most beautiful seduction."
Anonymous printmaker

"Just look around, print is everywhere."
Anonymous

"Younger, less experienced artists borrow from other artists. Older, more experienced artists steal from other artists."
Wayne Thiebaud, artist and printmaker

"As my life drains away, like water in a graining sink, all I ask is that I leave a ring."
Anonymous printmaker

Glossary of Printmaking Techniques

Listed below is a website that will provide you with excellent information regarding printmaking techniques. The International Print Center New York in their efforts to inform and educate, was kind enough to give us permission to offer their site for the readers of this book. I found their information clear, concise and thorough. We appreciate and thank them for their generosity. There are several other sites also available on the internet regarding printmaking techniques.

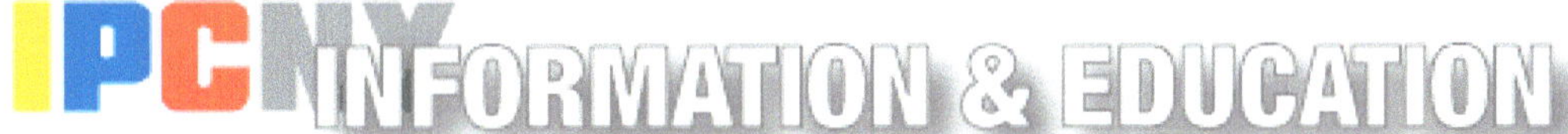

www.ipcny.org/info/FAQs/glossary.html

Alternative: Select IPCNY on your Search Engine; then click Education; then click Glossary

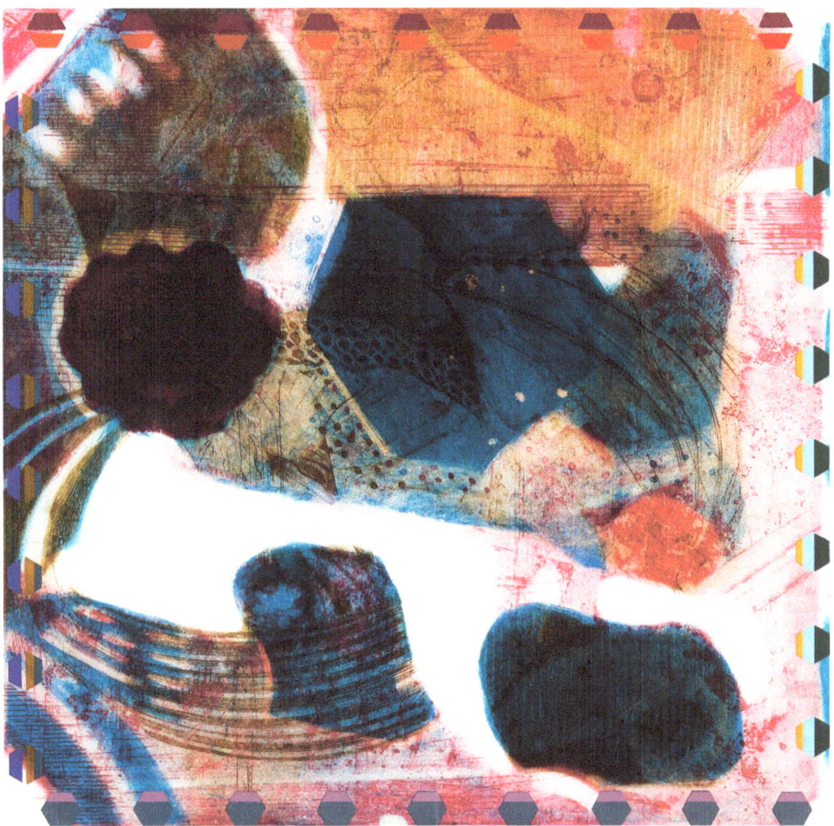

Marvin Lowe "Voodoo of the Western World" Intaglio Etching 24 ½ x 23 ½

www.ingramcontent.com/pod-product-compliance
Lightning Source LLC
Chambersburg PA
CBHW050720180526
45159CB00003B/1086
9780986110917